Danbury's Third Century:
From Urban Status
to Tri-Centennial

William E. Devlin & Herbert F. Janick

Published April 2013 by
Western Connecticut State University
181 White Street
Danbury, CT 06810

Printed by AM Lithography Corporation
694 Center Street
Chicopee, MA 01013

International Standard Book Number:
978-0-9889243-1-4

Library of Congress Control Number:
2013932099

FSC
www.fsc.org

MIX
From responsible
sources
FSC® C005009

The mark of
responsible forestry

Printed on 55% recycled and
30% post-consumer fibers

Cover: Aerial view of downtown Danbury and
Candlewood Lake in 2008. *Courtesy of Greater
Danbury Chamber of Commerce. Photo by James
Cordes, Cordes & Company.*

The Tricentennial celebration marks both the end and the beginning of
this history. From September 15, 1984, to September 15, 1985, proud
citizens celebrated Danbury's 300th birthday with the remarkable energy
and enthusiasm described in the final pages of this volume. While primary attention during this year-long event focused on the gigantic opening
parade and the path-breaking closing community party, key members of
the Tricentennial Committee, particularly Superior Court Judge Norman
Buzaid, and *News-Times* editor Steve Collins, felt strongly that the
Committee should promote the writing of a modern history of Danbury
that would supplement James Montgomery Bailey's still-valuable but
dated *History of Danbury* published in 1895. Consequently, the
Committee agreed to commission the publication of a history that
would give attention to the third century of Danbury's past. This book
is the result of the foresight of the Tricentennial Committee.

A skeptic might ask: "Why did it take more than twenty-five years to
produce this volume? To answer this question requires extending credit to
three important people who are no longer with us. A sudden heart attack

in 1986, shortly after his retirement from the newspaper, cut short Steve Collins' leadership of this effort to update Danbury's history. A key person recruited by Collins, Dr. Truman Warner, a trained historian and anthropologist at Western Connecticut State University, spent a number of years on this project before his death in 1997. After Clarice Osiecki retired in 1998 from her longtime position as president of the Greater Danbury Chamber of Commerce, she devoted the remaining years of her life to the Danbury history. Each of these dedicated Danbury historians made an important contribution to this book. The authors benefited from the wisdom contained in decades of Collins' newspaper editorials; the publications of, and enlightening conversations with, Warner; and the copious research materials gathered by Osiecki as well as her preliminary drafts of several early segments.

Despite the commitment of this trio of historians, the vision of a modern Danbury history that was meant to be an essential part of the 300th birthday celebration would have been frustrated without the dogged persistence of Mary Ann Frede and Barbara Susnitzy, two of the original members of the Tricentennial Committee who refused to be sidetracked by multiple frustrations and countless delays. When these two indomitable women asked us in the fall of 2007 to undertake the task of writing this long-postponed history, we quickly agreed for a number of reasons. Some were personal. We welcomed and trusted the sponsor's guarantee of support, autonomy and patience. The prospect of working together as we had done on a number of Danbury-focused academic and public history projects appealed to both of us. To be frank, enough time had elapsed since each of us had finished publication of book-length manuscripts for the memory of painful deadlines to have mercifully dimmed. However, the prime motivation came from the unique and somewhat puzzling history of Danbury itself. The opportunity to tell the story of a small, industrial boomtown that in less than a century faded to the status of a struggling backwater before reviving as a prosperous and progressive corporate center drew us into the project and kept us absorbed and enthused during five years of research and writing.

The central theme of this book is Danbury's unlikely transformation from

being the proud capital of the nation's hat manufacturing industry into the
hub of a region that *Money* magazine in 1983 ranked among the ten best
places to live in the entire nation. Part I, which begins in 1889 when the
city officially came into existence, examines the craft and business of men's
hat making in Danbury, tracing the decline of the industry that by the
time of the second World War had crippled the local economy and eroded
public confidence. Part II explores the burst of fresh energy that accompanied the introduction of high-tech industries in the postwar decades and
the corporate boom in the 1970s and 1980s. Though changed in many
essential ways, Danbury remained a middle-class community.

This story could not have been written without the help of many
people. The earliest and most crucial vote of confidence came from Western
Connecticut State University President James Schmotter. We approached
him shortly after agreeing to tackle the assignment in order to ascertain
whether the school had any interest in publishing the resulting local
history. He responded without hesitation, saying, "This is a project the
university needs to support." A professional historian himself, he never
wavered in his commitment to this position. When a manuscript began
to take shape, he asked WCSU Vice President Paul Steinmetz to supervise
progress. It was a wise choice. A transplanted Californian, Paul had participated in writing "the first draft of Danbury history" in an earlier career as a
reporter for *The News-Times*. In his university post, he made several crucial
decisions that removed obstacles and kept publication on track.

The staff of the Ruth Haas Library has been uniformly helpful. Serials'
librarian Jennifer O'Brien bent some regulations to ease our access to the
Danbury newspaper on microfilm. Mary Rieke responded quickly and
efficiently to every question about the contents of the Archives. But two
technologically challenged historians owe a special debt of gratitude to
archivist Brian Stevens for his generosity and computer savvy. Among
many acts of assistance, he introduced us to a program that enabled both
authors to work on the same manuscript from their homes; monitored our
use (and frequent misuse) of the system to avoid what he termed "version
confusion"; and calmly responded to our frantic phone calls with helpful

advice. Our work would have been much more hazardous without Brian's professional guidance.

A critical – and scary –point in the evolution of any literary composition comes after the authors have done their best to produce a coherent manuscript and are willing to submit their handiwork to criticism from outside readers. We were fortunate that three highly qualified colleagues were willing to perform this vital function. Senior Professor Ed Hagan, director of the writing program at Western; John Malone, retired chairman of the English Department at Somers High School in Somers, New York; and Jim Pegolotti, former dean of Arts and Sciences at Western and a prize-winning author, read every chapter and made many firm but gentle suggestions for improvements in style, structure and content. This is a far better book because of their substantial effort.

Two other talented historians and public-spirited Danbury residents generously performed a hidden but essential task at the end of the creative process. University of New Haven Professor of History Paulette Pepin, and Steve Flanagan, retired New Milford High School history teacher, under a tight time-schedule, checked the final manuscript for errors before it was handed over to the printer.

We decided at the start that the primary audience for this book would be intelligent but non-academic readers. Therefore, while we followed rigorous scholarly methodology, we concluded that most readers would find elaborate footnotes more a hindrance than a help. We hope that the "Notes on Sources" section at the end of the book will adequately indicate the nature and range of our research.

Unlike many publications about local history, this is not primarily a picture book. However, because illustrations provide an opportunity to reinforce interpretive points we decided to integrate them in the narrative rather than isolate them in a special visual section. While the photographs included come from many sources, the largest number are from the rich files of the Danbury Museum and Historical Society. We wish to thank Bridget Durkin, the director, and Diane Hassan, her able assistant, for their assistance in all stages of our research, but in particular for their help in locating appropriate photographs and then scanning them for publication. Despite a heavy workload, Carol Kaliff found time to track down important images from the sadly incomplete files of *The News-Times*. Where newspaper negatives no longer existed, Ruth Haas Library Archivist Brian Stevens and his student assistant Gillette DeBary coaxed clear prints from the newspaper preserved on microfilm. Steve Flanagan took the striking contemporary photographs. The Greater Danbury Chamber of Commerce provided the aerial photograph on the cover through the courtesy of James Cordes of Cordes & Company.

A talented team of professionals turned our manuscript into a handsome book. Jason Davis, the director of Publication and Design at WCSU set a tone of enthusiasm and commitment to the project that was shared by his entire staff. Copy editor Connie Conway helped eliminate awkward and confusing references in the manuscript. Peggy Stewart evaluated, selected, and then prepared all the photographs for publication. When Frederica Paine retired in April 2012 after 15 years as layout and design specialist at Western, we shuddered at the prospect of losing her skills and judgment. In reality we benefited as she was able to concentrate on our project from her retirement home in New Hampshire. We appreciate her smooth transition to an unfamiliar long-distance work relationship. Edwina Walker Amorosa of Access Indexing opened up the book to readers by expertly indexing its content.

Finally, we are grateful for the support and understanding of family and friends who, despite awareness of our inevitable long-winded response, continued to ask, "How is the book coming?"

William E. Devlin

Herbert F. Janick

Danbury, Connecticut

December 2012

Part I: The Hat City (1889-1945)

Part II: A Fresh Energy (1945-1985)

1889 to 1945
The Hat City

M. Burleigh's 1884 bird's-eye-view lithograph captures Danbury in the midst of the decade-long boom that led to its growth into a city. Main Street runs diagonally across the page. St. Peter's Church (no. 9) is in its present location, as is the Civil War Soldier's Monument (26) at the West Street intersection. Danbury's tallest building at the time was the First Congregational Church (1), while other churches shown include the First Methodist (4) on Main Street and what was then called the German Lutheran Church (6) on Foster Street. The Danbury & Norwalk Railroad passenger station (20) was on Main Street, on the site of the present downtown post office, while the Wooster House Hotel (23) sat at the corner of White Street. The oddly shaped factory on Maple Avenue later became the Turner Machine Co. (53). The view amply illustrates the nearby neighborhoods of homes owned by merchants, professionals and working hatters.

On April 19, 1889, Connecticut Governor Morgan Bulkeley officially brought the City of Danbury into existence with a few strokes of his pen on the city charter. A few days later, a spontaneous parade celebrated the event in what *The Danbury News* described as "a genuine blowout," marked by a crowd larger than any ever seen before on the downtown streets. Soon after, the new mayor posed with the eight members of the newly minted Common Council for the first official mayoral portrait. Forty-seven-year-old Mayor Legrand Hopkins can be seen at the center of the group, eager to take the helm of this new enterprise. He is surrounded by a mustachioed group of men who not only reflected the makeup of Danbury's population at the time, but also included the founder of the city's longest-running retail business and a future figure in one of the era's most famous U.S. Supreme Court cases.

Attainment of city status was a fitting climax to a decade of booming growth marked by industrial development in the four-square-mile core of Danbury. Beginning in 1879, improving economic conditions, new railroad connections to the West, and an aggressive program of reservoir building led to the number of the city's hat factories doubling in only six years. More than a thousand buildings of all types went up and the population of the thriving borough nearly doubled during the same time span, soaring to 17,000 and placing Danbury in eighth place in size among Connecticut's municipalities. Such rapid growth demanded a more appropriate form of government for the urban core. The borough government established in 1822 was meant to deal with the unique problems of the village, which were centered on its Main Street, without taxing rural residents. Within its boundaries, a warden, assisted by a board of burgesses, filled the roles of first selectman, sheriff and chief magistrate. But this neighborly form of government, whose most pressing concerns had once been fire protection and keeping livestock off the streets, found itself in 1888 responsible for a complex municipality with a bonded debt of nearly a half-million dollars – the result of building reservoirs to satisfy the hat industry's unquenchable demand for clean water – as well as paving Main Street for the first time and beginning construction of a sewage system. Borough governments were elected annually and often changed personnel from year to year, so no one knew exactly how so much money had been spent on these public works projects. The new city charter gave the mayor and 12-member Common Council – four aldermen elected at large and eight councilmen who represented the city's four wards – power to deal more adequately with water supply, fire protection, sewers and other public works that served only Danbury's densely built-up area around Main Street. However, they continued to share authority with a town government, an arrangement that remained in place until consolidation of the two local governments in 1965. The town retained most of the responsibility for providing many major services such as road maintenance, bridges, schools and care of the poor.

Most of Danbury's current institutions did not exist or were in their infancy in 1889. In September of 1889, Councilman Charles Halstead, head of the council's fire committee and pictured to the right of the mayor in the official portrait, organized the paid fire department with a hook-and-

Courtesy of Danbury Museum & Historical Society Authority

Mayor Legrand Hopkins (center front) and the elected members of the first Common Council of the City of Danbury, 1889. Top row from left: Matthew Scott; Henry W. Hoyt; William McPhelemy; William Jarvis. Bottom row from left: Oscar H. Meeker (founder of Meeker's Hardware, the longest-enduring city business); Charles Halstead; Hopkins; Dietrich Loewe (hat manufacturer and figure in the 1915 U.S. Supreme Court Case Loewe v. Lawlor); Cable Purdy.

ladder company and hose company housed in the fire headquarters on Ives Street, and authorized purchase of the very first steam-powered equipment. It was none too soon. A few years earlier, in 1885, volunteer firefighters hampered by low water pressure were forced to watch the William Beckerle & Co. hat factory, one of the town's biggest, burn to the ground as they waited helplessly for two hours for a horse-drawn steamer to arrive from Norwalk. The conflagration took five lives, destroyed five homes along with the factory, and left 475 hatters temporarily jobless. A paid police force of two or three officers, which had been organized in 1884, gradually replaced the borough's part-time constabulary. The Danbury Library was well established in a new and impressive 1876 building on Main Street, thanks to the benefactions of Alexander Moss White, a Danbury native and New York hatters' fur dealer, who had donated the family home and property for this purpose. A small community hospital was being organized. Schools, under the control of the town government, flourished in the three school districts within town limits, in contrast to the uneven quality of one-room schools in the 10 rural districts. New Street and Balmforth Avenue Schools were large and modern for their time. A small high school established in 1872 held classes initially in an area of the New Street School and later on the upper floor of the United Bank building on Main Street. Classes were small and the number of graduates low as students did not need a secondary education to thrive in business at that time.

The city's first mayor, Legrand Hopkins, had served a successful one-year term as borough warden, winning wide praise for his adept handling of the Blizzard of 1888, which occurred only weeks after he took office and cut Danbury off from the outside world for several days. Alone among the solemn group of men depicted in the first official mayoral photograph, Hopkins can be seen to have a twinkle in his eye and the hint of a smile, while the councilmen surrounding him affect deadpan seriousness. These nine men provide a cross-section of Danbury's changing population. As it grew into a small city, Danbury's opportunities had attracted a variety of new residents, and by 1889, descendants of the old families that had settled the town in the late 1600s – such as Councilman Henry Hoyt, a bookkeeper in the F.A. Hull Hardware firm who designed the new city seal modeled on Bridgeport's – were in the minority. However, Danbury's opportunities drew new Yankee residents, native-born Protestants like Legrand Hopkins, from neighboring farming towns. Hopkins hailed from New Fairfield, which he had left during an adventurous youth only to eventually return. He then settled in Danbury, where he started small businesses and worked as a hat finisher in the city's dominant trade. Indeed, so many people had moved to Danbury from surrounding towns that the city boasted a social club called the Sons of New Fairfield, with the mayor as a proud member. A councilman seated near Hopkins in the official photograph is Oscar Meeker, who'd moved from Bridgeport six years earlier to found a feed-and-grain business on White Street that would become the city's longest-running business. Other prominent figures in the city – hat manufacturers, ordinary hatters, builders, businessmen, the county sheriff, even Lyman Brewster, the lawyer who drew up the original city charter – had grown up on farms in Brookfield, Ridgefield and Redding, and in

Connecticut towns as distant as Salisbury. The city's main newspaper, *The Danbury News,* called itself "the journal of a Yankee Town."

Danbury had been founded by Congregationalists from Norwalk in 1684. By 1889, the Congregational Church building with its 200-foot steeple stretching into the sky had long been the most conspicuous landmark on Main Street. Not only did Danbury have thriving Episcopal (St. James) and Baptist congregations, it was also home to the biggest single Methodist membership in the state, numbering more than a thousand.

Though now a minority, descendants of Danbury's founding families were still numerous: Sixty-three Hoyts and dozens of Barnums, Benedicts, Boughtons and Wildmans could be counted in Crofutt's 1889 Danbury City Directory. But their numbers were being challenged and in some cases surpassed by names that were less likely to have originated in Fairfield County than in County Clare in western Ireland. The 46 Ryans, 44 Kanes and Keanes (both pronounced Kane) and 31 Gallaghers listed in the same book rivaled the time-honored names of Danbury's founders. By 1889, almost half of Danbury's population was foreign-born and of those almost half were Irish and Catholic. So numerous had Irish Catholics become that Legrand Hopkins may have been trying to seal his 1889 election victory when he donated the mourning bell that still hangs in the Gothic St. Peter's Church, the first Catholic church in the Danbury area. Abe Feinson, whose family moved to Danbury in 1908, would remember the Danbury of his childhood as being "an Irish-Catholic town." But by 1889, many of the first generation of Irish immigrants in Danbury were beginning to die out. Their children, like William McPhelemy, a member of the first Common Council pictured behind Hopkins in the mayoral photograph, had begun branching out in new directions. They now occupied places in business, government and the police and fire departments, and formed a large bloc in the hatting industry, where they gradually came to dominate in the union leadership. McPhelemy's father, Michael, had been an immigrant from County Tyrone. In addition to founding a successful bottling business, the elder McPhelemy had built one of White Street's most impressive business buildings, and helped start a club for the city's upwardly mobile

Courtesy of Danbury Museum & Historical Society Authority

Access to the railroad and a stream was key to the location of virtually all Danbury hat factories, including the William Beckerle Co. on Pahquioque Avenue. The building shown here is the one rebuilt after a fire in 1885. To prevent any future fire losses, Beckerle founded his own volunteer fire company, still in existence, whose original building is shown atop the hill in this view.

Irish residents when he found himself thwarted from joining mainly Protestant social clubs. The Irish had settled most thickly in the southern half of the borough. The Town Hill neighborhood to the east of Main Street and reaching along South Street towards Bethel was the heart of the new city's Fourth Ward and had become their stronghold. The concentration of so many Irish individuals with similar first and last names in the Fourth Ward produced both a bastion for the Democratic Party and a rich legacy of nicknames. Consider "Warrior" and "Shorty" Gildea, "Smoke" Gorman, "Squeak" McNamara, "Teke" Doran, "Peg Leg" Foley, "Spike" Hennessey, and "Wrong End of the Turnip" Blake, who must have had a memorable face. The nicknaming went on in later years to identify members of other Fourth Ward ethnic groups as well, including "Meatball" Torcaso, "Snake" NeJame, "Labor Day" Ziegler, "Lousy Lou" Sauer, "Jimmy Banana" Ferrandi, "Mops" Troccola, and, most recently, "Tweezer" Seri!

Other ethnic groups were beginning to set down roots as well. Like hat manufacturer Dietrich Loewe, seated to Hopkins' right in the official photograph, the largest group was German. This group had established Immanuel Lutheran Church on West Street, where Loewe worshiped, as well as a school nearby on Foster Street in the early 1880s. Mainly working in hat shops, their membership also included most of the town's barbers and tailors, as well as a variety of craftsmen and business owners. A small settlement outside the city limits called Germantown took shape as workers of the Beckerle hat factory built their own homes with financial help from their employer.

Other European nationalities were becoming numerous, as well. In 1889, a group of 20 Swedes crammed into a tiny kitchen on Patch Street and organized the Scandinavian Sick and Help Society for mutual support and social contact. The members soon began to meet monthly, later merging with other Swedish organizations in Connecticut to form a national body, the Vasa Order of America. There also was a mutual-aid society for the small French community. Italians had begun to settle in the city as fruit vendors, farmers, railroad workers and laborers on public works projects. They were the vanguard of what would become Danbury's largest ethnic community during the next 30 years. But whether it was an established Yankee or newly started European business, a single major industry generated the opportunities that drew them to Danbury.

HATTING

Danbury in 1889 was many things: a railroad town, a factory town, a steam town. But most of all, it was a hat town. When it came time for cities in the state to give themselves nicknames, Bridgeport expressed its pride in its parks, New Haven in its elms, Norwich in its roses; but there was no question that Danbury would be known as the Hat City. It had the facts and figures to back up that claim. The two dozen hat factories operating in the city in 1889 turned out about one-third of the men's hats made annually in the United States, totaling close to six million. Another 21 firms supplied those manufacturers' every need by providing hat-making machinery made in local machine shops as well as equipment and specialized tools, leather sweatbands, shipping cases and boxes, wooden shaping blocks, wire for stiffening hat brims, printed labels (called 'tips'), rolling racks for holding hat bodies, and the processed fur that was the raw material for felt hats. So many factories and shops were located within the city's boundaries that a 1906 report of the Connecticut factory inspector found Danbury the most industrialized place of its size in the state.

By 1889, hat factories had shaped every aspect of the city's life. Danbury, though, was not the typical New England mill or industrial town with tall brick mills surrounded by workers' housing. A visit to a Danbury hat factory in that year would begin at a jumble of two- or three-story wood frame buildings located on the banks of a waterway. In years past, the stream – usually the Still River but sometimes one of its tributaries – might have supplied water used in production. But with a growing reservoir system in place by 1889, the only remaining use of these waterways was for disposing massive amounts of dye materials, called dyestuffs, and the contents of the factory's privies. For over a century, the Still River downstream from Danbury was an eerie Technicolor show of whatever colors of hats were being dyed in the city's factories that day, a condition that endured into the 1960s and occured occasionally after that. The state board of health reported in 1886 that almost two-and-a-half-million pounds of dyestuffs, chiefly from tropical woods, spilled annually into the Still River system from Danbury's hat factories. The same report also estimated that "over 600 pounds of fatty and other organic matters washed daily from wool and fur" drained into the stream. Chemicals like acids, sulfates and mercury used in the hatting process also found their way into the river, settling in bottom sediment or drifting with the currents to the mouth of the Housatonic, where deposits of mercury remain to this day.

Some hatters believed that local water possessed a magical quality that accounted for the quality of Danbury-made hats. There is no evidence for that claim but plenty of evidence that the sheer quantity of water available was a deciding factor in locating hat shops here. Steam-powered processes in the hat factories demanded massive amounts of water; making a single hat from start to finish has been estimated to require from 50 to 84 gallons. By 1889, the source of the clean water used in the factory came not from the Still River but from reservoirs located in the hills northwest of the city. The borough government built the first of two Kohanza reservoirs in 1860, supplying water for drinking and fire protection as well as for hatting. This expansion of the reservoir system, though, was a direct result of a push for more economic growth in the form of more hat factories. In 1880, the borough's water commissioners recommended expanding the system beyond the two relatively small Kohanza ponds. Commissioner and engineer John W. Bacon saw it as crucial to creating an opportunity for dramatic growth with the coming railroad connection to the West, a judgment that turned out to be correct. "By furnishing an abundant supply of good water for manufacturing and other purposes," Bacon predicted, Danbury could see "an increase of business and population during the next ten or fifteen years, far beyond any former experience." The commissioners' 1880 plan recommended acquiring land around what is today known as Padanaram Brook for immediate use, and acquisition of Boggs Pond and its brook (sometimes referred to today as Middle River Brook) for future needs. During the 1880s, the borough constructed Padanaram Reservoir and the East Lake storage reservoir above it.

The typical Danbury hat factory of 1889 would also be located next to a rail siding or spur. Besides abundant water, the city's rail connections were indispensable to the hat trade. By 1889, hatting was already a global operation. Rabbit fur, the most common raw material for hats, came primarily from Australia where millions of rabbits ran wild, or from France or Belgium, where rabbits raised domestically for food were the main source. The best wool for hats came from the Cape of Good Hope in South Africa, with lesser grades imported from Mexico and California. Peacock feathers that decorated the hats arrived from South America. India was the source for most of the shellac used in hardening derby hats, the city's chief hat style produced in 1889. Leather hatbands, silk linings and colorful printed tips often came from Europe, although Danbury firms supplied them as well. Trains fed the production lines each and every day. In 1889, *The Evening News* reported:

> The hat manufacturer could order his fur and other stuff in New York, have it shipped as late as 5:30 in the afternoon, and it would be in this city at two o'clock in the morning. Under those conditions the fur could be in the different hat shops early enough for the employees in the blowing and forming rooms to work on.

Railroads brought salesmen and other business contacts from all over the country, especially New York City, the hat trade's wholesale and retail capital. Trains sent out thousands of crates of finished men's hats, neatly stacked in piles of a dozen each and packed into wooden cases (hat production was customarily measured in dozens rather than in numbers of individual hats). Most of Danbury's hats were destined for domestic markets, but some were shipped overseas, mostly to Europe and South America.

In 1889, multiple railroads served the city, making Danbury the main rail hub of western Connecticut. The Danbury & Norwalk had been the area's first railroad, a local effort completed in 1852 that set off a wave of industrial and population growth in the borough. In 1872, the line had constructed a six-mile extension through Bethel to connect with the Housatonic Railroad at Hawleyville. By 1889, the Housatonic absorbed the entire Danbury & Norwalk line. The completion, in 1880, of an east-west line named the New York & New England Railroad sparked Danbury's decade-long hatting and population boom. The New York & New England ran from Boston through Danbury into New York State as far west as Brewster. The road had been cobbled together from several failed projects that had been conceived thirty years earlier. Despite its dramatic impact on Danbury's growth, the New York & New England turned out to be a financial failure. After competing fruitlessly with established coastal lines for east-west business across southern New England, it succumbed to bankruptcy in 1893. The New York, New Haven & Hartford Railroad acquired it in 1895, three years after gaining control of the Housatonic line as well. The resulting combination was known locally as the Consolidated Road.

The hat factory's tall brick smokestack indicated the presence of the steam engine that powered its machinery. Coal fed the engines, some of which used thousands of tons a year, and coal also provided fuel for the stoves and furnaces in most homes. Delivered to the city by freight cars from Pennsylvania mines, it was then distributed by fuel dealers like Augustus Seifert, Emil Goos and John McCarthy, whose occupation elevated them to local prominence. The price of coal was a pressing concern for manufacturers and residents alike.

Fur was the principal raw material used in Danbury's hat production, although a few factories specialized in wool hats. Different mixtures of fur determined different grades of hats – beaver or nutria the most prized and expensive, rabbit the most common. Each rabbit skin supplied about an ounce of fur and it took three to four ounces – the skins of three or four rabbits – to produce enough felt for a single hat. The number of rabbit skins used in the city every year ran into the millions. They arrived in the city in great bales of between two and four thousand skins, each bale weighing up to five hundred pounds.

Some of the largest factories in the city did their own fur processing. However, in 1889, most fur was either prepared locally by W.A. and A.M. White or Peter Robinson in their large brick factories on the Still River, or it was purchased in New York City through the Hatters Fur Exchange near Washington Square in lower Manhattan and transported to Danbury factories by train. Fur workers spent their days in a whirl of dust and flying fur, plucking the bristly outer guard hairs from rabbit skins and removing the soft under-fur destined to be made into felt. Their job also required painting the fur with an orange-colored solution of nitrate of mercury, nicknamed the 'carrot' for its color, which reputedly helped the fur fibers bond together to form felt. Exposure to this chemical also threatened the health of workers, producing a palsy known as the "hatter's shakes." In later years, small fur shops sprang up in the midst of residential enclaves around the city sending "fur flying in the air through the neighborhood," in the words of one resident who grew up near one of these shops. The spent hides of the rabbits and other animals were not wasted; they were sold and made into glue. Fur processing was perhaps the dirtiest, most disagreeable job in the industry, and its workforce was often the most recently arrived immigrants who were willing to accept any job. Their plight was eased somewhat by the philanthropy of the White brothers, who provided boarding houses for their workers near the White factory complex on Beaver Street, and were known for giving away turkeys to their employees at Thanksgiving.

Within the clothing industry, hatting was unique. Hats were the only item of clothing for which both the textile – felt – and the garment were produced in the same facility. Making the felt used in hats required careful manipulation of fur or wool through dozens of steps involving heat and pressure to create a soft, light and flexible fabric. The individual keratin fibers of fur had tiny, barely visible overlapping scales, and when the mass of fibers was moved forcefully enough, fibers would eventually bond together to form a loose mass that could be tightened by exposure to hot water. But the fibers had to move in their own natural direction, at their own pace. If the hatter applied too much speed or force to move the fibers faster than they were inclined to go on their own at any stage of manufacturing, imperfections called "dags," "push," or "shove" marks could appear later and ruin the finished product. "It may look simple but it wasn't," recalled Robert Doran, who grew up in the industry at the Doran Brothers Machine Company. At every stage, the hatter, an authentic craftsman, had to know by feel and by experience how to work with the fragile material as it took shape. As Doran pointed out, " … no other sources [in the textile industry] had to learn 'hands on' … [It] made for a very tight-knit community. Everybody knew everybody on a personal basis and they were all engaged in felt-making."

Entering a Danbury hat factory in 1889 meant stepping into an alien world. There was no assembly line or conveyor belt, only a series of buildings or "shops" or "rooms" that the hats moved through on rolling racks. In parts of the factory, fur flew everywhere, and dust thick with toxic copper salts hung in the air. It was so hot and humid in the "back" or "make shops" where hat bodies were shrunk and shaped to approximate sizes through steam and hot water, that workers labored in rubber aprons and high rubber boots. "So much steam, you didn't only want to wear a rubber apron in front of you, but also over your head; there wasn't any ceiling; the steam rising from the rafters, condensed and came down like rain," remembered union leader Hugh Shalvoy, who first went to work as a hat maker in 1878. There could be an inch or more of water on the floor in a room so filled with steam that "you could barely see your hand in front of your face," said one 20th-century hatter. And in winter, a hat maker could be standing in freezing cold water on the floor, but with his hands and face enveloped in boiling-hot steam. To prevent moisture from ruining the hats, manufacturers built factories of wood that would absorb some of the great quantity of steam. As an industrial survey of the city noted in 1917, the presence of so many large wooden buildings packed densely in such a small area created a city full of potential fire hazards. Even in the drier front shop where hat bodies were finished off through shaving, sanding (known as "pouncing"), ironing and other processes, working conditions weren't much better: "It was 90 to 100 degrees, eight months a year," reported a hat finisher. "We were sandpapering where we worked, so there was a lot of dust. It was hard work." Hatters' hands were commonly stained black with dye (a point of pride) and in 1889, one might still see hatters sharing beer on the job and singing loudly to ease their burden. Within broad categories of production, hatters worked at specialized jobs such as pouncers,

Courtesy of Danbury Museum & Historical Society Authority

Hat factories such as those shown here, owned by John W. Green (later by George McLachlan), were really collections of shops and buildings where different processes took place. The large smokestack illustrates the importance of steam power to the operation. Built off White Street on the site of today's Western Connecticut State University parking garage, the factory was known locally as "Green's (or later McLachlan's) down in the swamp."

flangers, hardeners, and wetters-down. Workers could be seen operating "dag-tearing" machines, "devils," and "double-whizzers," to say nothing of "snip feeders," "tip" printers and other oddly named machinery like the "elephant's foot," a heated sandbag that dried out the finished hat.

The "former," the machine that blew the processed fur onto a revolving metal cone, which then fashioned the gathering felt into a rough pyramid shape, was the most important piece in the factory. The former made it possible to mass-produce great quantities of hats. Its operators, known as a coners-and-slippers, turned cones of felt over to a hardener and a wetter-down – the workers who began the shrinking and sizing processes of the "backshop." The number of formers in use determined the production capacity of a factory. Small shops employed one or two on lease, while giant companies like Tweedy, Mallory or, later, Lee, ran four or more. The other important operation in the backshop took place in the "make" shop, whose workers, called simply hat makers, tended at this time to be mostly Irish immigrants. Using machines like the Taylor Sizer, invented by Danbury's James Taylor, the makers turned out a crudely shaped hat body with only an approximation of a crown and brim.

A recognizable hat appeared for the first time in the finishing shop or "front shop," where the best-paid and most skilled workers in the factory, called finishers, gave these rough bodies their style and final appearance. Besides noticing that this area of the factory was drier than the steamy back shop, a visitor would not see much machinery in the front shop in 1889. Because this was such precise work, manufacturers were reluctant to introduce machines, perhaps chastened by the example of a leading hat company in Philadelphia that fully mechanized its finishing operations in 1877 and was out of business within a year. "The hand finisher was the prince of the operation," explained Doran. "He was an artist ... He had to blend in that hat so all surfaces looked exactly the same – the crown and the brim – everything had to be done with his eye and his hand." The finisher had to know by feel how to sand only the outer layers of the hat, where felt had bonded most strongly. Hit an interior layer of felt and the hat he was working on was ruined. Twelve hundred of the 4,000 hat finishers in the country in 1889 made Danbury their home. Most of them were native-born Yankees along with some immigrant Germans, though the Irish arrivals were starting to make inroads.

Finally, in its journey to becoming a finished product, each hat passed to the trimming room. Here, groups of women sewed on ribbons, crown linings and labels and applied feathers, if required, to the hatbands.

At a time when almost everyone, male or female, donned a hat to go outdoors, Danbury factories turned out two types of hats. Most American men of the era wore the fashionable piece made of soft fur felt, and this was the biggest seller. By the turn of the century, the average American man bought four of these stylish hats each year, and Danbury supplied a great portion of that market. Still popular in 1889, "stiff hats" or derbies would soon begin to fade in popularity, but the so-called Connecticut hatting district of Danbury, Bethel and South Norwalk, along with Brooklyn, New York, remained the national centers of their manufacturing. This familiar bowl-shaped headwear, known in Britain as the 'bowler' and made of hardened fur felt stiffened with shellac cut with wood alcohol, took four to five days longer to make than "soft hats" and sold for a higher price. Danbury continues to pay tribute to the derby on its city seal, where it appears as one of several emblems of Danbury's fame and growth.

Specially trained skilled labor was the irreplaceable ingredient in making a hat in 1889. Danbury's Hat Manufacturers Association admitted as much twenty years later, when it recalled that, during the 1880s, "machinery (was) little used and the work required thorough training, with comparatively long apprenticeship. It was difficult to find elsewhere a class of workmen who could carry on the industry as successfully as those of this town … There has been no other labor force from which recruits might be drawn, unlike most other industries." Even as machines made inroads into the factories, the experienced hands and eyes of individual hatters remained essential. Into the 20th century, it was still possible to find men in local factories who were capable of producing a hat from start to finish using the centuries-old methods and hand-tools of the trade.

Courtesy of Danbury Museum & Historical Society Authority

George Schweitzer, superintendent of the F.H. Lee Hat Co., inspects newly formed cones of felt for flaws and "dags." Mistakes in handling the felt as it formed could ruin a finished hat.

Their skills gave hatters a measure of power and autonomy that other workers lacked and therefore gave their unions leverage in negotiating with employers. Hatters thought of themselves as craftsmen who shared a unique and ancient culture, one that gave them special privileges and power in the workplace. Soon after the industrial era began, during the 1850s, hat finishers and hat makers organized some of the first national unions; Danbury's multitude of hatters were a vital part of those organizations. The role of these unions was not just to negotiate for the best wage possible, but also to protect the dignity and status of members as skilled craftsmen with a tradition of control over what happened in the workplace.

In Danbury's hat factories, in 1889, the shop foreman, not the boss or owner, hired the workmen. The foreman's great power in the shop extended to quality control. He decided what completed work would be accepted and therefore who would get paid. Hatters were assigned "stints," a set amount of hats set out for them to work on during a workday. They were paid by the piece according to the number of hats they'd worked on, not an hourly wage. Hatting was understood to be hard work; when hatters finished their daily quota, they could leave or choose to work on more hats if union agreements allowed it.

Sometimes all the workers in a shop would "turn out," or depart the factory, over a work dispute or simply to enjoy good afternoon weather by playing baseball or fishing. Or they might leave to attend one of the city's many impromptu parades. In 1886, the national trade magazine *Hatter and Furrier* reported that Danbury finishers regularly put down their tools and exited their factories for picnics – without their bosses' permission. And every manufacturer in town knew it was a given that a hatter could not be kept at work while the Danbury Fair was going on. Small wonder that by 1889, on the strength of hatters' union success, Danbury had become a leader in the trade union movement in Connecticut. A meeting in the city in 1882 established the state's Central Labor Union, with machinist Charles Peck of Danbury, who later became the city's mayor, as its first president.

Hatting was a world of insiders, and the trade spawned many secrets. Union locals kept only the barest of records, so we know little about what went on at meetings. Fur mixtures and dye formulas were a concern of manufacturers in the highly competitive industry. "It was hit or miss," judged Maclean Lasher, a chemist and dyer for years at several factories in Danbury. "No two factories made fur or hats exactly the same way." Most importantly, hatters had their own unique and time-honored language. In the factories of 1889, one could hear apprentices referred to as "snotts," an archaic form of British workingmen's slang. A hatter who asked a foreman for work was "on turn," while someone learning the trade was "on teach." When a union hat finisher was newly hired, he had to turn over his union traveling card, which allowed him to work in a unionized factory anywhere, to the local's financial secretary, who gave him a "local check." He got back his union card only "upon a strict compliance with trade rules."

Instead of being fired, hatters were "bagged." They worked not from a wage scale but from a "bill of prices" – piece rates they were paid for the hats they'd worked on. The bill would have been posted prominently inside the hat factory, but would be difficult for a visitor to read. So conservative was Danbury's hat trade that well into the 1890s these posted bills of prices used the old English currency terms of shillings and pence, which had been out of use in the rest of the U.S. since the Civil War. And the locations of factories were not generally publicized: An individual had to know the language and have an inside connection even to find them, let alone get a job in one. Some of the factories were known by nicknames like "the Twelve Apostles (a partnership of twelve working hatters), "The Jew's Harp" (a tongue-in-cheek reference to the plant's owners Simon and Keane, one of them Jewish and one Irish) or "Green's down in the swamp" (located off White Street, where a Western Connecticut State University parking garage is today). In nearby Bethel were "The Gold Mine" and "The Shanghai."

Indeed, breaking into the trade at all was a significant achievement for an outsider. As hatter George Thorne confirmed, "It was pretty hard to get into the hatting trade at one time." Thorne, a native of Dover Plains, New York, came to Danbury in 1887 and acquired a job as a hardener in the John W. Green hat factory – but only because of an acquaintance with the owner's sister. Once he became "well-known around town," as a reliable worker, Thorne said he was often able to get work at other shops "when someone went on a drunk" and didn't show up. Hatters of the period also related how young men who did odd jobs, called "buggy-lugging" and involving carrying materials around the factory, sometimes could get a prized union apprenticeship.

Once a member of the union, a hatter had many opportunities. "Fair" shops were those with union contracts that used the union label in their products, "open" shops had no union contracts but employed both union and nonunion workers but "foul" shops barred union workers entirely. Union workers could work in fair or open shops but "foul" men could only work in nonunion shops, which tended to pay less. In heavily-unionized

Danbury, union members had far more options to earn better pay. Unions worked to give their members equal work opportunities and to restrict membership. Danbury locals limited the number of apprentices that any factory could employ at one time to three. This rigid rule in particular caused friction with manufacturers as the size of the city's factories expanded to hundreds and hundreds of workers. In 1890, the unions were finally forced to bend this restriction as well as to reduce the duration of an apprenticeship from four to three years, in order to supply the constant demand for new workers.

The hatting unions valued their autonomy and made every effort to police themselves. Some rules of the Danbury finishers illustrate the union's determination to manage its own affairs and assert its independence. One rule required that any member aware of a violation of union rules must report the details directly to the president of the local. Another regulation stipulated in the union's constitution mandated that "all charges by one journeyman against another" had to be signed by the accuser, who had to make the accusation in person and could be fined for making a "malicious charge."

Hatting was a seasonal trade, based on a schedule set by city wholesalers who placed their orders for new hats in January and July. The big selling seasons were spring, keyed on Easter sales, and fall, which led up to Christmas. Early every year and again in mid-year, merchants from across the country came to New York City to see what was in the shop windows and place their orders. Danbury hat manufacturers would begin to ship out trial runs of new styles to Broadway dealers at those times, based on what they thought might become popular. Wholesalers, merchants and manufacturers took their cues about what style hat was going to be most popular from the young fashion setters of New York City. *The Evening News* would prominently feature predictions of "styles for the coming season."

Anyone entering a hat factory in the late spring or early summer would find, in the words of one hatter's report to the Connecticut Bureau of Labor Statistics, that "work in May is flat, June is dull, July is medium and August a boom." For hatters, that meant that their wages also fluctuated depending on the season. The hatter quoted above reported average earnings of $45.58 per month, but that varied between a high of $78.03 in August and a low of $19.96 in May. November was another good month, as were February and March. A female hat binder reported even greater fluctuations in income, from a high of $24 in one week, to a low of $2 in a particularly slow month. She described long stretches from one to six weeks as "unoccupied" or "on vacation."

Danbury's year followed this rhythm of the hat trade. During the rush season when production was high and hatters were earning money, downtown merchants prospered, while the "dull seasons" of late spring and late fall meant low sales. When work was scarce or "dull" in Danbury, hatters could take a train to Bethel or South Norwalk, or even to Newark or Brooklyn or Orange, New Jersey, to find work there. The seasonal routine also meant that hatters had time to maintain their homes, plant gardens and serve in local government. Unlike most industrial workers, hatters frequently served as members of the Common Council and in other local government roles alongside downtown merchants and manufacturers. It also meant that when labor-management struggles like lockouts and strikes occurred, as they did with increasing frequency after 1889, they tended to begin during the "dull seasons," when factories were doing minimal production and some were even closed. Once orders began pouring in for the next selling season, the pressure was on all parties to settle.

The seasonal breaks also inadvertently helped to protect workers' health. A visitor to a hat factory or simply to Danbury in 1889 would undoubtedly encounter someone with missing teeth, bleeding gums and shaking hands, arms or legs. These individuals had the "Hatter's Shakes," a palsy-like condition developed through long periods of exposure to mercury-laced vapors released into the steam in badly ventilated hat shops. Pioneering workplace studies done by Dr. Alice Hamilton of Harvard in the 1920s found that more than 20 percent of hatters had some form of mercury poisoning and as many as 40 percent suffered from lesser but measureable traces of the disease. Some hatters also faced the risk of poisoning from the alcohol used to cut the shellac that stiffened derby hats. Hatters could be seen wobbling home from their plant after a day of exposure to this potent hazard. Dyers had to work with chemicals like chromium, which was indispensable for "fixing" hat colors. But the effects of all these conditions could be ameliorated by minimizing exposure to the chemicals. So the slowdowns and seasonal fluctuations of the trade, the vacations and layoffs, actually helped prevent some hatters from being slowly poisoned in their work-places. To workers of the times, however, the risks taken were worth the rewards.

Those rewards were reflected especially in the nature and quality of their housing. When workers left the hat factory after completing their stints, they likely as not walked to a home in one of the city's residential neigh-borhoods that surrounded downtown. Though homeownership rate was not remarkably higher than in some other places, visitors were often struck by how little Danbury resembled other industrial towns and it acquired a reputation as a city of homeowners. With a few exceptions, it looked like a collection of middle-class neighborhoods. There were almost none of the

Courtesy of Danbury Museum & Historical Society Authority

To endure the tropical temperatures in the steaming backshop, hat makers in the Hoyt-Wolthausen factory, shown here around 1890, worked in their undershirts, wore rubber aprons and a variety of improvised foot-wear, including rubber boots and clog-like shoes seen here on three sockless workers (front row center).

brick tenements or rows of identical double- or triple-decker units of factory housing found in most industrial cities at the time. Instead, Danbury was "filled with comfortable homes of more or less elegance," wrote Susan Benedict Hill, who completed James Montgomery Bailey's *History of Danbury* after Bailey's death in 1893. "Nearly every residence has its well-kept green lawn ornamented with shrubs and flowers in their season." One reason for this was that it was possible for workers with top skills and who were working in a shop with the right contracts during good times to earn extraordinary wages. One hatter reported his earnings to the state as more than $1000 a year, double the annual earnings of virtually any other skilled workers in the country. Danbury hatters in the 1880s enjoyed "a wage level materially higher than that to be found in any similar community in Connecticut or elsewhere," the Danbury Hat Manufacturers Association asserted in 1909. "Wages were so high that the standards of living were high. The employees of the factory were able to enjoy a measure of the comforts of life, and even a degree of luxury."

As a result, many Danbury residents in 1889 seemed to have achieved an approximation of the American Dream. As Susan Benedict Hill's conclusion of Bailey's 1895 history reported, "The equality of condition in Danbury has always been remarkable. Few have been very wealthy, but almost no streets in the city exhibit signs of squalor or extreme poverty." *The New York Herald*, in a Labor Day story in 1892, went further. "Danbury is practically a workingmen's town," stated *The Herald*. "The houses are not cheaply constructed … They are artistic in design, surrounded by nicely kept yards. Many of the workmen own a horse and carriage. Not a few possess more expensive houses and live more generously than some of the owners of factories." Surviving records support most of *The Herald's* glowing description. They indicate that more than 90% of the city's housing in 1889 consisted of either one- or two-family houses. More than half of the new city's 2,055 dwellings were occupied by two families, and most of the rest by single families. Walter Fanton, a diarist who was a young man in the boom times of the 1880s, described how working class residents often became homeowners:

Many fine houses … were built on earnings between 12 and 15 dollars weekly wage. A good building lot [went for] $50 to $100, then you dug the cellar yourself with your neighbors and friends and then the foundation corner with money saved to pay the mason. Then a friendly farmer would give a cash loan … You built a two-family house, paid the lumber man and carpenters and plasterers and painter. A good home cost less than $2,000. You rented the upper floor, [which] paid your tax and interest on the loan. You saved every cent and soon the home was your own.

Plentiful among the homes in the city's neighborhoods was a type of structure not often seen elsewhere: a two-story clapboard workingman's cottage possessing a minimum of detail, with a front entry but also a one-story projection to the rear of one side, containing a secondary entry. Later houses became more elaborate and spacious. For those still needing to rent, there were 25 boarding houses in the city in 1889, as well as the many multi-family homes. However, because there were so many homeowners, places to rent were scarce in Danbury in 1889, a situation that would be equally true in 1946, 1963 and 1980. The city's first brick model tenement wasn't built until 1887, when it was constructed on Balmforth Avenue.

Hatters made up the bulk of the small depositors whose funds lifted the city's two savings banks, the Savings Bank of Danbury and Union Savings Bank, to prosperity. Although hat manufacturers and merchants made up the boards of directors of these institutions, they reported in 1892 that their nearly 11,000 depositors were "made up almost entirely of working people who, when they once begin, seldom close their accounts, and then only temporarily for the purpose of buying a lot or to make a payment on a house. 90 percent had less than $1,000 on deposit. Only about one-thirteenth of the taxable property on the city's Grand list was in the hands of manufacturers.

Not only were hatters homeowners, they could even realistically envision the possibility of becoming manufacturers. In 1909, the Danbury Hat Manufacturers Association asserted, "at least three-quarters of the employers have themselves risen from the ranks of the employed during the last twenty-five years." Most of them had begun working "on the bench" as ordinary hatters, then moved up to start their own firms. "Those who have started manufacturing accumulated their capital by depositing their weekly savings in [the town's savings] banks," noted the New York Herald in 1892. A knowledgeable hatter with enough capital could lease a shop building and a forming machine, hire a few skilled workers and begin production. Among the many workers who made this jump in the 1889 period were Thomas Meath and James McGarrigle, a pair of Irish immigrants who started their own firm. Major manufacturers of 1889, like Samuel C. Holley, Henry Crofut and Byron Dexter, grew up on farms in nearby towns and came to Danbury to work at the expansive Tweedy works, the city's first giant hat factory and an incubator for local hatting talent. When William Farrah Green, a silk hatter born in Yorkshire, England, came to the United States in 1853 he gravitated to Danbury to work at Tweedy's, where his son, John W. Green, pioneered the manufacture of the derby hat in 1876. The younger Green then became plant superintendent and finally started his own company, which became one of the city's largest firms.

But upward mobility in the hat industry carried challenges. Even though the financial cost of entry into management was low, it was hard to remain there. Though hatting was not a highly profitable industry, it was ultra-competitive. As a hatters' trade journalist put it, "Each manufacturer is sitting up nights in the effort to design some plan to circumvent his competitors." Changes in price of only a few cents per hat could devastate profits and affect a company's viability. As a result, hatting partnerships dissolved and companies reorganized frequently. Many of the firms listed in the 1889 city directory were out of business or operating under different names only two years later. Manufacturers large and small sought to cut their labor costs through a variety of means, particularly by introducing more and more machinery or turning to operating so-called "independent" – in reality, non-unionized – shops where lower wages could be paid and time-honored union work rules could be ignored.

DOWNTOWN

The good fortunes of the hatting industry supported a lively downtown focused on Main and White streets. The heart of the new city was, as one urban historian described places with a similar pattern of development, "the thickened spine of a New England village" that had grown incrementally in the same place since 1684. All roads in Danbury led into Main Street, which straggled along for two miles in the geographic center of the municipality, with no continuous side streets crossing it. The tree-like pattern, with side streets as branches sprouting off the Main Street trunk with no particular plan or forethought, inspired composer Charles' Ives' piece, "Tone Roads," in which different instruments follow different musical paths, sometimes in different keys, but in the end "the sun sets and all are [back] on Main Street."

In 1889, Main Street was a jumble of buildings of many eras. On the west side of Main Street, in the downtown area, elegant new banks designed by New York and Bridgeport architects and trimmed in brownstone or terra cotta alternated with the handful of aging clapboard homesteads of old Yankee families like the Ives' home that had survived. Elm trees, planted a half-century before by property owner William Starr, had matured into a lordly colonnade that practically formed a leafy canopy over the broad street newly paved with Belgian blocks. The east side of Main, from the landscaped Elmwood Park in the south to the bridge north of Wooster Square - the intersection of Main, White and Elm - and spilling over into White Street, was given over entirely to commerce. Scores of businesses, virtually all of them locally owned, occupied its storefronts. Owners were willing and interested volunteers for local governments: Among the councilmen included the 1889 official mayoral photograph were two grocers, a pharmacist, a bottler, a partner in a hardware firm and a feed and grain merchant. All were in business in the downtown area.

Indeed, downtown Danbury in 1889 boasted a wide range of businesses, including a half-dozen bottlers, two dozen grocery stores, two piano tuners, a business college, three pool halls, a host of cigar stores, a dozen laundries (all but one of them Chinese-owned), 13 law firms, nine dentists and 30 physicians, two of them women. The greatest number of people in any one trade was in dressmaking, usually a household occupation but also run on a larger scale. An example of that was the Norton sisters' operation. The sisters came to Danbury in 1865 from their native Somers, New York, and managed an extensive business employing helpers and turning out large numbers of fancy dresses, especially wedding gowns.

The upper floors of downtown's brick business 'blocks,' as they were called, housed not only such operations as the Nortons' but also professional offices and the clubrooms of scores of social organizations. These ranged from the conventional Masonic lodge to a branch of the Irish rebel group *Clan na Gael*. A number of clubs revolved around sports, including two fishing clubs, a croquet club, a lawn tennis club and a "wheel" club for bicyclists. Veterans had the Grand Army of the Republic and a number of other "guards" companies ready to parade in uniform. Six temperance societies were active but were arrayed against some 37 saloons, most of them on White Street, that vied to slake the legendary thirst of hatters. Henry Dick, founder of one of the city's longest-lived and most successful furniture businesses, actually moved to Danbury in 1908 after a relative suggested it would be a good place to open a saloon.

On paydays at the hat factories, well-dressed hatters and trimmers were said to have promenaded down Danbury's broad main thoroughfare. Danburians seem to have responded to any excuse to stage a rally or a parade – elections and holidays in particular prompting crowds of participants, sometimes colorfully costumed, and spectators. As election results rolled in or when news events were breaking, crowds gathered in Wooster Square outside the Danbury News building to listen to up-to-the-minute dispatches being read. Charles Ives found inspiration in the memory of such events, recreating in one of his most famous works, "Memorial Day," the sounds of the progress of a parade down Main Street to its end at Wooster Cemetery.

This was a horse-drawn world, and Danbury's downtown offered several large livery stables and a dozen blacksmith shops in 1889. One resident of the era remembered "the smell of a livery stable's open doors with its mixture of hay, feed, well-oiled harness and equipment added to those of the horses, liniment and manure pile out back, all recognizable even in the dark." Watering troughs for the city's horses were landmarks at such locations as the center of Wooster Square, the end of Balmforth Avenue at North Street, and on South Street at the end of Main. Runaways or bolting horses were common and their misadventures appeared regularly in the newspapers. A horse represented a considerable investment, and a group called the Anti-Horsethief Association remained active. Horses offered an avenue for recreation as well: A signal event of every winter was the amassing of enough snow to allow horse-drawn sleighs to travel down North Street, the favored straightaway, or explore country roads like Sugar Hollow where riders could enjoy hot cider and donuts at the Maplewood Inn.

RURAL DANBURY

Outside city limits, farming was the lifeblood of rural Danbury. Its landscape was a typical Connecticut quilt of meadows with lengthy stone walls, cultivated fields, scattered woodlands, swamps and barren, rocky hillsides. Despite its agrarian character, a long, slow decline in local farming begun after the Civil War continued in the town as hatting enjoyed its reign in the city. In the 1870s, Samuel C. Wildman of Danbury painted a bleak picture of local agriculture in a letter to the state Bureau of Labor Statistics. "Many farms in this locality," he wrote, "have been abandoned and our hills, where once roamed thousands of sheep and cattle, are now covered with wild vines and weeds." Area farmers like Wildman blamed the lack of farm laborers for what was called at the time "rural abandonment." According to state statistics, Danbury's farmland declined in value by 15 percent during a ten-year period in the late 1800s, and the amount of land under cultivation decreased by 20 percent during the same period.

The picture of local farming was not uniformly gloomy. Rail connections to urban markets caused most local farmers to turn increasingly to commercial production of milk. In 1917, over 50 percent of Danbury's total acreage remained in agricultural use, and close to 200 Danbury farms produced 8,000 quarts of milk a day – far more than any of the neighboring rural towns. At the same time, grain shipped in by train from the fertile prairie states supplanted locally grown feed sources. By the late 1880s, Oscar Meeker's and three other large feed-and-grain operations were providing local farmers with much of their feed, while several big hardware stores downtown – Danbury Hardware, Hull & Rogers – kept them supplied with tools and their other needs.

The fortunes of dairying determined the course of agriculture and rural life in Danbury, where most local dairy farms were small operations. On remote King Street in the early part of the century there were at least seven farms of 15 cows each. Small commercial dairies supplied the city with milk and dairy products, while surplus milk was shipped out of town by railroad, usually to Bridgeport. Paul Ruffles described the daily routine on his family's King Street dairy farm in the period before 1920, an account that would be equally accurate for 1889:

> We used to get up at 3:30 every morning to milk the cows, then load five milk cans after we had finished milking … hitch up the horses and drive a half mile across the fields and into the woods to a cold bubbling spring with a cement vat built around it. After placing the cans in the water to keep them cool, return to the barn to clean up. By 7 my father would be back at the spring to reload the cans on the wagon. This time he would drive [the wagon] back through the fields and then out on the roads to Danbury. It used to take him half an hour – if the dirt roads were in good shape – to reach the railroad station on White Street, six miles away. There he would see his cans aboard the baggage car of the 8 a.m. to Stamford, where a dealer would pick them up. During the winter when snow blocked the roads, he put the cans on a sled and drove across the fields and over the stone walls to Danbury. [You could because] all of King Street was open pasture land then, except for the woods.

Farmers in the Mill Plain area had a slightly easier trip than Mr. Ruffles. They brought their milk to a small railroad depot originally built on the New York–New England line that operated there until 1927.

Necessarily, the main crops grown in Danbury were the hay and feed corn consumed by dairy livestock. Haying was an early summer chore on all the farms. It required the help of strong farmhands to pitch machine-mown hay into heaps then haul it to the barn, where ropes and pulleys lifted the 400-pound bales into the mow, or hayloft. Horses drew the mowing machine, the hay rake and the wagon that moved the hay.

A few farmers in northeastern Danbury cultivated tobacco, which was grown in the open sun throughout the upper Housatonic Valley, and there was even a tobacco warehouse in the city at one point. However, tobacco had little local impact. For some farmers in fertile parts of town like the Great Plain district, where the Howard Shepard family made a living growing vegetables and berries for sale in city markets for more than 60 years, there were opportunities to grow and sell crops.

In enterprises scattered throughout the town, people made a living from other products of the land. The Danbury Lime Company operated an extensive quarry near what is now Rogers Park, and there were other lime quarrying and burning operations in the Beaver Brook district. A granite quarry on Brushy Hill supplied stone for several well-known local buildings – St. Peter's Church and Hearthstone Castle among them. In Westville, O'Brien's sawmill produced railroad ties, bridge parts and fence posts from trees that were slid down the surrounding hillsides on ice. Six different ponds around the town, including Oil Mill Pond off Lake Avenue and Doyle's, Sanford's and Merson's Ponds, provided ice in winter, supporting several ice-cutting firms that supplied households who needed it for refrigeration. A number of mills harnessed the Still River in the Beaver Brook district east of the city limits. McArthur's paper mill produced strawboard dried on the hillside for hatboxes and wrapping paper used in hardware stores.

For most area residents, rural or urban, the Danbury Fair was the highlight of the year, celebrating the city's connection to a large and productive agricultural belt that encompassed northern Fairfield County, lower Litchfield County, and adjacent parts of Dutchess and Putnam counties in New York State. Held in early October, the fair had grown steadily since its beginnings in 1869, when local interests withdrew from the Fairfield County Agricultural Society after that organization chose Norwalk as a permanent site for its fair. By the late 1880s Danbury's own fair, run by the Danbury Agricultural Society, had grown to the point where it outdrew the combined attendance of all similar events held in the state. Its physical nucleus was largely in place by 1889: a grandstand and race track for trotting horses, livestock buildings, stables, three big tents, a main building – and what came to be referred to in later years as a midway. However, the fair's widespread fame as a "Big E" style amusement-park/ old-time agricultural fair would not come until the 20th century.♦

Two early buildings of Danbury Hospital: the original wooden building from 1890, and the brick "Center Building" completed in 1908. The hilltop location of the new institution was thought to be therapeutic.

The Price
of Progress

Danbury sailed into the 1890s on a wave of civic pride. Scarcely a month went by without an announcement in the pages of *The Danbury Evening News* of the formation of some new social club or the completion of an additional downtown business block. Immensely proud of their young municipality, Danburians sought to keep pace with long established Connecticut cities. Having already erected a series of respectable and up-to-date public buildings, including several schools, a City Hall and a hospital, residents demanded similar high-quality facilities from major organizations operating in their newly chartered city. In the 1890s, Danbury business and civic leaders petitioned the United States Congress for a modern post office; the state government for a fitting courthouse; and the New York, New Haven & Hartford Railroad for a more suitable railroad station. In all these campaigns they were both patient and persuasive.

As if to celebrate the buoyant mood of the time, Danbury businessmen displayed their wares at the famous Chicago World's Fair in 1893. Hardware merchant and capitalist Frederick A. Hull sponsored a presentation that promoted his Kentucky coal mine investments. Reclusive violin-maker Lucius Wildman, whose combination home and workshop was a small converted farm building in the remote reaches of the Stadley Rough district, exhibited some of his imaginative "bird violins," which featured exquisitely carved singing birds perched atop each instrument's neck. Hat manufacturer John W. Green secured an exclusive franchise to market souvenir ladies' fans decorated with scenes of the "White City." A number of Danburians made the trip by rail to Chicago.

However, life in the young municipality involved more than celebration. During the 1890s and the early 1900s, Danburians struggled to respond effectively as their city transitioned from an easy-to-govern, semi-rural town to a tightly packed city of nearly 20,000 people with complex environmental and human needs. The boomtown mentality had to give way to a sober search for courses of action on a number of fronts: establishing new institutions and reforming old ones, expanding or creating a physical infrastructure, absorbing growing numbers of immigrants arriving from distant and unfamiliar places, and dealing with ever more frequent disruptions of the local economy because of growing conflict between management and labor in the hat industry. Elected governmental officials and dedicated private citizens shared responsibility for facing these challenges rooted in the city's rapid growth, just as they shared both credit and blame for the mixed record of success in their efforts.

For the first time, it was the city's women who provided the momentum for the creation and administration of a system of social services that encompassed the hospital, an orphanage known as the Children's Home and an organization called Associated Charities, which was established in the late 19th century to provide assistance to the poor. Connecticut's first licensed female doctor, homeopath Sophia Penfield, was a key figure in charity work and at the hospital, where she was admitted as a staff physician in 1908. But most of the women involved in these efforts were wives and daughters of the city's elite who had the necessary leisure time along with the motivation to serve the larger community. Most belonged to the Congregational Church, where the teachings of the Social Gospel were influential.

The Mary Wooster Chapter of the Daughters of the American Revolution (DAR), chartered in 1893, became the incubator for several creative reforms. The group resorted to an unorthodox approach to raise funds for a local history museum. In 1895, the women of the DAR persuaded the owners of the *Danbury Evening News* to let them publish a special issue of the newspaper which they hoped would call attention to their project. Although in their own words the DAR members "didn't know business from birdshot," they turned out a more-than-respectable product, at 20 pages longer than any previous Danbury newspaper. The amateur editors advocated physical fitness – bicycling – and freedom in dress. They used wry humor to chide male readers, such as featuring a "Man's Page" instead of the "Women's Page" common in the newspapers of the day. The experiment was a huge success, resulting in two sold-out runs. Sale of the first copies at auction generated enough interest that thousands more were ultimately purchased, many by out-of-town customers. As a result of the issue's popularity, the organization was able, in 1900, to finance an historical room

Courtesy of Danbury Museum & Historical Society Authority

Broadview Farm, completed in the midst of a depression in 1894 atop Hayes' Hill. Built to reform Danbury's care of the poor, it proved expensive to equip and operate, never came close to housing its capacity of 150 residents before it closed in 1962, and came to be regarded as a boondoggle by some. The crops shown in this view furnished provisions for the town's other poor residents from a "town store" located in City Hall.

Courtesy of Western Connecticut State University Archives

One of Danbury Normal School's first professors, Lothrop Higgins. Higgins taught at the school from 1905, the year after it opened, until he became its principal in 1923. Here he is lecturing in the then-state-of-the-art science facility in the school's single building at the time, known today as Old Main.

in the new courthouse building. The Danbury chapter of the Red Cross also came into existence at a DAR meeting in 1906, primarily through the efforts of DAR member Julia Brush and Dr. William C. Wile.

With the model of a small village hospital in England as their ideal, another cluster of women took steps in 1882 to establish a similar facility in Danbury. Early backers like Jennie Tweedy, Mrs. Theodore Tweedy and Sarah Ives were members, by birth or marriage, of elite families that had long been at the forefront of civic improvement efforts. They wisely enlisted powerful male allies, particularly *Danbury News* publisher James Montgomery Bailey, who lent indispensable editorial muscle to the project and also served as the hospital committee's first president. All local physicians voiced their support, but the generosity of one of them in particular was crucial – Dr. Alpheus Adams. Adams donated two adjoining cottages that he owned on Crane Street as a site for the hospital, which opened there in 1885. Surprisingly, the first years were difficult as many citizens shunned the tiny institution they judged to be exclusively a refuge for the poor. In an effort to reverse this negative image, the hospital's board of managers, with financial support from the state, built a larger and more impressive Queen Anne-style structure that could accommodate 30 patients. Erected on town-owned land atop Hayes Hill, it was only a short distance from the Crane Street buildings.

The public now embraced the attractive facility that opened in January 1890. Organizations like the hatters' and trimmers' unions donated furnishings for hospital rooms. Women, who held a majority of the positions on the board of directors, plunged into fundraising. An annual "charity sociable" became a fixture at City Hall. With public acceptance, the facility, now called Danbury Hospital, began to grow, adding a training school for nurses in 1903. Six doctors approved by the Danbury Medical Society and headed by veteran physician Dr. William Wile constituted a competent staff. In 1908, the first brick building, known today as the Center Building, replaced the wooden hospital, doubling the number of beds to 60. However, by World War I, admissions had risen to 1,500 a year, forcing the institution to convert public solariums to patient rooms. The hospital planned to undertake an urgent major expansion in the postwar years.

A decade after the hospital opened its doors, other reform-minded local citizens, concerned that most young women in the area who wanted to be teachers could not afford to travel to, or board at, the distant existing training facilities in the state, managed to snatch the honor of hosting the fourth state normal school from Waterbury in a harrowing duel played out in the Connecticut General Assembly. Led by John Perkins, the young principal of Danbury High School, the community mobilized to effectively present, at the 1903 session of the legislature, the city's case to be the host for the first teacher-training school in the western part of Connecticut. A special town meeting approved spending $10,000 to purchase land for a school building to help counter the arguments of influential Waterbury interests that it (Waterbury), not Danbury, should be the home of the next normal school. Danbury Representative Charles Hoffman, a Republican, introduced a bill to locate a state school in Danbury. When legislative hearings began in March 1903, organized groups of Danbury citizens sporting blue badges bearing the slogan "Normal school for Danbury" jammed morning trains to Hartford. They overflowed the Connecticut State Capitol hearing room and forced the session to be moved to the nearby Supreme Court building. So well-prepared were the Danbury forces that they were able to present completed architect's renderings of a proposed school building when challenged by a Waterbury loyalist. The final state Senate votes on the measures affecting Danbury's candidacy produced a tie that Lieutenant-Governor Henry Roberts broke in Danbury's favor, earning him the distinction of having a street near the college named in his honor. Octogenarian fur manufacturer Alexander Moss White, donor of the Danbury Public Library, solved the problem of a proper site for the school, which had to be convenient to trolley lines and the railroad station, by offering three acres of his 300-acre farm on White Street for this purpose.

The Danbury Normal School opened in 1904 with classes held on the top floor of the high school while the building, now known as "Old Main" on the Western Connecticut State University campus, was under construction. Perkins, named the first principal of the new school, held that position for the next 20 years. Most of the students were women from working-class backgrounds, including a sizable number from the families of hatters. A minority of students lived at a distance far enough to prohibit them from commuting to classes by train. Instead, they lived with local women like Mary Howarth, a member of the school's first class. Howarth regularly boarded 20 female students in her house on White Street.

Students at the Danbury Normal School received special preparation for teaching in rural schools. Danbury's was the only state training school to require that all students devote 20 weeks of their training to service in one- or two-room country schools like Danbury's own Miry Brook, King Street or Beaver Brook schools. By 1918, one-third of the schoolrooms in the Danbury system, including the entire 14-room Balmforth Avenue and eight-room Locust Avenue schools, were operated as practice facilities for Danbury Normal School students.

While the volunteer spirit provided momentum for advances in social services and education during these early years, town and city governments carried most of the burden of managing the transition from semi-rural town to small industrial city. In the city's earliest days, mayors tended to be manufacturers or downtown merchants while councilmen and town selectmen were mostly hatters or operators of small businesses. Each of the city's four wards developed a political character that persisted for decades. The patrician First Ward in the northwest section, home of many factory owners, reliably voted Republican while the Irish working class residents made the Fourth Ward on Town Hill and South Street a Democratic bulwark. Particularly striking from today's perspective is the almost complete absence of lawyers, doctors and other professionals from participation in city or town government. Few members of either party in Danbury other than J. Moss Ives, who served as Judge-Advocate General of the Connecticut National Guard during the terms of four governors, held statewide positions. The only Danburians to run for state office between 1890 and 1920 were Republican Charles S. Peck, a candidate for lieutenant governor in 1912, and Charles T. Peach, a printer who was the Socialist Party nominee for lieutenant governor in 1908 and for Congress in 1910. Neither of these candidates was successful.

Both town and city governments shared responsibility for creating and updating the complex physical infrastructure required after decades of booming growth. Elections held every other year encouraged frequent changes in power that continued to handicap implementation of long-range projects. For the sake of economy and expediency, city officials regularly ignored the advice of engineers and consultants in planning major improvements. It's not surprising that officials and voters often shied away from big infrastructure investments during a time when there was little state or federal aid available. With few exceptions, citizens and officials alike usually adopted a gradual approach, spending only what was necessary to solve immediate problems as they occurred. Despite these daunting obstacles, Danbury completed several major public works projects conceived during its borough days, including expanded reservoirs and a sewer system.

The creation of West Lake Reservoir illustrates the pitfalls of this gradualist approach. First proposed in 1880 by a borough committee as part of a master expansion plan, it was meant to take advantage of Boggs Pond, a prized body of water located just northwest of the city. The pond was estimated to be 150 acres in size and to contain about 200 million gallons of water. With its great size, and its water believed to be so free of vegetation, Boggs Pond could be used immediately. But when controversy arose over the cost and a local physician challenged the water's quality, worried borough voters rescinded the appropriation for it and approved instead a reservoir on Padanaram Brook. A decade later, when a serious drought caused the water levels in all the city's reservoirs to plunge to a two-week supply, the desperate officials again decided to tap Boggs Pond despite the extra expense of building a pumping station on the Rundle & White farm (today Ridgewood Country Club). The following year, 1892, Republican Mayor Charles S. Peck once again recommended construction of a large reservoir on Boggs Pond.

Almost immediately, heavy spring rains created a false sense of security and enabled newly elected Democratic Mayor Charles S. Andrews to drop the plan. Finally, in 1904, another water emergency occurred that was so severe that some residents couldn't get water during the daytime when demands of factories were heavy. At this point, city officials persuaded the General Assembly to issue $200,000 in bonds to pay for what became West Lake Reservoir on Boggs Pond. Before construction, however, another change in administration prompted the hiring of a new engineer whose faulty blueprints delayed the project's completion for more than a year. By the time West Lake finally came on line in 1907, not only had the initial acquisition expense increased dramatically but the frequent design changes had inflated the total cost as well. In their 1908 report, the city's water commissioners felt compelled to practically apologize for the reservoir's fitful history while at the same time boasting that the town reservoirs for the first time contained over a billion gallons of water. The 1914 report of the superintendent of water works went even further. "Our supply is ample for a city of 75,000 people; in fact we now store more water than most of the other cities in the state; with waste eliminated entirely we [will] have water enough to make the City of Danbury one of the most beautiful cities in the country," he asserted.

The piecemeal and least expensive approach proved to be disastrous in the case of the city's sewage system. In 1880, growing awareness that sewage-contaminated water spread diseases like cholera and typhoid fever led the Village Improvement Society to propose building sewers in the borough.* A survey done a few years later in 1885 found that of 2,800 families then residing there, only 600 had underground cesspools; the rest discharged their waste either directly into a stream or into outdoor privies. In June 1886, after a devastating state board of health report about conditions in Danbury, borough residents voted to build 18 miles of sewers in a "combined" system where both sanitary waste and ordinary street drainage would be collected and discharged into the Still River at a distant outfall point. As more sewers were added, the plan called for moving the discharge location farther out of the settled part of the borough and, if necessary, to provide some minimal purification at an indefinite future time.

This approach represented a deliberate decision to break the law. Fouling a river was a violation of the rights of downstream property owners, referred to in the law as holding 'riparian rights.' The borough rejected the recommendation of its own eminent consultants, Rudolph Hering, the father of modern environmental technology, and George Waring, founder of New York City's Department of Sanitation, who advised Danbury officials in no uncertain terms to treat the sewage before discharging it into the Still River. Stunned by Hering's estimate that it would cost a quarter of a million dollars to build a proper sewage treatment plant, officials refused to change their approach. Prominent Danbury attorney Arthur Averill predicted that the borough was inviting litigation from every property owner on the Still River downstream of the outfall sewer. Ammon T. Peck, a civic gadfly, chided in a letter to the *Evening News*, "see the statutes and read them carefully, you open sewer men, who seem to be deficient in the sense of smell!"

Opponents of the plan were advised to "never cross a bridge until you get to it," Peck later recalled, but his warning proved to be prophetic.

---

* This group of old Yankee families concerned with the aesthetic effects of their former village's rapid growth was also responsible for three small triangular parks at Division Street, Franklin Street and Jefferson Avenue, and for placing statues at some of them.

Construction of the outfall sewer to the Still River at Cross Street began in the summer of 1891. Just as Peck anticipated, it wasn't long before downstream property owners began to complain. The river's water was so fouled with untreated sewage and industrial wastes from the city that dark brown scum covered the surface of the water impounded behind milldams. Workers in mills located in the Beaver Brook district could not go outside without becoming nauseated. George W. Morgan, owner of a Beaver Brook cider mill, joined by an informal "alliance" of over 70 mill owners and farmers who owned land or used the Still River along its northeasterly course through Danbury and Brookfield, brought a lawsuit (Morgan v. Danbury) to require the city to stop polluting the river. Even the normally tight-fisted Town of Brookfield voted a $300 appropriation to support the litigation, and at least one cash-strapped farmer offered to pay his contribution to the legal fees with livestock.

Hoping to bolster its case after the suit was filed in 1893, the city installed a rudimentary treatment system that merely deodorized the sewage with lime during the summer months when the river level was so low in some places that people could cross its bed by jumping from stone to stone. The city defended its actions by arguing that it had a governmental duty to provide sewers, that the river had been systematically fouled for years by the hat industry, and that it planned to filter the waste. Superior Court Judge George Wakeman Wheeler didn't buy any of it. In August 1895 he issued a sweeping permanent injunction against municipal pollution, ordering the city to build a filtration plant by 1897. As for the disinfecting plant the city had already built, Wheeler saw it not as a remedy but as an admission of guilt.

The decision made headlines as the broadest injunction ever issued in such a case up to that time. It had ramifications far beyond Danbury. Connecticut cities that were located on small, sluggish streams, or even on Long Island Sound or on major rivers now all faced the threat of similar court action if they did not treat municipal sewage before discharging it. The winning legal team, which included Probate Judge Leonard McMahon of New Milford and a young Danbury lawyer, Charles W. Murphy, soon pursued a similar suit against the city of Waterbury for polluting the Naugatuck River.

Wheeler's decision withstood appeal in Connecticut's Supreme Court, forcing the city to settle the damage suits from downstream property owners. In addition, Danbury purchased a farm on Plumtrees Road where it constructed the mandated sewage treatment plant with its filter beds, and in later years established a town dump. But it was not the end of litigation over Still River pollution. In 1902, attorney McMahon threatened to sue the city again, claiming it was not operating the filtration plant properly. More lawsuits made their way to court in 1933 and 1947, again from property owners in Beaver Brook and Brookfield. In the end, the ill-considered decision to disregard its consultants' advice in 1886 cost the city dearly.

In dealing with social problems connected with poverty, a responsibility the state assigned to each community, Danbury leaders took a more generous, though not necessarily more effective, course of action. By the early 1890s, the town almshouse on Osborne Street – since 1869 the only facility set aside to assist so-called paupers – had become a scandal, sheltering mostly indigent elderly men in conditions labeled "wholly inadequate" by the Connecticut State Board of Charities. In 1893, a town meeting during which participants ignored a looming depression, yielded a decision to build an almshouse that would be a credit to the young city. An appropriation for this purpose was as large as the one the town had authorized for construction of City Hall eight years earlier. As one proponent explained, Danbury wanted "a new building and care of the poor that would not be a shame on Christianity." Voters rejected an unobtrusive location on King Street in favor of a hilltop expanse perched above the hospital with a commanding view of the city, now the site of Broadview Junior High School. The selectmen visited existing poor farms in other parts of the state and then hired a well-known architect, Warren Briggs, to design a massive, three-story Romanesque dormitory building surrounded by fields of vegetables, apple orchards, and a barn. Danbury proudly opened Broadview Farm in 1894.

Although attractive and comfortable, the model institution was also expensive to operate. As shocked selectmen discovered, the original appropriation covered only the cost of the building. When equipping the farm was added, the total outlay for the project more than doubled. In 1899, a bipartisan committee headed by Republican hat manufacturer D. E. Loewe sought to determine why each year the operation of the farm and other expenses of caring for the poor consumed up to 20 percent of the town budget, even though Broadview never came close to housing its capacity of 140 residents. One answer the Loewe committee found was that the $3.35 per week it took to lodge each person was the highest in Connecticut, almost double the state average.

With so many unexpected expenses coinciding with national economic depressions in 1893, 1897 and 1907, it is not surprising that Danbury's government sought ways to economize. For several reasons, assistance to the so-called "outdoor poor" – people who lived independently but needed temporary help with food or shelter – was a vulnerable target. The primitive aid process, suited to a small town but not to a growing city where selectmen investigated each appeal case-by-case and issued a voucher on the town to merchants, was time-consuming. One can sense the frustration in the official report about efforts to help the needy in the difficult depression years of 1894-95. "We can only say we have done the best we could," selectmen pleaded. This antiquated system was also expensive. Small grants to those in distress regularly totaled 10 percent of the town budget, a figure close to the sum spent on the public schools. Even more irritating, as a procedure without adequate recordkeeping it invited waste and – even worse – fraud. The Loewe Committee found that, with the cooperation of unscrupulous storeowners, town funds bought a variety of nonessential items like cigars and whisky. By 1904, a series of reforms, including establishment of a town store at City Hall (stocked with produce from Broadview Farm) as the exclusive source of provisions for the needy, reduced the amount spent on the outdoor poor by one-half.

Between 1890 and 1920, Danbury also struggled to provide school buildings worthy of its rising status. The way the town government, responsible for education policy, met the emerging need for an adequate high school illustrates the perennial conflict between an ideal solution and available resources. During the 1890s, the principal and four teachers offered only a three-year program to tiny classes. The graduating class of 1893, for example, consisted of 12 students, eight of them girls.

But by the early 20th century, a state law that raised the age of mandatory school attendance, combined with growing opportunities for middle class occupations that required a higher level of preparation, fueled parents' and progressive educators' demands for construction of a separate high-school building. Debate over the best location for the facility, along with heated town meetings over the proposed cost, dragged on for several years before Danbury's first high-school building opened in September 1903 at the corner of Main and Boughton Streets. Boasting two floors of classrooms and a third-floor assembly room that could seat 500, the building was clearly intended to meet the city's needs for the foreseeable future. It was ample enough to accommodate students from Danbury's public grammar schools and St. Peter's and Immanuel Lutheran's parochial schools, as well as children from area towns like Brookfield and New Fairfield whose towns paid their tuition because their towns lacked high schools. In 1905, the high school introduced a four-year course. A year later, enrollment broke one hundred for the first time.

However, to the chagrin of education authorities who had not anticipated the city's 20 percent population spurt between 1900 and 1910, the facility reached its capacity in just six years. Two classrooms needed to be carved out of attic space and by 1910, the still-new high school was so crowded it had to resort to double sessions. As members of the town school committee weighed a solution, they realized that they had to simultaneously cope with the bigger problem that all Danbury schools were now filled to capacity. In fact, congestion was severe enough in 1914 that a desperate Danbury made an unsuccessful proposal to acquire St. Peter's School to provide more space. Four years later authorities opened a temporary elementary school in a former butcher shop on White Street. In this frantic atmosphere, a chastened school committee proposed, in 1918, a massive expansion that would triple the size of the high-school building and also house a junior high school. "We wish to avoid the mistake we made in 1904," a board member confided to the *Evening News*. Wartime circumstances, however, prevented any action on this radical plan.

The privately managed Danbury Fair also faced a serious challenge during these years, when fire destroyed many of the fair's original buildings just after the season ended in October of 1897. The Agricultural Society, which ran the fair, used the occasion to re-grade the grounds, cutting off the top of a knoll to accommodate an enlarged amphitheater that stretched more than 800 feet from end to end (but would burn down in the early 1920s). The investment paid off as the annual October event continued to grow. In 1910, the fair attracted a record crowd of over 70,000 – more than three times Danbury's own population.

Apart from providing a fundraising opportunity for most of the city's churches, which fed the crowds at competing food stands near the race-track, the Danbury Fair introduced Danburians to new technology at the same time that it reinforced traditions based on rural life. Parades of decorated automobiles dazzled crowds during the early 1900s, when only a handful of people owned the new machines. Auto races joined trotter races as a feature at the fair's racetrack by 1910, when an automobile spun out of control and tore through a fence, injuring several spectators. The flatness of the fairgrounds site made it attractive for early barnstorming aviators, who began appearing at the fair only a few years after the Wright Brothers' pioneering flight in 1903, and within a decade Danburians began training to become aviators. Despite difficulties, the Danbury Fair prospered because it bridged the gap between two eras: While new-fangled airplanes buzzed overhead, local farmers continued to display their prize vegetables and livestock.

Nevertheless, the boomtown era that brought the city into existence was definitely over. In November 1903, when Revered Harry Meserve visited Danbury for the first time, the city still struggled to emerge from the devastating depression that began a decade earlier. The 35-year-old minister was also at a crucial point in his career. After graduating from Yale Divinity School in 1894, and having served churches in Springfield, Massachusetts, and Indianapolis, Indiana, for the five years thereafter, he spent 1902 traveling extensively in Europe. The post of pastor of the First Congregational Church in Danbury offered a promising opportunity for personal influence and security for his growing family. Yet Meserve refused to commit to the church for longer than a year. Looking back at this decision from a later vantage point, he explained his hesitation: "At that time there were too many vacant houses in town, and men were walking the streets, some business men too, knocking the town and knocking it hard. They said it was a dead town." But Meserve stayed in Danbury for more than ten years and helped the city become a more prosperous and progressive place.♦

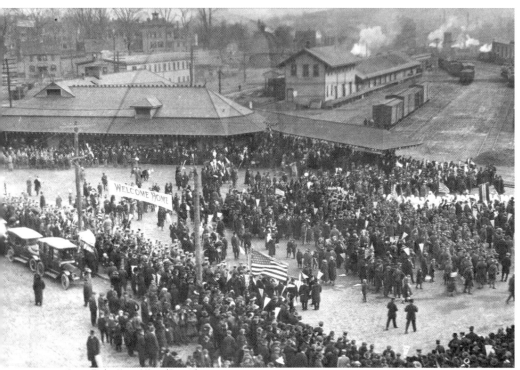

A crowd welcomes troops returning home from World War I at Danbury's Union Station on White Street. Completed in 1903, the New York, New Haven and Hartford station was architecturally unique in that it had more roof than floor space. Behind the station are the extensive yards of the "Consolidated Road," including buildings of earlier lines that had operated in Danbury.

Making
Connections

Danbury's crossroads location is its primary geographic asset. The flat terrain where the Still River collects in wetlands near the Danbury Fair Mall and begins its twisting flow east, finally turning northeast through soft limestone bedrock to the Housatonic River, marks the major break in the rampart-like hills that line the Connecticut-New York border. From the time of Danbury's settlement, east-west travel passed through this gap, intersecting with an ancient Indian path, the distant ancestor of today's Route 7, which progressed northward from Long Island Sound all the way to Canada. Because of this geographic situation, Danbury's growth has always depended on the community's ability to take advantage of improvements in transportation. Between 1890 and 1920, the city made the transition from a largely frustrating effort to expand its rail and trolley systems to a more promising opportunity offered by automobiles and trucks and the emerging network of state highways being built to accommodate them.

In the early 1900s, the railroad was still king. By the 1890s, the completion of its three separate rail lines had made Danbury the rail hub of inland western Connecticut. More than a hundred trains each day stopped or passed through the city. With a scattered mishmash of frame buildings representing passenger and freight depots of the different lines in the sprawling White Street rail yard, the city did not give the appearance of a thriving rail center. The oldest passenger depot, that of the Danbury & Norwalk built in 1852, was by this time well on its way to becoming a Main Street eyesore that many hoped to replace.

During the summer of 1893, rumors swirled that the Consolidated line (the New York, New Haven & Hartford Railroad) was acquiring property in the area of Canal Street after a company official announced that a new station would be built in the city, but nothing substantial came of it. By 1894, Danburians were dispatching petitions to the railroad requesting a new station. Finally, in 1901, the railroad realigned the tracks and con-structed the new Union Station (so-called because it served several separate lines) on the former site of the New York & New England line's passenger depot, which was moved a few yards west to where it still stands.

Completed in 1902, Union Station was meant to serve as the epicenter of the city's life. Architecturally, it was an eclectic product of the railroad's design office, resembling earlier stations in Stamford, South Norwalk and Torrington. However, the L-shaped Union Station on White Street was larger than most, and the sweeping lines of its platforms created a dramatic impression that today is not shared by its more contemporary sister stations. Its roof area is more than twice its floor area. A grand waiting room, entered through a soaring arch, at the time left little doubt about the railroad's importance to Danbury's life. Besides serving as the lifeline of the hatting industry, rails had additional economic importance to the city. Some Danburians, like composer and insurance executive Charles Ives, traveled by train to work in Bridgeport or New York City. An influx of summer boarders, bound mostly for nearby country towns, arrived by rail, as did an even greater invasion of outsiders who visited the Danbury Fair each autumn. Handling them necessitated a dedicated train and earned the fairgrounds a station of its own on the line. Underscoring Union Station's role as the doorway to Danbury, in 1913 the Danbury & Bethel Gas &

Electric Company erected an electrical sign bearing the slogan "Danbury Crowns Them All" – on the nearby property that overlooked the station – property owned by coal dealer John McCarthy. The Consolidated Road also recognized Danbury's role as a regional rail hub when it began construction of a large roundhouse and repair shop in the middle of the rail complex in 1916.

One could travel easily by train all over the northeastern United States and beyond during this period. A trip from Danbury to New York City by train took little more time than it does today. Still, some hoped to make the trip even quicker by building new connections to the city. The most promising alternative was "the Ives link," so-called because it was vigorously promoted by Isaac Ives of Danbury, uncle of the composer. A busy lumber merchant, patent-medicine peddler and promoter of entrepreneurial schemes, Ives was a flashy character who was a favorite of late nineteenth-century Danbury. Schooled in business in New York City, Ives knew firsthand the value to Danbury businessmen of speedy train transportation to the metropolis. He believed that 15 minutes or more could be shaved off the trip to New York by building a new line southwest from Danbury to connect with the Harlem Railroad (today's Metro-North Harlem line) in New York State. He promoted the idea to investors for years, but one scheme after another fell through. Finally, in 1904, a group obtained a charter from the two state legislatures and began work on the Danbury & Harlem Railroad. Though not involved financially in the line, Ives was important enough to deliver an address at its groundbreaking ceremony and to dig the first shovelful of earth. But the railroad backers were only able to construct a powerhouse at Backus Avenue and several miles of track before going bankrupt. The New York, New Haven & Hartford retained its monopoly.

Fixed-rail transportation played a key role in directing the course of Danbury's internal growth. Following the example of larger Connecticut cities like Bridgeport and New Haven, local supporters organized the Danbury & Bethel Street Railway in the mid-1880s. Tracks were laid in the middle of Main Street and horses slowly drew the enclosed passenger cars along a set route. Use of the public road by the privately owned streetcar company generated multiple episodes of friction between the city government and the railway. In 1890, the turf battle between them became so intense that Mayor Hopkins had a railway labor crew working on White Street arrested for ignoring an agreement with the city over the proper handling of granite paving blocks.

In 1892, a group of New Haven investors led by ex-Connecticut Governor Thomas M. Waller acquired Danbury's horse railway. The following year the new owners petitioned the city to convert the horse-car line to electric power as most Connecticut cities were doing at the time. Surprisingly, considering the past friction, the Common Council embraced the idea and the public eagerly purchased shares of stock to finance the $355,000 project. The retention of a prominent local businessman as president of the new company helped smooth the approval process. Hat manufacturer Samuel C. Holley, president of the Union Savings Bank and one of the organizers of the local electric company, guided the transition to electricity.

Courtesy of Danbury Museum & Historical Society Authority

A project of the Danbury & Bethel Street Railway, Kenosia Park operated from 1895 until 1924. Its centerpiece was the Hotel Kenmere, surrounded by gingerbread-trimmed balconies that were built around live trees. In the foreground is the bandstand, where concerts were held every night during summer. Here an open "summer car" of the trolley line discharges passengers.

Unexpected obstacles delayed the opening of the electrified line and its transport vehicle, now properly called a trolley, for a full year. The first electric streetcar, festooned with flags, traveled through the streets on New Year's Day, 1895, meeting with enthusiasm all along the route. Curious onlookers just getting out of church gawked at Car No. 1, built at the J.G. Brill Co. factory in Philadelphia. Passengers packed the small, enclosed car to overflowing by the time it reached the corner of White Street. *The Evening News* trumpeted, "Danbury has a trolley that is second to none in this state."

The trolley line's headquarters was on South Street, near the Bethel line in a building that today is the site of the Party Depot store. It housed a compound 250-horsepower steam engine with two steam cylinders that powered a fleet of two to three dozen cars, as well as three big sweeper cars that kept the tracks clean and free of snow in the winter. Trolley cars ran every forty minutes at first and the fare was a nickel no matter how far a rider went even if a transfer was required, as it was on some routes. By agreement with the city, the cars were allowed to travel no more than eight miles per hour. The trolley's original route followed Main Street and branched off to carry travelers all the way to the city limits in most directions. A generator on West Wooster Street and Park Avenue at Fry's Corner propelled the cars on to the Danbury Fairgrounds and Lake Kenosia via Backus Avenue.

Looking to increase ridership and revenue, the trolley company accepted the offer by an entrepreneur named Leo Lesieur, originally a carriage painter from Worcester, Mass., to build a park on six acres of the lake's southwestern shore. For his stake, Lesieur put up a gas-powered merry-go-round that he owned. The line to Kenosia opened six months after the initial trolley run, on May 24, 1895. The park was an immediate hit. "Trolley parties have become a craze," *The Evening News* reported three months after the trolley's initial run. "There is hardly a night when one or more cars full of merry men and women are not to be seen and heard being sent over the road." Most of these excursions appealed to trimmers from different local hat factories, who excitedly laughed, sang or blew horns along their way to a supper on the lakeshore after work.

Lesieur operated the park along with his wife and his brother-in-law, William H. Jarvis, until his death in the 1920s. Lesieur's nephew, C. Irving Jarvis, grew up in the park, where his first jobs were peddling popcorn and other treats to audiences in its open-air theater. The entertainment know-how the young Jarvis absorbed later helped him transform the Danbury Fair into a regional attraction as John Leahy's assistant manager in the 1950s and '60s.

Kenosia Park in its heyday was located on a six-acre wooded property (later expanded to 12.5 acres) near Kenosia Avenue that is now the site of Lake Place condominiums. At its heart was a grand, three-story hotel, the Kenmere. A thousand-seat, open-air theater was nearby, surrounded by a high wooden fence. Here summer-stock theater companies, particularly Mabel Day's Operetta Company from New York City, would perform every night during the season with a matinee on Sunday for a 25-cent admission. The Gilbert and Sullivan operettas that once constituted an entire season were especially popular. The bill often featured W.C. Fields' brother and a young ventriloquist named Edgar Bergen with his dummy, Charlie McCarthy. Below the theater, a pier anchored a fleet of 36 steel boats, all with female names, and dozens of canoes and rowboats available for hire. A bandstand stood on the shore for nightly concerts. The grounds were lavishly landscaped with exuberant Victorian favorite flowering plants like roses and hydrangea. Lesieur's merry-go-round also cranked away and later an old icehouse on the property was replaced by a small roller coaster near the lakeshore that thrilled riders. A highlight of the park was a trip on a 10-passenger motor launch named "Venus." In newspaper reporter Robina Clark's words, the Venus "plied the lake with silk flags flying and a striped awning overhead." A romantic moonlight excursion on the little lake also cost 25 cents. The summer season ended with a harvest supper hosted by the trolley company for its employees and those who worked at the park. The feast featured all the chicken and corn-on-the-cob the guests could eat.

A later addition to the lake's attractions became a "white elephant." Sometime in the early 1900s, head chef Perrie of the Hotel Green purchased a paddle-wheeled, steam-powered, Hudson-River-type day boat that seated 30, which he hauled to the lake from Norwalk by horse and wagon. Named the "Montgomery" after *Danbury News* founder James Montgomery Bailey, the craft featured a three-piece band that played during short trips around the little lake. The boat was much too big for Kenosia, and its pilot, Elmer Barnum, frequently ran it aground in the shallow waters of the former swamp. After damaging the hull in these accidents, Perrie anchored the boat in the middle of the lake for use as a floating dance hall. Finally, unable to float, it was beached and left to be used by swimmers as an improvised diving platform. The cost of a trip to this earthly paradise was a nickel trolley-ride from City Hall – although for the same price one could travel all the way from Bethel, with a free transfer of cars at City Hall.

During the summer, traveling to the lake in open trolley cars thrilled riders. There were no windows on these special cars and instead of a center aisle, benches stretched across the interior. "Riders climbed aboard by mounting the double running boards that ran down the length of the trolley on both sides," remembered George Orgelman, who lived along the trolley line on West Street and rode the cars in the mid-1920s. Orgelman observed that convenient public transportation influenced the dimensions of houses built along the route. With mass transit readily available, people needed smaller home lots, as they no longer kept horses that required a small barn or carriage house in the back yard.

The electric trolley proved profitable at first, paying dividends every year until 1908, when it began floundering. That led to another, albeit short-lived, impact the trolley had on Danbury life. To promote ridership, the company turned to sponsoring semi-professional baseball teams between 1912 and 1914. Their field was located adjacent to the company's barns on South Street, and could accommodate 1,800 fans. The teams – known of course as the Hatters – played in the loosely organized and often financially unstable minor leagues that were common before the development of major-league farm systems after World War I. Since the 1912 team mainly played teams in the Hudson Valley that refused to travel to Danbury, the local schedule offered only three games. But this setback proved temporary. When the 1913 season opened, Mayor Anthony Sunderland declared a town holiday and then led a parade to the stadium before the game. The next two seasons the team did well, drawing an average of a thousand fans each home game. Adult admission was a quarter, children paid a dime, and bleacher seats cost only a nickel. Factories closed during the summer months just before game time at 3:30 in the afternoon. The teams played a hundred-game season that ended on Labor Day when some of the best minor league players were elevated to the major leagues. One Danbury native, John "Bony" Blake of the Hatters, seemed headed for a promising future, but many of the players were nearing the end of their careers in 1914. However, financial woes brought on by a national depression forced the local team to disband after this season.

The Danbury street railway's problems, though, were bigger than baseball. In 1903, Charles Mellon, president of the New York, New Haven & Hartford Railroad, began buying up trolley and steamboat lines in southern New England, putting together a virtual monopoly on transportation in the region. Danbury and Bristol were the only lines in the state to resist a takeover and to remain independent. It may have been a fatal choice.

Perhaps the fate of Danbury's trolley might have been different had the monopoly come to control it. Most trolleys in Connecticut became part of an interurban network of light rail that connected cities and larger towns. However, the Danbury service area was small, predominantly rural and geographically isolated. Despite an expansion up Franklin, Hoyt and Davis streets, the Danbury & Bethel Street Railway was the shortest trolley line in the state, with only 15 miles of track. There were several attempts to break this isolation. The most ambitious route proposal, backed by manufacturer N. Burton Rogers and Danbury High School Principal John R. Perkins, would have begun near the Danbury railroad station and continued up North Street into New Fairfield, Sherman, Gaylordsville and Webatuck, New York. Spurs would have taken passengers to the summer destinations of Ball Pond and Squantz Pond. This plan never got through the General Assembly.

Courtesy of Western Connecticut State University Archives

Auto races such as this one at the Danbury Fair helped familiarize and popularize the new form of transportation to Danbury-area residents during the early twentieth century.

The city fervently hoped that the impressively named Bridgeport and Danbury Traction Company might deliver the local trolley system from its isolation, but the line never came close to reaching Danbury. Starting construction from southern Connecticut in 1912, it was only able to lay five miles of track before going bankrupt. The feeble line owned only two cars, whose dark green paint inspired sarcastic references to "grasshoppers." It never made a profit and ceased its abbreviated operations in 1915.

The struggling Danbury & Bethel Street Railway made other attempts to boost profits besides operating a baseball team and an amusement park. In 1914, it expanded its power station to sell surplus electricity to Danbury and Newtown. At the same time, the company began to economize, adding less expensive but more problematic Birney safety cars, which had a reputation for riding roughly and derailing easily. When economic hard times hit during World War I, the trolley line was vulnerable.

In 1895, the same year the electric trolley debuted in Danbury, the city got its first glimpse of its successor. Startled city residents gawked as A. Homer Fillow tooled around the streets in what he called his "contraption," an automobile he pieced together at a time when cars were still in the experimental stage. Fillow, at the time chief engineer of the Danbury and Bethel Gas and Electric Light Company, would go on in later years to open one of the city's first commercial auto garages on Crosby Street and to serve two terms as mayor of the city between 1927 and 1931. Other tinkerers, mechanic Matthew Barber of Westville district and machinist William Bacchus, are also credited with crafting home-built automobiles that they took for spins around the city during the same time period.

The introduction of the automobile and the highway construction that accompanied it provided the connections to the outside world that once again made Danbury another kind of transportation hub. The motor vehicle would come to dominate life in the Danbury region, though that process took decades to complete. It had an impact on everything from the condition and paving materials of local roads and streets to the location and style of buildings. It ushered in new types of businesses as service stations, car dealerships and auto repair shops began to replace the city's many blacksmith shops and livery stables.

But most of that would not begin to occur until decades after Homer Fillow's jaunt through the streets of Danbury. In their infancy, automobiles posed little threat to the dominance of rail and horses. Danburians had plenty of opportunities to admire early automobiles displayed as futuristic curiosities at the annual Danbury Fair, but cars remained enough of a novelty that the sight of one parked at a livery stable or on the streets attracted hundreds of onlookers. At the turn of the century, only a handful of city residents actually owned a car. Among the first to embrace the automobile were doctors, who found them ideal for traveling to house calls. The police department's first motor vehicle was a motorcycle, only added in 1912, and the fire department resisted motor apparatus until 1910. So impressed was Mayor William Gilbert with the test runs of the fire department's new 40-horsepower Pope-Hartford chemical and hose wagon that year that he arranged a test race to a bonfire on South Street. The new engine roared out of the Ives Street headquarters at the same time as a horse-drawn hose wagon charged out of the Boughton Street station. Despite the discrepancy in distances traveled, the auto engine passed the horse cart as they turned onto South Street, arriving there in just under two minutes. The stunt helped promote public acceptance of the motorized age.

Although Connecticut adopted strict traffic regulations for automobiles in 1901, city officials regularly dealt with complaints of cars "speeding" in the business district at up to 15 miles an hour. At first, owners parked their cars in existing barns and carriage houses. There were stories told of people who tried to control the unfamiliar vehicles by crying "whoa!" as if the car were a horse, before crashing through the rear wall of their barn. By World War I, the first tiny garages and narrow gravel driveways began to appear as appendages to newly built homes. In 1904, there had been only 62 automobiles registered in the city, and acquisition of a "horseless carriage" would prompt a mention in *The Evening News*. Ten years later, an array of brands – dominated by the relatively inexpensive Ford Model T but also including long-vanished makes – could easily be spotted. Even the battle over a power system hadn't yet been settled, with gas, electric and even steam-powered vehicles vying with each other on the streets.

In 1908, Connecticut began construction of what would become Route 7 by improving historic Sugar Hollow Road. At the same time, Stony Hill Road and a section of Mill Plain Road also became part of the state system of "trunk highways" that connected major population centers. As in the past with turnpikes and railroads, Danbury's Main Street became the local hub of this system, the focal point where all sinews converged. Other downtown streets like White Street and North Street also became part of these state routes, adding to growing local automobile traffic. As early as 1916, an inspector for the street railway counted more than 200 automobiles an hour passing Danbury's City Hall on a Sunday afternoon in June – many of the "machines" traveling two abreast from Main up West Street. Frustrated motorists began to call for the removal of the Civil War Monument from its position in the middle of West Street at Main. The police department was compelled to add traffic duty officers to the force.

Street paving evolved to accommodate the automobile and became a source of public debate. In the late 1880s, the parts of Main and adjacent streets that made up the busiest parts of the downtown business district had been surfaced with granite blocks, which provided excellent footing for horses in slippery weather. During the first days of city government in the early 1890s, remaining city streets adjacent to the business area were 'macadamized,' covered with an eight-inch bed of tightly-packed gravel that tapered to six inches at the curbside gutters and were sprayed with oil. Remaining streets in the town and city were dirt-surfaced, and had to be sprinkled frequently (daily in the heavily-traveled city) by horse-drawn sprinkler carts. In the early years of the 20th century, the town government extended macadam or gravel covering to major dirt and mud country roads including Great Plain, Beaver Brook and Padanaram, providing even these rural areas with reliable roads.

By 1915, thanks to the militancy of automobile owners, the topic of paving materials on downtown streets consumed hours of contentious debate in meetings of the City Council and Board of Aldermen. New homeowners and operators of businesses demanded more paved roads and better maintenance of graveled ones. The newly organized Chamber of Commerce in 1915 recommended replacing the granite blocks on Main Street with wooden ones more suitable for automobile travel. City government ultimately responded by approving a major street resurfacing program in 1919, the same year that the last livery stable in the city ceased operation. To emphasize that the age of the automobile had begun in Danbury, authorities removed the horse-watering tank that had stood in Wooster Square for half a century.♦

The Frank H. Lee Hat Co. factory on
Leemac Avenue, the biggest in the
country when it was built in 1906,
employed upwards of a thousand
workers.

A Bloodless
Civil War

What the *New York Herald* had once called "America's model union town" didn't last. Major lockouts or strikes disrupted all or part of Danbury's chief – and only – industry four times between 1890 and 1909, rightly or wrongly earning the city a reputation as a place of "labor troubles." Some of these struggles grabbed national attention and had nationwide ramifications, but all of the clashes created division and bitterness within the community. By 1917, labor-management relations had deteriorated to the point that a visiting industrial consultant observed, "It is very noticeable in Danbury that there is a strong class feeling."

There were several reasons for the growing discord. Pressure from middle-men to cut costs, cutthroat competition among manufacturers, and the introduction of more and more labor-saving machines led to manufacturers' anxiety about dealing with unions. So did a growing inclination of both unions and manufacturers to maximize their strengths by joining national organizations, which tended to be less accommodating in reaching agreements than one's neighbors. In Danbury, all these trends coincided with determined efforts by manufacturers, usually led by Charles H. Merritt, and later his son Walter Gordon Merritt, to break union control in the trade once and for all.

Behind the bickering over bills of prices and union-label campaigns that triggered local incidents, the hatters' role in the shops was the root of the real conflicts. As Alson Smith, son of a Methodist minister who grew up in Danbury during this time, wrote in a memoir, "The [hatters] were fighting losing battles on two fronts: against the mass production methods that were making simple jobs out of a once-great craft, and against the immigrants who flocked into town to take the simple jobs created by the newfangled machinery." Would hatters still be able to see themselves as independent (and independent-minded) craftsmen, their skills indispensable, their dignity intact, as manufacturers came more and more to consider them as mere machine tenders? By the early 1900s, Danbury hat factory owners, convinced they were fighting their own losing battle with non-union competitors in other cities, concluded that to survive they had to free themselves from what they saw as arbitrary union rules and customs – from what they called the unions' "monopoly of labor." However, they could never form a united front against labor. None of the major conflicts closed down every hat shop in the city. The most severe outbreaks affected the vast majority of the workforce, but some hatters were still at work during each of these episodes.

Labor-management conflicts in Danbury had some common characteristics. National depressions regularly led to breakdowns in normally peaceful relations. Disruptions usually took place between the production seasons, when new contracts were being negotiated and when many shops were partially or entirely shut down anyway. When disputes boiled over into lockouts or strikes, each side had its weapons of choice. The unions took advantage of their strength in numbers through use of the union label, the nationwide boycott, and the local ballot box. Manufacturers turned again and again to the lockout, the lawsuit, and threats to leave town. Victory in a strike or lockout simply meant that one side was able to outlast the other. Union locals faced challenges in raising strike relief funds for their members, so benefit performances and fundraisers of all kinds abounded in the city during lockouts and strikes. Manufacturers had greater access to funds but could not afford to allow stoppages to drag on for too long lest they lose seasonal orders, which could cost half a year's profits. In the words of a hatters' ballad of the time, it was "a game of bluff." But no matter how long and bitter these battles became, Danbury "set a record for deportment," as *The Danbury Evening News* crowed at the end of a six-month "tie-up" in 1909. Not a single verifiable incident of violence in Danbury was recorded between 1890 and 1909 despite four major conflicts. During a big lockout in 1893, the crime rate actually dropped. Violence, even toward workers called scabs for working during a strike and considered despicable excuses for men, was not a part of the traditional culture of hatters. "Visitors to Danbury," *The Evening News* reported after the long strike of 1909, "marveled at the quiet and tranquility that they found. Men who have made a study of great strikes have said that they never had found better conditions existing under similar circumstances. Danbury and its neighbors are justly proud of all these things."

There were good reasons for such equanimity. Of the major hatting centers in the country, Danbury was perhaps the only city whose economy was completely dependent on the product. Most believed that "the prosperity of employers and employed must in the long run be inseparable." Danbury was a small city, its manufacturers and workers crossed paths daily, attended the same churches and lived near one another if not in the same neighborhood. Employers, as many as three-quarters of whom were former "bench hatters," had a natural sympathy for their workforce and might have friends and relatives in the unions. A statement by manufacturers in 1909 declared that "in this town there has never been that separation of employer from employed, which is getting to be characteristic of large industrial organizations … The employers in this town feel they have a fairly complete understanding of and sympathy with most of the difficulties of their operatives." Accommodation and compromise solved most problems, as both unions and manufacturers were willing to turn a blind eye toward violations of agreements as long as that kept the factories moving. But strikes and

Courtesy of Danbury Museum & Historical Society Authority

The determined face of Frank H. Lee, owner of Danbury's largest hat factory during the twentieth century.

lockouts, when they did occur, became a kind of bloodless civil war. "Troubles" in the hat shops affected everyone and were a disaster for the whole community, especially its business owners. The community's sympathies usually lay with the hatters and their unions; when tie-ups dragged on, community political and business leaders did their best to try to end them.

The employers in these conflicts tended to belong to a new generation. In the years between 1889 and 1920, leadership of Danbury's hat industry underwent a gradual turnover rather than a drastic change. The Tweedy, Benedict and White families, and those of other local pioneering Yankees, departed. In their places, in the 1890s, new firms and new titans of the industry emerged. Reflecting the makeup of a changing city, they were more often than not Catholic and from immigrant backgrounds. The face of the city's elite would change accordingly, with St. Peter's Roman Catholic or Immanuel Lutheran becoming as common a home church for prominent manufacturers as the First Congregational. One of the few constants in this period of turnover was Mallory's, Danbury's oldest firm. But even at Mallory's, its guiding patriarch, Ezra Mallory, retired in 1897 to be succeeded by his sons Charles B. and Harry. This younger generation of industry leaders would largely guide and shape events in the local hat industry and would have an even more significant impact on the development of the city itself.

Most prominent among this cohort of leaders were Frank Lee and Harry McLachlan. Lee's father died in 1889, a 79-year-old laborer named Bernard Lee who'd immigrated to the United States four decades before from the hilly country around the tiny town of Drumshanbo in the Irish county of Leitrim, then in the process of losing two-thirds of its population during and after the great potato famine of the 1840s. Bernard Lee and his wife had made their way to the Danbury area, where relatives were already living. He found work and lived on the farm of one of Brookfield's oldest families on Longmeadow Hill, where the potato crop never failed. Two of his sons would later buy part of the farm. But Bernard Lee's seventh and youngest son, Frank H. Lee, found a different route to move up in the world. The family relocated to Bethel in the 1870s. Frank, born in Danbury in 1868, learned the hat trade in a Bethel shop. Frank Lee's own children would attend private schools and topnotch universities, his products would be worn by presidents and he would become the city's biggest employer. He would also become the single most important individual in shaping Danbury's future during the entire 20th century.

Lee, like most of the manufacturers of his time, started out as a "bench hatter," serving a three-year apprenticeship, then spending four years as a journeyman. He even belonged to the union, and served as an officer at one point. Later he opened his own shop in Bethel and then in Danbury's Mill Plain district, where he produced derbies. There he was said to have drawn water for his operation directly from a stream, which flowed underneath his shop, by pulling up a loose board in the floor. Lee was part of several partnerships beginning in the 1890s. The earliest incarnation of what became the giant Lee Hat Company appears in Danbury incorporation records in 1897. By 1917, the firm was producing a thousand dozen (12,000) finished hats per day in the largest hat factory in the country, and employing over a thousand people.

According to a profile in the American Hatter trade magazine, Lee possessed "a desire to work and a grim determination to (succeed)," a quality plainly visible in his portrait photograph. But he also had the respect of his workers. As Hat Makers Union President Jeremiah Scully told fellow hatters in the midst of a bitter strike in 1917, "Lee has gone away from us, but in every dealing with me he has been fair and honest."

Despite a somewhat retiring disposition that manifested itself in a love of the outdoors and fishing and a devotion to family, Lee was involved in virtually every sphere of Danbury's life. He was on the boards of banks, Danbury Hospital, the American Legion, and the Knights of Columbus. In 1927, he began a newspaper, *The Danbury Times*, which operated for eight years. He belonged to Ridgewood Country Club, the Danbury Club and the Danbury Agricultural Society, which ran the Danbury Fair. And yet, despite the roll call of activities, Lee and his family spent time during most of their summers in a primitive cabin on Bantam Lake in Litchfield.

The ultracompetitive environment in the hat trade of the 1880s and '90s could not spawn too many Frank Lees. At the same time that Lee was advancing in his trade in 1883, Harry McLachlan, a 15-year-old Scottish immigrant, came to Danbury to clerk in a retail store. He left that job after a year to become an apprentice in one of the local "backshops." He would remain a man of the backshops for the rest of his life. A precocious talent, he caught the eye of manufacturer Byron Dexter, who made the youth a foreman in his own backshop. In the early 1890s, McLachlan noticed a new trend of small hat finishing and trimming shops around the country and decided that money could be made supplying rough hat bodies on demand to these small establishments. He opened his own shop in 1897, at that time only the second shop in the country to concentrate on rough hat manufacturing. McLachlan's strategy of nimble flexibility proved successful enough during the decade to attract his brother George as a partner until George left to open his own factory on Thorpe Street. Others followed their lead and by 1914, rough hat bodies had become one of Danbury's major products. Ultimately the city became responsible for 75 percent of the rough hat bodies made in the United States, and about half the factories in the city specialized in them. Only big firms like Lee, Mallory and a few others continued to make completed hats.

Harry McLachlan belonged to many of the same clubs and served on many of the same boards as Frank Lee. But he also became a figure in the national hat trade, serving as the first president of the National Association of Hat Manufacturers and, for 20 years, leading a committee on tariff protection for the organization, which later became known as the Hat Institute. While he was its leader in the 1930s, the Hat Institute began a national campaign to combat the new trend among young men of going hatless.

In 1906, Lee and Harry McLachlan teamed up to create one of the country's largest hat firms, the Lee-McLachlan Hat Company. On a new street that would be named Leemac Avenue in honor of the two partners, they built the largest hat factory in the country. A complex of attached buildings, it used the wood-frame construction that was traditional in the hat trade. As the town's largest employer, it became an important part of the lives of many Danburians. Like many of the larger shops, it had both stiff and soft hat departments that could respond to future style changes but continued to produce Danbury's sentimental favorite, the derby.

The partial shift to rough hat production also had the effect of lessening the need for the proud hat finishers – traditionally the best paid of the hatters. Although manufacturers were cautious about replacing finishers with machines, the introduction of the hydraulic press in 1890 is said to have put approximately a third of American hat finishers out of work. The machine sold so well that Turner Machine Co., Britain's oldest hat machinery firm, sent Arnold Turner, one of its owner's four sons, to Danbury to build a factory for manufacturing the devices. The factory opened on Maple Avenue in 1892. Turner remained in Danbury until his death, becoming a part of the community and playing a role in several important developments. Demand for the pressing machines was so great that, a year later, Turner had to build a large addition to the factory. Turner's peculiar, wedge-shaped facility was built adjacent to the railroad tracks on Maple Avenue and remained a local landmark until it was destroyed by fire in the 1980s. Other machinists also settled in Danbury – mainly immigrants from England and Ireland, creating the basis for precision metal production that would become a pillar of Danbury's post-hatting economy. Among the most prominent of these was Charles H. Reid, son of another potato famine immigrant from Ireland, who applied his inventive skills to making hat machinery and to founding the firm continued by his nephews as Doran Brothers. This innovative company developed specialized machines that further revolutionized the process of hat finishing.

Fur processing, the other significant branch of the trade, experienced major changes as well. Charles Darling Parks, an orphan from New Jersey, came to Danbury to live with relatives and decided to make his fortune in the city. Beginning in 1890, when he and a New York partner formed the American Hatters and Furriers Corporation and took over the big White Brothers fur processing complex on Beaver Street, Parks branched out into the sideline hide and tallow business and into fertilizer production. Finally, in 1903, he founded the Connecticut Glue Co., utilizing the rabbit skins discarded by his plant to make rabbit-hide glue. But Parks didn't confine himself to the messy manufacture of fur and its byproducts. He founded a fuel oil dealership, served as a director of the Danbury National Bank, and, with partner Warren Mercier, became one of the biggest owners of commercial real estate in the city. In 1910, he bought the Tarrywile estate from the heirs of its founder, the prominent doctor and medical publisher William Wile, and began purchasing additional land nearby. According to his obituary in *The Danbury Evening News*, Parks "acquired property adjoining (his farm) on both sides of Southern Boulevard and made many improvements that converted the locality into a garden spot." On the Tarrywile estate, he built up one of the city's largest dairy farms, planted corn and orchards, dammed a stream to create Parks Pond. Indeed, at the time of his death, Parks owned about two percent of Danbury's entire land area.

With the exception of Arnold Turner, all of these new industrial leaders had come up the hard way, learning the trade and working "on the bench" in steaming hot and wet "make shops" or dangerous machine shops. Despite this background, many of them – though personally generous – took a harsh line with unions but were benevolent toward their individual employees. Lee and Harry McLachlan are said to have paid, or helped to pay, for a significant number of employees' and others' higher education. Lee alone helped 37 of these people. According to his daughter, Lee even assisted the families of employees who were serving time in jail because he'd fired and prosecuted them for stealing hats! But these new leaders differed from those of the past in one important way: where they lived. The major nineteenth-century manufacturers lived in downtown neighborhoods among their workers. The next generation of industrialists often lived on the outskirts of town, harbingers of the suburban move-ment to come. Frank Lee and Charles Darling Parks assembled farms that dwarfed even the Rundle & White and Beckerle stock farms of the previous century. Between the two, they amassed well over 1,000 acres of farmland and forest. Others followed suit. Their accumulation of land would prove to be significant to Danbury's future economic growth, as many of the important corporate and open-space acquisitions of later years would involve these large parcels.

Another important figure among the manufacturers was not a newcom-er. The story of Danbury's labor-management conflicts revolves around Charles H. Merritt and his attorney son, Walter Gordon Merritt. Implacable foes of the unions, for a quarter century one or the other would be at the center of every major local conflict. Their efforts to break union power in the hat shops amounted to a kind of crusade.

When Charles H. Merritt died in 1918, some spoke of him as Danbury's "leading citizen," according to his obituary in *The News*. A relative on his mother's side of Danbury's philanthropic White family, Merritt grew up in a Quaker household in upstate New York. In 1868, he moved to Danbury and started a shoe factory before succumbing to the prevailing economic winds in the young city and converting to hat manufacturing in 1879. In 1872, he had become president and chief executive of the local gas company, a position he held until his death in 1918, setting a record for longevity in that industry despite changes in the company ownership. But his many contributions to community causes were even more impressive. An originator along with its female founders of Danbury Hospital and the Danbury Relief Society, he helped create the Associated Charities, a forerunner of the Community Chest, and was one of the organizers of the Chamber of Commerce. In addition, he was president of Danbury Library and worked behind the scenes for the establishment of a state trade school in Danbury that would become Henry Abbott Technical School. Merritt also contributed to the welfare of his own employees; in 1886, he set up a reading room in his factory stocked with 200 books from his personal library.

But Charles Merritt regarded hatting as strictly a business, not a way of life as did Danbury's hatters. Unlike other manufacturers in the city, he never learned the trade "on the bench." To most hatters, he was a rich outsider who didn't understand their culture. For his part, as a businessman of his day, he felt he enjoyed an absolute right to control all matters in his own plant. He "deeply resented" what he regarded as outside union interference in his factory, and after "more than a decade … could (still) tick off his grievances against the unions," according to labor historian Daniel Ernst. Merritt's cousin, the village bandmaster George Ives who was working for Merritt at the time, referred to him as a "monopolist." However, despite – or possibly because of – his autocratic stance, Merritt seems to have strug-gled in the hat business. He produced hats for the low end of the market, advertising them strangely as "Just a little bit better than the next best." His wages consistently ranked among the lowest in the city, and his anti-union positions may have earned him what Ernst termed a "quietly pursued boycott" by labor. In 1905, the United Hatters brought a lawsuit against him for allegedly putting fake union labels in his hats. Merritt retired from hatting in 1907, at the age of 64, after spearheading no less than four lockouts.

However, in 1889 Danbury's unions and its hat manufacturers were enjoy-ing a delicate truce. The first recorded local labor dispute occurred in 1882, when three of the city's manufacturers – Merritt, William Beckerle and

Edmund Tweedy, the latter two the city's largest employers – rebelled against what they regarded as union restrictions such as the three-apprentice rule and imposed a lockout on union hat finishers that threatened to lead to intervention by the state militia. That crisis ended after the unions flexed their numerical strength at the ballot box and elected a slate of hat finishers in the borough election.

Three years later in 1885, hat curler and businessman Granville Holmes came up with a plan that was embraced by both sides. The terms of the settlement optimistically referred to as "The Accords" offered substantial benefits for each side. Unions were pleased that all factories would operate as "fair" (fully unionized) shops. Manufacturers, long plagued by division and rivalry, were authorized to organize a trade association and operate as a unified entity. The "bill of prices" (piece-work rates) would be set by a committee chosen by the unions and the new employers' organization and would be binding for a full season, instead of having workers plead for higher wages if sales turned out to be brisk. The unions would eliminate "shop calls" (work stoppages over prices or other disputes). All firms could display the union label in their products, and both parties agreed to utilize arbitration, then a novel process, to settle future disagreements. No wonder Danbury's arrangement was praised by British Prime Minister William Gladstone on the floor of Parliament! And *The New York Tribune* was able to write in its Labor Day profile in 1892: "there is no place in the country where there is such perfect and friendly understanding between proprietors and employees as at Danbury. It is proclaimed by workmen, as well as proprietors, that Danbury is the model union town of the United States."

THE TRIMMERS LOCKOUT (1890)

Danbury's workforce – both in and out of the hatting industry – was now totally unionized. Because of the 1886 Accords, many of the manufacturers' annoyances disappeared. The number of hats made in and shipped out of Danbury continued to grow, and the city flourished. Between 1886, when the Accords were signed, until 1892, the city's output of hats increased by 20 percent. According to reports from the credit agency Dun & Bradstreet, local hat firms were financially healthy. The pact clearly benefited the manufacturers and the union hatters who had signed it.

But the agreements did not help one important body of workers. The city's hat trimmers were one of the previously unorganized groups that unionized as a result of the 1886 Accords. The female union amounted to about 20 percent of the local hat industry's workforce, the largest single category of employees. Trimmers were a source of fascination for Danburians at that time. A mix of married women and young single women, trimmers sewed in the factories sitting in circles. They could socialize while they worked, and seem to have developed real bonds of fellowship as well as a sense of fun. Working in what were the cleanest rooms in the hat factories, it was not uncommon for some trimmers to bring their young children with them to play while their mothers worked. Some of the younger single women reportedly "made great sport" by sewing their names and addresses into the linings of hats and then hearing back from interested men from far reaches of the country. The trimmers' genial comradeship frequently brought their activities to the attention of the local press. They held social events and took an active interest in the city's charities, raising funds and furnishing a room in the new Danbury Hospital.

Despite the 1886 agreements and their congenial working atmosphere, the hat trimmers found their pay dwindling and their union toothless. The rules that were working so well for male hatters had "never protected the trimmers from unjust acts of the manufacturers," wrote one trimmer in a report to the Connecticut Bureau of Labor Statistics. Arbitration, she complained, "does not arbitrate." There were widespread abuses by some manufacturers designed to curb union strength, she declared, including management spies at shop meetings; reduction of work crews when new bills of prices were made so that those who remained were "such as could be molded"; the discharging of "kickers" – girls who had "too much to say about the bill of prices"; and the issuance of blacklists of outspoken union members.

"No one has seen one of these lists in black and white," the unidentified trimmer asserted in 1890, " … but it is claimed that notification is sent by every manufacturer by telephone or otherwise as soon as one of the active members of the union is discharged" to prevent them from finding a new job.

When the new president of the Trimmers' Union, Ellen Foote, sought a modification of the 1886 Accords to accommodate the needs of her members, Merritt's manufacturers' association responded by initiating a lockout and organizing a new trimmers "society." He blamed the election of Foote for the disruption, along with "the constitution of the feminine mind, which causes it to regard any obstacle to having its own way as not worthy of respectful consideration." Merritt's consternation was more likely the result of "Queen Ellen's" tough negotiating style. "I have to be sharp and upright and stare grimly into their eyes every time I go into conference with these factory owners," Foote once told a reporter. "I have to act that way, for I find that they are not to be trusted. They take advantage of every loophole which we may overlook."

Courtesy of Danbury Museum & Historical Society Authority

Trimmers at work in the trimming room of the Mallory Hat Co., circa 1900.

A manufacturers' lockout began on November 17, 1890, shuttering 17 shops that employed about half of Danbury's workforce. Nonetheless, the male unions offered little support to the locked-out trimmers. Meanwhile manufacturers and foremen waged an energetic, but unsuccessful, campaign to recruit members for a rival management-backed trimmers society; they even resorted to a condescending offer of "thirty pounds of bonbons" to foster defection in one shop. A proposal by the manufacturers association that would have removed Foote from her position and made her ineligible for office in the future did draw support for her from the male unions, but it also provoked such division among manufacturers that the meeting in which it was discussed lasted until five in the morning and saw some manufacturers almost come to blows. As a compromise, the Trimmers Union had to accept an advisory board of male makers and finishers in order to retain Foote, who was re-elected president annually until 1911. Her talent for public speaking, which in later years could captivate hard-bitten male hatters for hours at a time, made her the city's single most dynamic union leader.

THE GREAT LOCKOUT (1893-1894)

Hat manufacturers and the men's unions at least were happy with the 1886 Accords. "The success of this system," one manufacturer wrote in 1890, "has fully justified the faith of its founders ... The experience of the past five years in Danbury has certainly demonstrated that the relations between labor and capital can be adjusted and maintained on a basis of justice and amity."

But the manufacturers were quick to abandon the agreements a few years later, when a double crisis hit the local hat industry. First, in 1893, a new trend in soft hats inspired by the Prince of Wales' adoption of a German mountaineer's soft hat as his favored headgear sliced deeply into sales of Danbury's dependable staple, the stiff hat or derby. Subsequently, a national financial panic delivered a second blow, causing production in Danbury's hat factories to plunge by a third during 1893. With orders in free-fall, the manufacturers panicked and sought to salvage profits by scrapping the accords. Lengthy negotiations failed, and with hat orders for the fall declining even further, the Danbury Hat Manufacturers Association, led by Charles Merritt, issued an ultimatum. The unions agreed to most of its points, but balked at demands for massive pay cuts and for opening shops to non-union labor. The Association had little to lose, as many shops were already running at half or even quarter-time, so its 19 firms, with one exception, declared the Accords dead, pledged an end to all ties with the unions, and proclaimed that they would reopen only as independent shops.

Danbury's first experience with a protracted and general labor-management conflict began on November 25, 1893, and dragged on for nearly two months, much longer than anyone had expected. Union leaders immediately posted pickets of six to ten men at the locked-out factories to watch for strikebreakers, and they held daily shop meetings in rooms secured at City Hall for their headquarters. To most hatters, the exercise was "a game of bluff," its winner determined by which side could stick together and outlast the other. The union leaders' first problem was providing for their 3,000 locked-out members. They belonged to the Knights of Labor, a national organization that offered them moral support but little else. On their own to raise strike funds for the three-quarters of the city's hatters who were now unemployed, the union members jammed a town meeting called after a petition was circulated by downtown merchants. Those in attendance took all of five minutes to vote a huge amount in town relief funds for themselves. This action brought Danbury national attention, particularly from anti-union newspapers, which ran stories on how the unions "owned the town," and planned to "milk" it for support. Although the hatters won an important moral victory, it proved empty because their resolution didn't include a means of financing the appropriation, and thus couldn't be enforced. To help their many unemployed members, the unions turned to raising money by sponsoring daily entertainments at City Hall featuring bands, singing and humorous recitations.

The locked-out workers enjoyed considerable sympathy from the community, which saw the noble hatter as an honorable "victim of his employer's desire to grow rich," as one observer opined in the pages of *The News*. The unions insisted in a statement published in the city newspaper that their struggle was only to establish "a reasonable co-partnership, to promote the feeling of equal rights, without which the best skill of the mechanic cannot be obtained." The Rev. F.A. Hatch of the Second Congregational Church and Fathers Kennedy and Lynch of St. Peter's, encouraged them from their pulpits. Father Lynch urged the workers at three masses on one Sunday to "starve before going in" to independent shops. Downtown merchants, who stood to lose the most from the double blows of a depression and a lockout, supported a quick settlement. *The Danbury News* set up a relief committee that for the first few weeks after the lockout began collecting contributions from local merchants. The manufacturers couldn't even count on City Hall. Mayor Charles S. Andrews, a recently elected Democrat, remained on friendly terms with the union leadership throughout the conflict. There was even some speculation by *The News* that the Democrat's victory in the mayoral election of 1893 had been a factor in bringing on the lockout, as "the hat bosses, all of whom are Republican save two, were very angry at this turn of events."

Longtime president of the Trimmers Union, Ellen Foote was profiled in newspapers all over the country during the 1893-94 lockout. This portrait appeared in the Columbus, Georgia, *Daily Enquirer.* Known to both trimmers and bosses as "Queen Ellen" for vastly different reasons, she continued serving as union president even after becoming matron of Broadview Farm in the early 1900s.

Courtesy of Danbury Museum & Historical Society Authority

The stalemate continued into the new year, something neither side had anticipated. The protracted struggle had begun to wear on both sides, as a hatter calling himself A.J.B.D. revealed in a ballad in the *Evening News* titled "A Month Ago Today":

> *We little dreamed of trouble,*
> *We little dreamed of strife,*
> *As we sought our bench*
> *Thinking most of home and wife.*
> *We little thought that hunger*
> *And want would come our way.*
> *But sang or whistled some sweet song*
> *A month ago today.*
>
> *We never thought our bosses*
> *Could turn on us and sting*
> *After giving them the lion's share*
> *And doing the right thing.*
> *We never thought we'd live to hear*
> *Our children cry and say,*
> *"Give me bread. I'm hungry,"*
>
> *A month ago to-day [sic].*
> *We have thought the whole thing over*
> *The one conclusion is, we fear*
> *It's the same old greedy motives*
> *With its [wage] cut-down year by year*
> *But let us stick together lads*
> *And from our "union" never stray*
> *And we'll have those times again boys,*
> *A month ago to-day* [sic].

The manufacturers were the first to break ranks when Beltaire, Lurch & Co. reopened as a union shop on January 1, 1894. Orders for spring began pouring into Beltaire's and the handful of Danbury firms not involved in the lockout. But the manufacturers association stepped up the pressure as two of the city's biggest companies announced plans to relocate in New Jersey or Yonkers. William Beckerle & Co., then Danbury's largest employer, with 450 employees and two big factories, went so far as to begin loading equipment onto railroad cars. But the action was a bluff. A few weeks later, *The News* reported that the equipment was still "on a siding in Redding, waiting for orders to return." Soon after, a crudely worded note arrived on Mayor Andrews' desk, signed "Avenger." It threatened that several factories would be blown up and warned that five prominent manufacturers would "dye." Although police and fire departments kept a close eye on the threatened factories and the two sons of lockout leader Merritt stayed up all that night guarding their Main Street mansion, authorities quickly determined that the note, executed in the handwriting "of a woman of some education," was "nothing more than a ... hoax."

In mid-January, 1894, with the trade's spring buying and ordering season approaching, negotiations between the two sides re-opened, but the community's hopes for a settlement were quickly dashed when the more militant manufacturers quashed a tentative deal by introducing new demands. This stalemate actually led to the end of the lockout when half a dozen manufacturers offered to break with the Association and make their own settlement. The Makers and Finishers locals quickly agreed, but the Trimmers local, left off the negotiating committee, balked. It took three meetings over several days before the Trimmers would agree to settle with the six breakaway firms. During the course of the meetings, Ellen Foote garnered national attention as an orator with her strong calls for continued resistance. Addressing a packed City Hall rally, she called for a place "where hungry members of the trade can call and get a hot cup of coffee and a lunch." The need turned out to be greater than anyone realized. The following day, the unions opened the city's first-ever soup kitchen for the locked-out hatters at 68 White Street, funded by donations from downtown merchants and hatters. During the four weeks it operated, the hatters' soup kitchen served between 500 and 800 dinners a day.

Meanwhile, the 12 remaining locked-out firms prepared to re-open as independent shops and appealed to Mayor Andrews to provide them with "the strong arm of the law" for protection. The mayor assured the manufacturers that any wrongdoing would be punished, but he also chastised them for invoking the possibility of violence. "You know as well as I do," the mayor wrote in reply, "that your former employees are citizens of this city, most of them property holders, and all are interested in the prosperity of Danbury." In fact, throughout the 10 weeks of the lockout there was not a single complaint against or arrest of a hatter. Arrests actually decreased, and during the first two weeks no police court had to be held for the first time in the police department's brief history. Connecticut's governor, Luzon Morris, was reported to be "really delighted with the Danbury hatters, (whose) conduct is worthy of the highest commendation." Taking place at a time of great conflict between capital and labor, the lengthy Danbury lockout was remarkable for its lack of violence. Unlike its chronological neighbors, the Homestead, Pennsylvania, steel strike of 1892 and the Pullman, Illinois, railroad strike of 1894, which were both bloody events, Danbury's Great Lockout was a heated but law-abiding affair.

As the quieter Danbury lockout "dragged its weary way along" to the end of its second month, manufacturers blew their factory whistles in celebration when eight locked-out firms attempted to re-open as independent shops. The unions picketed the approaches to the shops, and less than 20 prospective employees showed up. Nevertheless, union leaders condemned the tiny contingent of scabs as "poor, crawling substitutes for men, without sufficient character to stand for their rights as individuals." Union leaders promised to publish their names in the newspapers, but never carried out the threat.

Finally, on January 31, the unions' executive committee advised workers to take whatever work they could, effectively ending the lockout and leading to a scramble for jobs. Hatters who applied to E.A. Mallory & Sons found work arrangements offered them so offensive that a hastily convened town meeting strongly condemned the firm. The event marked the last time that union hatters used their numerical strength in local government to directly advance their cause.

Even though neither side won a clear-cut victory, nor remained fully united throughout the struggle, the locked-out hatters experienced the greatest short-term losses. Only about half were initially taken back by employers and by mid-March, a quarter of them were still unemployed. The soup kitchen remained open, supported by a 10 percent assessment on union hatters' wages, until three weeks after the lockout had ended.

The protracted test of wills chilled labor-management relations for years to come and tarnished the city's reputation, morale and economy. Locals believed that it took Danbury more than a decade to recover from the Great Lockout. Some believed it never fully recovered; but by the early 1900s, Danbury's hat factories were humming once again. However, the foremost legacy of the Great Lockout was to be further conflict.

LOEWE V. LAWLOR: THE "DANBURY HATTERS" CASE (1902-1917)

Divisive and bitter as the Great Lockout was, it represented only the opening battle in a bigger struggle. Increasingly, decisions involving Danbury's industrial affairs would no longer originate locally and the local tradition of accommodation and compromise would come under mounting strain. In 1896, Danbury's hatters' unions, already part of national associations in their own trade specialties as "finishers" and "makers," became part of the United Hatters of North America. The new national union abandoned the Knights of Labor and joined the fledgling American Federation of Labor. The national organization led by Samuel Gompers was on the rise, enrolling two million members by 1900. It wielded considerable influence by sponsoring nationwide boycotts that targeted non-union manufacturers. A key element of its clout was use of the union label in products, which guaranteed to the buyer that they had been made by union labor. In the years after 1896, the United Hatters enjoyed its greatest period of success, unionizing all but a dozen of the country's 190 hat manufacturers. One by one, Danbury's former open shops, among them the prominent Mallory's, renegotiated with the unions and reopened as "fair" or unionized shops. By the turn of the century, only three non-unionized holdouts remained in Danbury, including Charles H. Merritt's factory and a firm headed by former City Councilman D.E. Loewe.

Dietrich Loewe immigrated to the United States as a young man in 1870. After working on the railroad for several years, he found his way to Danbury where he learned the hatting trade in local shops. By the end of the decade, he joined two local men to found D.E. Loewe & Co. The company grew steadily through the 1880s and 1890s and, by the turn of the century, had become a profitable mid-sized, soft-hat business with 240 employees, albeit one that survived on a thin profit margin. It was a logical target for unionization when, in 1901, the United Hatters sought to complete its closed-shop campaign.

Like many immigrants, Loewe lived in two worlds: the English-speaking world of Danbury at large and the predominantly German world of his church, workplace and home. He belonged to Immanuel Lutheran Church and, according to one former employee, hired primarily Germans in his factory. But unlike many immigrants, Loewe quickly integrated himself into the life of his adopted community. His home was on Stone Street, in a strongly Irish-Catholic hatters' neighborhood in the middle of the 4th Ward. By the mid-1880s he was serving as town tax assessor, followed by a term in the state legislature from 1887-89, several terms on the Common Council (he appears in the group photograph of the first mayor and council described earlier in this book), and finally some stints in town government. Later he would serve as president of Danbury Hospital during a period of its growth.

Loewe opened his "foul" (non union) shop during the Great Lockout. While he customarily employed more than the allowed number of boys in his factory, the local unions, who never filed a grievance against him, turned a blind eye to the violation. His objection to unionization was economic, a conviction that it would lead to higher labor costs that would drive him out of business. In fact, Loewe, motivated by the paternalistic German philosophy of "taking care of one's own," had good relations with his workers. As late as the 1950s, decades after he went out of business, former employees met annually to dine and socialize. His first business partner, Edwin Targett, became president of the Finishers Union local.

Courtesy of Historical Society of Wisconsin

Walter Gordon Merritt provided the intellectual heft behind management's drive to break the power of the hat unions. A Yale-educated attorney, Merritt's work for the American Anti-Boycott Association gave him a nationwide reputation.

Ironically, Loewe first took issue with the United Hatters over the threatened denial of union cards to some of his employees.

In November of 1900, United Hatters' Vice President James Maher, a Brooklyn native who at one point had worked and lived in Danbury, met with Loewe at the Groveland Hotel on Main Street to inform him of the national union's intention to unionize his shop. Loewe balked at this discussion with someone he considered not a local person, so the following March, Maher returned to repeat the demand accompanied by the secretary of the United Hatters, Martin Lawlor. A native of County Kerry in Ireland, a region that also produced the noted New York union organizer Michael Quill, Lawlor had settled in Bethel, where he became an active and enormously popular leader in hatting unions while still in his teens.

An adamant Loewe broke off negotiations with the United Hatters in April 1902. "I knew that all the employees were satisfied – and we as a firm were satisfied – with the way the business was running, and I felt Danbury as a town was satisfied," he insisted. "I couldn't see why it should be necessary to change the conditions. I wanted to be left alone." Loewe should not have been mystified. Years later, Makers Union leader Jeremiah "Dee" Scully bluntly summarized what was going on when he explained, "Maher wanted to unionize all the hat shops and Loewe wouldn't go along."

On August 20, 1902, the United Hatters finally called on Loewe's men to strike. All but ten of his 240 employees walked out, realizing they could be blacklisted by the union if they stayed and thus jeopardize their future employment. Those who walked out included the son of one of Loewe's partners, who was a union member. Several eyewitnesses, including a shop foreman, passed down stories of a tearful Loewe begging them not to leave. Tom McNally, a "rounding boy" in the sizing room of Loewe's backshop, observed the scene and reported, "I can remember Al Ackerman (a foreman) taking off his canvas apron and laying it down on the bench, and I went upstairs to the dressing room to get my coat and hat. I said to Mr. Ackerman are you going, he says 'yes I'm going with the men.' Loewe came in and he was crying. And he says 'I don't know what it's all about' and he says 'I wish you wouldn't go.'"

It took the manufacturer several months to hire and train a new crew mainly made up of recently arrived immigrants. Meanwhile, Loewe was placed on the AFL's "unfair" list. All over the country, union agents visited hat retailers to dissuade them from continuing to order from Loewe. Loewe's striking employees tried hard to find work – most, but not all of them, successfully. During the first year of the AFL boycott against Loewe, his company's sales reportedly declined by $33,000, a huge sum for those days.

But Loewe found a way to fight back. Since the initial meetings with Maher, he had been collaborating with fellow open-shop manufacturer Charles H. Merritt, who knew he would also eventually become the target of a boycott. In long talks in the woods south of his home, Loewe discussed tactics with Merritt and his Yale law-student son, Walter Gordon Merritt. They agreed to form a nationwide association of employers to be called the American Anti-Boycott Association, which would fight the unions in the courts. In February 1902 they issued a formal call to employers all over the nation to join them in a legal battle to destroy the unions' boycott weapon.

By April 1903, the group had a hundred charter members and had raised a substantial war chest. With Charles Merritt at the helm, the American Anti-Boycott Association hired attorney Daniel Davenport, a Wilton native working out of New Haven who had developed a legal theory that the Sherman Anti-Trust Act of 1894 could be applied to unions. The Sherman Anti-Trust Act had actually been passed by the United States Congress with the intent of curbing trusts and monopolies that restricted interstate trade. Davenport argued in essence that unions were "labor trusts" that interfered with "the liberty of the trader."

In support of Loewe and using his name, the Anti-Boycott Association filed a lawsuit against the striking United Hatters simultaneously in U.S. District Court and in Fairfield County Superior Court. The suit, formally designated as Loewe v. Lawlor, became known as the Danbury Hatters Case. Although the legal question at issue was whether the boycott fell under the Sherman Act, the plaintiffs' strategy provoked wide attention. Davenport decided to sue individual union members for the actions of the union in the AFL boycott of Loewe hats. To do this in a dramatic manner he assigned Merritt's son, Walter Gordon Merritt, a recent Yale Law School graduate, to search property and bank records to find 240 local members of the United Hatters whose property could be attached, a figure that matched the number of Loewe's employees. Gleeful at the opportunity to strike a blow at organized labor in his first major assignment, the young Merritt wrote later that he was "trembling with excitement" as he unobtrusively compiled this list.

Even before his men went out on strike, Loewe's lawyers convinced him to have a notice printed in the *Evening News* warning union members that they would be held individually responsible for any damages his company suffered from the strike, whether they worked for him or not. Two-thirds of those named in the suit lived in Danbury; the rest were from Bethel and Norwalk. Only a handful of them, like Hugh Shalvoy of the Makers' Union, were union officials. The lawsuit would tie up their property for the next 15 years. Some of these hatters whose properties were attached were called to attend federal District Court trials in Hartford, where they were grilled about the extent of their knowledge of the boycott. Most, like Eugene Mulkin and Jacob Prince who testified in 1912, claimed to have no knowledge of the boycott or even, in Prince's case, to know what the word "boycott" meant.

The Anti-Boycott Association sued for damages of $80,000, which under the terms of the Sherman Act, was automatically tripled. Holding individual union members financially responsible was a novel legal twist that eventually brought the case to the United States Supreme Court. But, as Walter Gordon Merritt claimed much later, the possible seizure of working people's homes and bank accounts was intended to be a threat designed to weaken union resolve. "I never imagined that a union like the AFL or the United Hatters would not run to the rescue of its members when they were held liable for union activities," he insisted. "Workmen battling together for self-protection … could hardly be found wanting to a handful of fellow members in such a crisis."

Because the United Hatters attempted to delay as long as possible, it took three years before the U.S. District Court in Hartford rejected Davenport and Merritt's arguments that the Sherman Act could be applied to unions. This setback didn't deter Davenport, who, thanks to the national Anti-Boycott Association, had the funds to bring the suit to higher courts. Finally, in February 1908 the U.S. Supreme Court ruled that the Sherman Act did pertain to unions. Two years later, a federal jury awarded Loewe $74,000 in damages which automatically more than tripled to $252,000. At this point the AFL took over the case from the United Hatters, appealing the judgment but losing again on January 5, 1915, when the U.S. Supreme Court upheld the original decision.

With the judgment now due, the homes and bank accounts of the original defendants were technically at stake. The AFL turned to its membership. On December 29, 1915, the *Evening News* printed a three-page letter from Samuel Gompers, president of the AFL, calling upon its members to contribute an hour's wages to pay off the judgment. "Dear Sirs and Brothers," Gompers' letter began. "Will you give an hour? Not an hour to read this, but an hour of your labor in a righteous cause, on Hatters' Day,

January 27, 1916. The Danbury hatters have performed a service of historic importance in the struggle for industrial freedom." The effort coincided with the beginning of the 1916 presidential campaign, in which former Supreme Court Justice Charles Evans Hughes was the Republican candidate. One unverified story is that during the campaign a newsreel film was made of the attached hatters' homes in Danbury and shown in strongly pro-union California. Hughes lost California and with it any hope of the presidency. Democrat Woodrow Wilson's surprising re-election sparked a spontaneous parade down South and Main streets by Lee Company employees and other hatters in the thousands, led by hastily appointed marshals on horseback and the officials of the local unions.

During a second "Hatters' Day," the AFL raised the rest of the amount required by the court judgment. Walter Gordon Merritt, who had become the lead attorney for the Loewe forces by this time, pressed for full payment, including interest. Before an auction of the hatters' homes could be held as scheduled on July 1, 1917, the AFL paid the initial $80,000 award while continuing to negotiate the interest, which amounted to $20,000. Merritt later explained, "I did not wish to end what seemed to me a noble battle with an anticlimax of haggling; and so, surrounded by glowering glances of disapproval from the banking fraternity [who wanted to settle for less than the full amount], I announced to the union attorney that there would be no compromise. That ended the negotiation. It looked like an impasse." But on July 14, 1917, Martin Lawlor of the United Hatters paid Merritt the full remaining amount. According to Jeremiah "Dee" Scully, head of the Hat Makers local, who was present at the exchange, Merritt "almost hit the ceiling" when Lawlor handed over the check with the words, "Here's your blood money."

Over 15 years, the Danbury Hatters' Case cost organized labor $420,000, a fortune at the time. Many of the local hatters whose homes were attached were dead by the time the case reached its end. The boycott had to be abandoned as a weapon to force employers into establishing closed shops. James Maher, the union officer who had initially called on Loewe, was elected to the U.S. House of Representatives from Brooklyn in 1910 and, in 1914, was instrumental in pushing for an amendment to the Sherman Antitrust Act, known as the Clayton Antitrust Act, which exempted organized labor from the provisions of the Sherman Act. The American Anti-Boycott Association, formed in Danbury to fight the Loewe case, became an important national organization that continued for decades to battle organized labor. It was headed by Charles Merritt until his death in 1918, when his son took over and renamed the organization the League for Industrial Rights. Continuing his family's tradition of public service, Walter Gordon Merritt would become an important figure in local affairs in later life, particularly as a major donor to Danbury Hospital. He also gave a large tract of land in northern Danbury and New Fairfield to the state of Connecticut for a forest preserve.

As for Dietrich Loewe, he eventually went out of business. Dee Scully and other former hatters claimed that he survived in his old age on annual contributions from grateful manufacturers around the country.

Even before the Supreme Court handed down its decision in Loewe v. Lawlor, the United Hatters' drive to unionize all of the country's hat shops had gone into reverse as the number of unionized shops dropped. In 1907, the United Hatters relaxed some of its rules on machines and the use of boys who were not registered as apprentices. Finally, an assault on the use of the sacrosanct union label itself took place in 1909.

THE 1909 "TIE-UP" AND THE "FATHER KENNEDY ACCORDS"

In mid-January 1909, a dispute over use of the union label in a small hat shop in Philadelphia escalated into a full-scale tussle between the national union and management organizations and led to the local hat industry's longest strike. After arbitration failed, Walter Gordon Merritt persuaded the National Association of Hat Manufacturers to announce that its members would discontinue use of the union label in their hats. That move prompted the United Hatters of North America to order an unexpected nationwide hatters' strike against companies that were members of the National Hat Manufacturers Association, which included all but ten firms in Danbury. About 3,500 union hatters walked out of hat factories all over the city, leaving "quietly and with that calmness and order that is

Father John D. Kennedy, a local hero for his key role in arranging a local settlement to the nationwide 1909 hat strike. Kennedy was also highly influential during his time in Danbury as curate at St. Peter's and as the first pastor of St. Joseph's Church on Main Street. He helped to organize St. Peter's School and establish the Kennedy Guards, a marching company that had its own band. Work was suspended in the city on the day of Kennedy's funeral in 1911, and more than 500 Danbury residents made the trip on a special train to his burial in New Haven.

Courtesy of Danbury Museum & Historical Society Authority

characteristic of the members of the hat trade in this city under such circumstances," according to the newspaper. For the first time, a dispute that idled Danbury's hatters had no real local connection. However, because Danbury's factories employed about a quarter to a third of the United Hatters' national membership, the yearlong action severely affected the small city. Local figures played leading roles in the dispute, and while the hat strike was hardly noticed in the economies of large hat manufacturing centers like New York, Philadelphia, Boston and Newark, or even Norwalk, a shutdown of most of Danbury's hat factories amounted to choking off the small city's lifeblood.

The strike followed the pattern of earlier labor-management conflicts, with manufacturers issuing ultimatums, attempting to re-open as independent shops and threatening to leave town. All the while, union hatters held rallies and meetings and sponsored benefit events like baseball games and concerts to raise funds for the unemployed trimmers, who still lacked a national union to support them with strike funds. After six long months, the strike also ended in a familiar way when both sides in Danbury reached a separate peace by agreeing to a new set of accords advanced by a team of clergymen, the Rev. John D. Kennedy, pastor of St. Joseph's Roman Catholic Church, and Rev. H.C. Meserve of the First Congregational Church. This team was backed by local business and political leaders and had worked toward a local solution from the strike's onset. The so-called "Father Kennedy Accords" recognized the United Hatters as bargaining agent for the unions and reinstituted arbitration of disputes. Local manufacturers agreed to resign from the national association, but won a concession from the union allowing a fair trial period for introducing new machines. Nationwide, the strike continued for another six months but thanks to this community intervention all of Danbury's factories were back in business.

Despite the appearance of tranquility, hatting in Danbury had reached a turning point as many in the industry had lost patience with traditional methods of production. During the strike manufacturers published, in the *Evening News*, a long and articulate analysis of the local situation. Their analysis criticized "the monopolistic position of the hatter." Since the 1880s, the statement's authors wrote, "machinery has been introduced and the work has been so divided that a long apprenticeship is no longer necessary. Any bright boy can learn in a few weeks all that is necessary for carrying on any given part of the work of the factory." A case in point was the finishing machines developed by Doran Brothers. "All of our machinery did the work that [the hand finisher] did by hand," said Bob Doran in an interview, "and we could actually do it better … Our machine had the operations controlled as to pressure, speed, surface contact, and could do it consistently all day long with one completely unskilled worker (who) could run four machines." Many manufacturers contended that because of mechanization, hatting could be done successfully anywhere, so that the concentration of skilled workers (and their unions) in Danbury was no longer necessary. While manufacturers generally did not strenuously object to bargaining with the more flexible and accommodating locals, they were exasperated with the big national labor organizations, the AFL and particularly the United Hatters, who they characterized as "a few radicals … intent on gaining the nearest pennies for themselves."

The Father Kennedy Accords kept labor-management peace locally until World War I, an accomplishment that the priest's alma mater, Niagara University, recognized by granting him an honorary degree. Grateful townspeople accorded him the largest funeral procession ever seen up to that time after his untimely death in January, 1911.

Though Danbury's manufacturers yearned in vain for the return of the formal (and high-priced) derby, manufacturers adapted by either concentrating on the production of rough hat bodies or keeping both soft- and stiff-hat departments in their factories. Despite the predictions of doom, old firms that went out of business were quickly replaced by startups. New factories were built and older ones expanded, and in 1916 the city reached a milestone. With 60 forming machines in operation, the city's hat factories set a record for the most hats produced in a single year. In 1917, the Industrial Survey of Danbury reported that the volume of production in its hat factories had increased by more than 20 percent in the previous decade. The value of hats made in Danbury every year was surpassed only by the value of those made in Philadelphia, whose giant Stetson plant poured out the most expensive hats. Well into the 20th century, Danbury remained America's Hat City. ♦

Courtesy of Anna Marques Amerigo Ventura

Virtually all of Danbury's Portuguese
population at the time is pictured in
this Frank Baisley photograph of a
community get-together in 1931.

Diversity

In 1915, agents of the Connecticut Bible Society, a private organization, canvassed Danbury to learn the religious preferences and national origins of its residents (and present them with a Bible if they didn't already have one). The results of the survey highlighted the rich diversity already developing among the city's 22,000 people. These divided into 27 distinct ethnic groups and represented 20 religious faiths. Almost half the population was foreign born. While people from Ireland, Italy and the Slavic regions were the most numerous, the developing Danbury mosaic contained sizable concentrations of Greek, Syrian, Lebanese, Portuguese and Hungarian immigrant families. The canvassers even located a family of Egyptian Muslims in Danbury – the only Muslims they found in the entire state. The number of churches in the city would triple between 1900 and 1930, and most of the their congregations would be made up of members of these new groups.

Not everyone in Danbury welcomed the massive and surprising influx represented in these figures. Many longtime residents saw the newcomers as a threat to traditional community values. While the alarm of Judge J. Moss

Ives, described by the *Danbury News* as "one of Danbury's best-known citizens," may have been extreme, he expressed the fears of the Yankee establishment in a long and blunt letter he sent to Governor Rollin Woodruff in 1908. Asked by the governor in a confidential memorandum what he thought was the most serious problem facing Connecticut, Ives replied that the huge number of immigrants was the chief source of difficulty. The wave of foreigners, with their high birth rate, lack of education, and criminal tendencies, he asserted, threatened to overwhelm fundamental American beliefs. In Ives' judgment, the urgent question was: "Will old New England, her standards of living, her ideals, her customs and her laws, survive the constantly increasing influx of alien blood?"

The immigrant's perspective was different – a mixture of ambition coupled with awareness of their inequality. Lina Novaco, born in Danbury in 1897 to Italian parents, expressed both of these characteristics when she was interviewed by her grandson, a Western Connecticut State College student, in 1975. She stressed that her parents believed America was a land of opportunity that encouraged them to work hard to better themselves. However, her interview also includes references to discrimination. Immigrants "lived wherever they found a place," she said. "They had to be satisfied with the smaller homes and with homes in different sections." And in her final comment, she noted, "They weren't looked upon too good by the townspeople ... they were foreigners that's all."

During prosperous times in the period from 1890 to 1920, Danbury attracted job seekers as it had in the past. These continued to include hatters from other industry centers as well as people looking to start businesses in the thriving downtown. But as the dwindling populations of rural towns like Brookfield, New Fairfield and Sherman dropped below the thousand mark, this nearby source of new residents dried up.

The new immigrants, like the earlier Irish who had abandoned the poor parts of that island's rocky and difficult west coast, frequently came from the margins of their societies in Southern and Eastern Europe and the Middle East. Frequently they left hilly or mountainous regions of their home countries only to find the topography of the Danbury area familiar.

Mere surplus population in their homelands, most of which were part of large empires to which they owed no particular allegiance, they found in Danbury an opportune place to settle down and advance. Some came to Danbury after having avoided the military draft in Europe.

While their reasons for leaving their homelands were diverse, almost all mmigrant groups arriving in Danbury followed similar stages of settlement. A few pioneering individuals inspired further migration from their families and home regions, a process known as serial or chain migration. Larger numbers often were attracted by jobs on the railways or on town or state roads. Some started unique businesses (the first reported Italian in Danbury was an organ grinder; the first reported Syrians were peddlers). Later arrivals filled the dirtiest and most dangerous niches in the dominant hatting industry or on farms. Ultimately a few talented and ambitious individuals – often members of the second generation – would start businesses or enter professions, becoming visible to the entire community and sometimes serving as spokesmen for their whole group. As the city's new ethnic groups grew in size, they would form organizations – mutual aid societies at first, then social clubs, drama associations, and finally organizations that would preserve and carry on aspects of the group's heritage, such as the Sons of Italy, the Sons of Portugal, the Ancient Order of Hibernians, the German singing societies, or the Slovak Sokol. By the 1920s, numerous groups had built their own spacious lodge halls, including the German Concordia Singing Society with a handsome building on Crosby Street, and the Sons of Italy with an imposing modern center at 32-52 Elm Street.

During the 1890-1920 period, the group growing the fastest in Danbury was made up of those who had emigrated from Italy. The only Italians recorded in Danbury by the 1880 U.S. Census were 20 members of a railroad work crew living in a camp near Lake Kenosia. Only five years later, in 1885, the city directory listed 18 Italian families. In 1887 a small item in the *Evening News* reported that "there are 147 resident Italians in town, including women and children," evidence that a community was beginning to put down roots. In February 1890, town officials were startled when 20 Italian men walked into Danbury's City Hall and asked to begin the process of becoming citizens. The officials' surprise was due to their expectation that Italians would move along after completing jobs. Just a few years later in 1894, two Catholic priests who conducted an eight-day mission for Italian Catholics at St. Peter's Church counted an unexpectedly high 680 attendees. They quickly made arrangements for an Italian priest to come to St. Peter's for special services every month. By 1916, 497 Italian families living in the City of Danbury, comprising almost 2,300 individuals and accounting for more than 10 percent of Danbury's total inhabitants. During the next decade Italian immigrants overtook the Irish as the city's largest group of foreign-born residents.

The immigrants came mainly from the hilly southern Italian province of Catanzaro, in the Calabria region near the boot of the Italian peninsula, from the area of Decollatura (today a sister city of Danbury) and especially from a nearby region centered on the town of Pietropertosa. In January 1900, people from that area incorporated the Societa Aperaja Di Mutuo Soccorso Sei Cittadini Di Pietropertosa, or Pietropertosa Society, one of several Italian mutual-aid groups. Within its ranks could be found many of the best-known Italian names in the city: Valluzzo, Vaccarelli, LaCava, Define, Torraca. Other families, whose names are among the most common in Danbury today – Gigliotti, LaPine, Melillo, Scalzo, Scozzafava and Tomanio – were also early settlers.

Italian-American organizations proliferated almost as rapidly as the population, far more than those established by any other immigrant group. A second mutual-aid society, called Societa Cristoforo Colombo, incorporated in 1900. It joined the Italian Social Club of Danbury, which was open to "any person speaking the Italian language"; the Italian Military Society, started around 1894; the Societe Napolitano, a music and drama group; the Torquato Tasso Society, started around 1900; the Amerigo Vespucci lodge; and two lodges of the Sons of Italy, Mario Blanco and Eleventh of November, 1918. In 1924 these last three organizations, together with the Cavalieri Colombo lodge, united to form what was reputed to be the largest single lodge of Sons of Italy in the state, with 400 members.

The first Italians were mainly laborers who replaced the Irish on the railroad construction crews and would themselves be replaced some decades later by the Portuguese. Some remained in Danbury to take difficult and dangerous manual jobs, as evidenced by repeated newspaper reports, beginning in 1889, of accidents at the Danbury Lime Company in the Beaver Brook district, in which Italian laborers were killed or injured. Others stayed on in Danbury to work in the construction trade as masons and laborers, or in the hat factories. But frequently they started small businesses. Most commonly, these were fruit stands and small groceries or meat or fish markets. During the 1890s, the terms "Italian" and "fruit stand" became practically synonymous in Danbury. But there were other small-business people and tradesmen at work as well by the 1890s: shoemakers, barbers, cigar makers. Members of one of the oldest Italian immigrant families in Danbury, Eugenio and Achille Torraca, began a tailoring business on Main Street in 1893, and became a Main Street fixture for over 50 years. Achille claimed to have originated several innovations in men's dress – peg-top trousers for one – that later became common. At a time when most Italian parents withdrew their children from school at seven or eight years old to work in stores and factories, Achille kept his in school; his son Ralph, who later graduated from the University of Pennsylvania and became a doctor, was reputedly the first Italian graduate of Danbury High School.

John Capellaro, another of the earliest Italian immigrants, came to Danbury in 1883, and, along with a partner, set up a fruit stand there. The following year he sent for his bride in Italy. He was ambitious and flexible, making several upwardly mobile economic moves. For a number of years he operated a shoemaking shop on White Street. Then, in 1911, he purchased the 1785 homestead of "Aunt Sally" Beebe in the rural Stony Hill district of Bethel near the Brookfield line, where he used food preparation as a route to advancement. Capellaro opened an outdoor dining space on the property after coming up with the idea of cooking game that he saw hunters bringing back from hunting trips to Canada. By the 1930s, Capellaro's Grove had become a town fixture as a popular spot for outings, clambakes and company picnics with all the food prepared by the Capellaro family, sometimes for crowds of upwards of a thousand.

Some Italians were able to break into the hat industry in the factory of John B. and Mark Beltaire, natives of Palermo, Sicily, who were known to employ fellow Italians in their work force. Longtime figures in the hat trade, they came to the United States as boys and learned hatting in Newark, New Jersey, before moving to Danbury and entering into a partnership with Samuel C. Holley in 1888.

Italians lived in all parts of Danbury, but their heaviest concentration was in the so-called "Barbary Coast" neighborhood, the multi-ethnic environs of lower Liberty Street east of Main, which acquired a reputation as a rough-and-tumble place. Some immigrants were attracted to the more rural parts of Danbury, and so many transplanted Italians lived on upper Franklin Street that they formed the Kohanza Club there.

Another Italian outskirts-dweller was Giovanni Zarcone, the operator of a 59-acre orchard and fruit farm on Hospital Avenue, who was the victim of a shocking crime. On a hot night in July 1909, he was murdered in front of his home by a band of men suspected to be members of the "Black Hand," an early incarnation of the Italian Mafia. Despite a massive manhunt by Danbury police and even the local National Guard, the perpetrators were never found. Months later, three rusty shotguns, including one weapon that had belonged to Zarcone himself who had sent it to New York for repair, were dredged up from the bottom of Neversink Pond. It is striking to note that the Danbury police department already included an Italian-speaking officer, Paul Pope – their only avenue of communication with the farmer's distraught family whose members spoke little English. The incident, dramatically labeled by the *Evening News* as "the most sensational homicide that this city has ever known," was one of Danbury's few brushes with organized crime.

People from the Slavic-speaking countries of eastern and central Europe, mainly from what is now Poland and Slovakia but also including several other nationalities, established a visible presence in Danbury at the same time as the Italians. Natives tended to lump these nationalities together as "Polish," but official documents listed them as "Slavic." In reality the Poles were a cohesive group, many of whom came to Danbury after living earlier in Pennsylvania coal country or in New York, where they had already picked up a few words of English. Workingmen were said to hear of jobs in hat factories and then travel by train to Danbury, carrying a card printed only with the name of their destination. Once in Danbury, inquiries were made at the police station in their best English for the location of other Polish people. Often the newcomers were directed to the Kieras family's boarding house on State Street, not far from the station, or to the Kurjiaka farm on Lincoln Avenue. After acquiring jobs, they would send for their families. Like other groups, their numbers were dispersed but their main center of settlement was the Town Hill neighborhood east of Main, where they joined the dominant Irish. The city's first Roman Catholic national parish, Sacred Heart of Jesus, was established atop Town Hill on Cottage Street in 1925. There, church authorities permitted the Polish language to be used as the primary vernacular language outside of the Latin mass.

Slovaks were more diverse religiously. Many helped to establish St. Paul's Lutheran, the Holy Trinity Russian Orthodox and St. Nicholas Byzantine Rite Catholic churches, while others belonged to existing Roman Catholic and Lutheran congregations. Most were Slovak peasants from the Tatra and Carpathian Mountains, attracted to Danbury by jobs in the hat industry or in farming. Some came to Danbury after settling first in the hatting center of Yonkers, New York, where they may have learned rudiments of the trade, and moved into the small houses and tenement buildings on Danbury's River and Rose streets, near the hat factories where most of them worked. However, members of different religious congregations tended to live close to one another in different parts of the city: Slovak Lutherans lived mainly on Crofut, South Well, Peace, Highland and Henry streets, while members of St. Nicholas Catholic Church were in the North Main Street-Golden Hill area, as well as in Westville.

Wherever they settled, Slovaks (and the Czech families among them) shared a common culture. In their neighborhoods, the compact yards of old hatters' homes allowed them to grow much of their own food, keep small livestock and plant grape arbors, fruit trees and gardens. This pattern was common among Polish, Italian and Portuguese immigrant families as well. However, the Slovaks brought with them from Europe the Sokol, a unique social organization that stressed physical fitness through gymnastics. Danbury's Sokol Lodge 30, organized in October 1902, began physical training in 1908. Within a few years, Danbury teams were competing with other lodges and performing impressive gymnastic feats for local audiences, their membership stocked with people bearing now-familiar names like Halas, Jurenka and Repko. The group produced one national Sokol gymnastics champion, Thomas Balash, in 1941. In 1939, the group purchased more than forty acres of property in the Hayestown district for a summer camp, and two years later opened the Lakeview Restaurant on the site, as well, to take advantage of its proximity to the newly built Candlewood Lake. By 1915 the Poles, Slovaks and members of other Slavic nationalities numbered almost 1,500 people, an estimated eight percent of Danbury's population.

A number of other ethnic and religious groups that would later play major roles in Danbury life were only beginning to set down roots. Although they had been a familiar presence in the city long before 1890, Jews were one group still seen by many as culturally "foreign." However, the first chief of Danbury's paid fire department, Morris Meyers, was Jewish, and he also served as a town selectman and councilmen. Danburians were familiar with a long list of Jewish downtown merchants, particularly clothiers, with names like Levy, Spiro, Werner and Plaut. Meyers was the nephew of Samuel Zarkowski, who had introduced ready-made men's clothing to Danbury in the 1860s. Abraham Spiro also served in the General Assembly. The small number of early mercantile families, mainly of German origin, seems to have assimilated quickly, but newly arriving Jews of Eastern European origin swelled the local community's numbers, during the early 1900s, to more than 400 – about two percent of Danbury's population. Like other immigrant groups, they carried old traditions with them. When David Susnitzky laid the cornerstone for his new building on the corner of

White and Canal Streets in 1910, he did so by custom with his own hands, then distributed a silver dollar to each one of his workers. At the conclusion of the time-honored ceremony all present drank a toast of wine.

Jews had no institutional religious presence in the city until the organization of the Children of Israel Society in 1897. Among the founders are the familiar names of Susnitzky, Heyman, Landsman, Levy and others. The congregation held services in the apartment of a White Street shop-owner but had no resident rabbi. Its spiritual leader, Abraham Krakow, ran a nearby grocery and deli, and the Hebrew school classes he conducted there were often interrupted when the teacher had to leave to take care of a customer. The congregation's forty families made for a close-knit community. But for Jews growing up at that time in a city full of Christian churches and churchgoers, "We felt a little out of place," Benjamin Heyman remembered in 1980, "We had playmates among the Gentiles but were never invited into their homes." However, he continued, "Even though we were always aware of our Jewishness, we were very happy because we had a strong family unit." In 1907 the congregation achieved a new prestige in the community when it purchased the old Universalist Church on Liberty Street. Its dedication was an important public event, with town dignitaries and leaders of Christian churches in attendance. Reform Jews organized their own congregation around 1920, meeting at first in rented quarters in the Odd Fellows Hall on West Street, then moving to Concordia Hall on Crosby Street. This new group hired the city's first rabbi and formally organized the United Jewish Center in 1926.

Two of the largest segments of Danbury's current population – those of Lebanese and Portuguese extraction – consisted of small, embryonic clusters before 1920. "Syrians" was the collective term used to identify immigrants from both Lebanon and Syria. Those who came to Danbury from Syria originated for the most part in a small fishing village called Souedieh and practiced the Orthodox Christian faith. Most of those from Lebanon came from the Christian areas around Mount Lebanon and Beirut and belonged to the ancient Christian communities of Maronites and Melkites, which are affiliated with the Roman Catholic Church. Families often used

St. George's Church
Danbury, Connecticut
Courtesy of St. George Church

After worshipping for several years in a Russian Orthodox chapel in the Great Plain district, immigrants from the northern coast of Syria founded St. George Antiochian Orthodox Church in 1920 and completed a church building on Elm Street in 1924. The first Antiochian Orthodox Church in the state, it attracted worshippers from as far away as Waterbury and Bridgeport.

Christian first names like George or Michael or Charles as surnames, and families of Haddads, Shakers, Jabers, Saffis, Rameys, Jowdys and Nejames or Najamys became as familiar in 20th century Danbury life as Benedicts and Hoyts had been in the 18th and 19th. The earliest, and in many ways the pioneering, family in this community was the Buzaid family, which began a peddling business in Danbury in the 1890s.

The unpleasant business of processing hatters' fur gave most of this group of immigrants their entry point into the American economy – a surprising move because fur-bearing animals were uncommon in Lebanon. In 1910, William Buzaid followed this path, starting the first Lebanese-run fur-processing shop on Oil Mill Road. But the Lebanese sprang from an ancient commercial culture, and by the early 1900s, many among them were founding businesses – grocery stores, fruit stands (where they succeeded the Italians), as well as fur-cutting shops, a business in which they soon dominated. In 1906, Thomas Antous established the Light Rock Water Company on Balmforth Avenue to sell drinking water to Danbury factories. The Lebanese and Syrians tended to Americanize quickly but did not forget their roots. In 1908, David Charles opened a small grocery on the Keeler Street corner of Main and had a tile inscribed in English and Arabic lettering with the Arabic version of his name, Daoud Bocharhe, along with the date. The first Syrian-American club featured strong Turkish coffee along with Arabic food.

By 1915, there were about 250 Syrians and Lebanese in Danbury, comprising 46 families. Many Christian families worshipped at first in St. Ann's Melkite Church on William Street, founded in 1910. By 1924 the Orthodox among them had built St. George Antiochian Orthodox Church on Elm Street in the heart of what became the "Little Lebanon" area around Spring, Elm and New streets. It was the first Syrian Orthodox church in the state, attracting worshippers from as far away as Bridgeport.

World War I drove many Christian Lebanese to America in order to avoid being drafted into military service by the Ottoman Turks. Between 1900 and 1916, even more left this region because of desperate shortages of food. Those who came to Danbury told stories of people dying of starvation. An even larger number of Lebanese moved to Danbury in the 1920s when textile mills in Lawrence and Fall River, Massachusetts, closed. The most numerous of the city's three Middle Eastern Christian groups, the Maronites, did not build their own church until 1932, on the corner of New and Stevens streets.

The Portuguese influx into Danbury was also in its infancy. The 1910 U.S. Census revealed a dozen laborers, farm hands and a single hat maker of Portuguese origin in a boarding house at 176 Beaver Street run by a Portuguese fur-shop worker and her Italian husband. Names of the boarders included Botelho, Simao and Henriques. The situation hadn't changed by 1916, when the Bible Society's canvass showed a similar number. But shortly after that, a large number of Portuguese men began working in the hat factories and joined local road construction crews, so that by 1925, Danbury's Portuguese population numbered over 800.

Most of these arrivals came from the southeastern Massachusetts and Rhode Island textile mill centers of New Bedford, Fall River, Taunton and Pawtucket. These cities had the highest concentration of Portuguese people in the country, but their textile mills were closing. Some of the first Portuguese to settle in Danbury in 1914 and 1915 took jobs in hat shops, and almost certainly Frank Lee hired a number of them to replace striking workers in 1917. But within a few years, the contracting firms of Osborne & Barnes and Bernard J. Dolan became the major employers of Portuguese manual laborers, who made up the bulk of the initial flow into Danbury. It was said that both of these contractors went to the docks in Boston to meet the boats from Portugal in order to recruit workers. As with the Italians they replaced, some of these immigrants had skills as masons and carpenters that they went on to utilize in the local construction trades.

A deep desire to escape poverty motivated the Portuguese immigrants. Most who arrived in Danbury came from mountainous areas northeast of Lisbon, from the regions of Lausa, Tres Montes and especially from in and around the town of Gouveia, today one of Danbury's sister cities. Another sizable contingent originated in the offshore islands of the Azores and Madeira. As a general rule, the vanguard of immigrants were young men in their twenties, strongly motivated to work hard and, for the most part, without union experience. Their level of education and literacy was rudimentary. Working hard and saving money was their key to financial security and a hedge against the poverty they'd left behind. The example of older generations, who shunned any display of wealth, was a powerful guide. Although some came with skills as barbers, tailors or shoemakers, most had to learn new occupations in the hat, fur and glue shops and other factories once they got here. Married men sent for their wives once they'd gotten established, while others often married Danbury's Italian women, who they regarded as compatible in culture and language. The family structure was patriarchal and traditional, but men worked such long hours that women commonly made most household decisions although they, too, frequently worked in hat, fur or glue shops, sometimes with their older children. Families tended to rent large houses, so they could take in boarders. Most of the single male immigrants lived either in boarding houses, usually run by women who prepared meals and did laundry –

services that were included in the rent – or in one of several so-called casas de malta, where clusters of men would rent a house together, building their own crude furniture and cooking their own meals in a bare-bones environment.

Almost from the first, the Portuguese population was concentrated in the side-street neighborhoods off Liberty Street: Nichols, Comstock, Chestnut, and Pahquioque Avenue, an area that eventually earned the local nickname of "Little Portugal." By the mid-1920s, businesses like Ventura's grocery and a popular bakery on Liberty Street catered to the growing colony. However, the first Portuguese grocery was established in 1924 by a woman, Maria Jose Santos, who specialized in making chourico sausage, a staple of the Portuguese diet. In the same year, the Danbury Portuguese community established the Sons of Portugal, the first organization of their nationality in the state.

In many ways, the success of these immigrant groups in Danbury seems to have been the result of a smooth and inevitable process. Indeed, the city did have some special characteristics that promoted assimilation. Old and new stock worked together in the hat factories, and their children attended the same public schools. Downtown Danbury was a particularly effective mixing bowl. In such a small and compact city it was easy for all residents to walk or take a trolley to buy goods, go to work, participate in organizations or simply take part in the active life of Main Street. Thanks to the central location of employment in the hat industry, all groups tended to live near one another. George Lepper, son of German parents, who grew up in the Division Street neighborhood at the turn of the century, remembered that "there were no ghettoes as such, though people from the same country did tend to live in close proximity." Eventually, people from different groups began to socialize and intermarry.

But a nativist backlash fueled by suspicions about "foreigners" occasionally erupted. Some outbursts were local manifestations of national movements. As early as 1890, the American Protective Association, a group that believed Catholicism and Catholic schools were a beachhead for papal imperialism, attracted a "healthy membership in this city," according to *The Danbury Evening News*. Alson Smith, son of a Methodist minister and descendant of a Revolutionary soldier, recalled in a memoir how immigrants "in my childhood were treated [sic] with a combination of contempt [sic], amusement and hatred. In our Methodist Sunday school we whispered excitedly about the guns that the Irish were supposed to have stored in the basement of St. Peter's Church against the day when the Pope should step ashore at New Haven."

Immigrants faced sporadic discrimination in housing and in other aspects of life. Lina Novaco's Italian immigrant parents had to purchase their home on a prominent section of Liberty Street near Main by resorting to the ruse of having a real estate agent buy it first, then sell it to them. The *Evening News* regularly highlighted the nationality of suspects in its police reports, subtly equating ethnicity with criminal behavior. It was reputed that union hatters despised certain groups of newcomers who they believed had been imported to work as strikebreakers. Irish-American boys from the Town Hill Avenue neighborhood tormented equally any outsiders who appeared on their turf. Members of many ethnic groups remembered how, as children, they had to line their pockets with stones when on their way to play baseball on South Street so they could ward off attacks.

Enforcement of the state's obscure blue laws forbidding certain forms of commerce on Sundays became a flashpoint of tensions between Yankee city authorities and small immigrant businesses. In 1903, authorities targeted Italian fruit stands that opened on the Sabbath, and in 1908, Syrian-owned fruit stands found themselves in their sights, as well. The owners complained of biased law-enforcement and stated in an open letter to Mayor William C. Gilbert their belief that they had the support of the general public in the matter. "From the conversation and expression of the large majority of citizens," the letter declared, "we are of the opinion that the public believes that every business man is entitled to be treated alike no matter where he was born or what he deals in." The growing climate of intolerance even provoked a mini-international incident in 1911, when a Danbury police officer tore down an Italian flag flying next to an American flag in front of August Mangani's store on White Street on September 20, Italy's Independence Day. The officer contended the flags were not displayed properly and removed them even though the merchant had agreed to correct his mistake. Alerted by the angry Mangani, the Italian consul in New Haven came to Danbury to investigate. A handshake ultimately settled the matter, but Danbury's Italians felt deeply disrespected.

At about the same time, the city's labor struggles took a xenophobic turn. In 1909, the local Fur Hat Manufacturers' Association issued a veiled threat to striking unions that they would, with reluctance, "import a lower grade of workers – likely to be mainly foreigners, having a different standard of living and content with a scale of wages much lower than the Danbury standard." Such a step, the owners emphasized, would "transform the character of the town." Eight years later, union men themselves echoed these statements when they accused manufacturers of bringing in "the scum of Europe" to work as strikebreakers at Lee's and other striking plants in 1917 and 1918.

World War I heightened pressure for national unity. Not surprisingly, J. Moss Ives led a campaign to speed assimilation of immigrants even though the city's Italian and Lebanese societies, the town's evening school, and the local Daughters of the American (DAR) chapter were already sponsoring programs that taught the English language and prepared immigrants for citizenship. The Mary Wooster DAR effort to help immigrant women, directed by the influential Mrs. John C. Downs, even hosted an annual "Ellis Island" party to raise funds for gifts to arriving immigrants. Ives brought speakers to the city to lecture on the nature of "Americanism" and the menace of Bolshevism. In 1919, the city responded to state and federal initiatives by instituting an Americanization department in the school system with a full-time director, the Rev. Elliott Barber, a Universalist minister who had some experience working with immigrants. The program aspired to "acquaint [immigrants] with the ideals and something of the history of this country, its institutions and its standard of living." In the early 1920s, Barber organized "real American" Independence

Day events that included speeches by Barber and Americanization directors from other parts of the state, as well as band concerts, baseball games, boxing matches and – one year – a gymnastic performance by the Slovak Sokol.

During the 1920s, federal quota laws drastically reduced the flood of immigration from southern and eastern Europe and the Middle East, areas of the world that had sent many citizens to Danbury. As those immigrants proved their loyalty and continued on the path to integration into American life, formal Americanization efforts faded. However, fear of ethnic and racial difference did not disappear from Danbury life.♦

Courtesy of Danbury Museum & Historical Society Authority

The 1928 wedding of Paul Tallman and Pauline Kearney. Henry Kearney, father of the bride, stands behind the bridegroom and is the only person in the photograph with a mustache.

Chapter Four Spotlight

African-Americans

One group of Danburians little affected by the massive influx of newcomers and immigrants was the city's small population of African-Americans, which numbered around 150 people in 1915. A scant handful of these individuals were working hatters who owned their own homes, a few others, mostly older, were former circus performers, and still others worked in the city hotels. So many worked at the Ridgewood Stock Farm as grooms and in other capacities that there was an organized Ridgewood Social Club that held a "cake walk" dance in 1896. Many of the oldest of these families, such as the Tallmans, had originated in New York; but increasing numbers of new families were arriving from Virginia, Maryland and other Southern states. By 1896, two black churches were in existence in Danbury, the older Mt. Pleasant A.M.E. Zion church having been joined by New Hope Baptist church, founded by newcomers from the South.

Danbury's African-Americans lived in an ambiguous world characterized by mixed messages from the larger community. Since the 1870s, blacks possessed full citizenship rights in Connecticut, the men able to vote and serve on juries. However, they could experience almost daily acts of casual discrimination, such as being prohibited from sitting anywhere but the balcony at the popular Taylor Opera House, or from skating at the public rink except on special days when the rink was reserved for them. Occasional items in the newspapers reveal cases of wretched poverty: two families made homeless when the former brewery they were living in burned; others living in near-shacks on the city's outskirts. Some streets originally known informally for the African-American families that lived on them were renamed, such as Crane Street (originally known as Freeman Street) and Seeley Street (originally called Tallman Street), while Moses and Tom Mountains also reputedly took their names from earlier African-Americans, who were supposedly slaves of a local landowner.

Unlike the South, though, where legal segregation enforced a rigid caste system based on race, individual black Danburians could and did earn the respect of the entire community. When Samuel Brooks, son of a successful Elm Street barber originally from Maryland, became the first African-American graduate of Danbury High School in 1893, he earned the honor of reading the essay at graduation. His selection, school authorities hastened to assure the public, was based on merit rather than "sentiment." Brooks' future looked bright; he went on to attend Philips Exeter Academy for a year before going to Yale, but he never completed college and spent most of his life waiting tables at an exclusive Hartford club. Another Danbury African-American who made the news during this era was Henry Kearney, who had found his way to Danbury from Virginia. In 1898, with African-Americans in the South being lynched at the rate of one every three days, so many residents of the rural Great Plain district showed up at Kearney's murder trial as character witnesses that the prosecutor dropped the murder charge and proposed a plea bargain. Kearney had shot the estranged and enraged husband of a woman who had taken refuge in a farmhouse Kearney was guarding for his employer. Kearney argued that he had shot blindly out a window to scare the man off, but had hit him by mistake. He ended up serving only two years in state prison, and went on to have a successful life as an employee of the Rider Dairy and a pillar of New Hope Baptist Church. His daughter married into the Tallman family, whose members have made many contributions to Danbury life. ♦

Photographer Frank Baisley's image of the emotional sendoff for troops leaving for training camp from the White Street railroad station in the summer of 1917 captures Danbury's enthusiasm for the war.

The Great War

Between ten and twenty thousand people – approximately three-quarters of the city's population – gathered on July 28, 1917, to send the first contingent of troops from Danbury to their training camp on Long Island. The crowd lined the parade route from the new National Guard Armory on West Street down Main and White streets to the passenger station there. One hundred members of Danbury's Eighth Company of the Connecticut National Guard marched past, accompanied by two bands and two drum-and-bugle corps. It was the biggest parade thus far in the history of this parade-obsessed city.

Prominent among the troops was Mayor Anthony Sunderland, who took a leave of absence from the mayoralty to join the military, an offer rebuffed by the Army until near the end of the World War I when he was accepted for aviator training. By the end of the global conflict in November 1918, the city's wholehearted support for the war effort was to be overshadowed by a crisis in its economy that put an emphatic end to the boomtown mentality begun in 1889. At this critical juncture, Danbury's leaders willingly sought a more promising path to prosperity.

The first contingent of Danbury soldiers in the American Expeditionary Force left for France in December 1917. By the time fighting ended in November 1918, the number of young men from Danbury who had been killed on the Western Front was 31, and 50 more were injured. George Hawley, who grew up in the rural Great Plain district, gave his life in the conflict. Frequent letters written to his parents from the front lines, now in the archives at Western Connecticut State University, reveal that his hometown was frequently on his mind. He expressed gratitude for receiving his first copy of *The Danbury Evening News* since arriving in Europe, regret at missing the local Memorial Day parade, and joy at chance encounters with other soldiers from Danbury. Tragically, Hawley contracted meningitis and died in a military hospital in France just a month before Armistice Day. The American flag at City Hall flew at half-staff in his honor. Raymond Walling, another casualty of the war, received a different form of posthumous recognition when the Veterans of Foreign Wars named its Danbury post for him.

Danburians supported the war enthusiastically. Twenty-six hundred men between the ages of 18 and 45 registered for Selective Service. Each week a fresh contingent of draftees left for Fort Devens, Massachusetts. Men unable to qualify for military service joined the Home Guard, who protected key installations such as railroad bridges and factories. A series of Liberty Loan drives raised nearly $6 million from the sale of "liberty bonds." The local chapter of the Red Cross played a leadership role, collecting cloth that could be used for dressing wounds, one shipment alone providing 15,000 pieces of bandage material. The Red Cross also sponsored parades to promote the war effort, which included knitting blankets, sweaters and countless pairs of socks for the troops. The organization even shipped two tons of jam canned by Danbury women to the front.

Other home-front experiences were more challenging and less psychologically satisfying. Because military needs held first priority, civilians faced a serious food shortage. Staples like flour, potatoes, onions and sugar were in short supply and commanded high prices. The federal government mandated conservation, and local bakeries had to use less flour to produce so-called "war bread." The State Council of Defense went further, asking residents to go without white bread two days a week. Hat executives joined the war effort by offering a cooperative way to produce more food for home consumption. The Mallory Hat Company leased an 80-acre farm in the Miry Brook district – rechristened the Mallory War Farm – where 150 employees worked during off-hours and on Sundays to plant and cultivate potatoes. For their labor and a modest fee, workers shared in the harvest. Even though Frank Lee, the city's biggest employer, was embroiled in a bitter strike, he set aside a portion of his own farm on the edge of Danbury, where his employees grew potatoes. Their efforts were recognized that July by state officials who credited Danbury with the largest increase in potato production in the state.

The combination of a brutally cold winter in 1917-18 and the growing military demand for fuel created a dangerous shortage of coal. In order to cope with the subzero temperatures that froze Danbury in January 1918, residents swamped local coal dealers seeking small quantities of the scarce product. Dozens of high-school students cut wood on farms in the King Street and Ridgebury districts on weekends for the city's fuel committee to distribute to needy residents. Factories and businesses operated for 10 successive Mondays during midwinter without any heat. The school system resorted to a different tactic, cancelling classes for a week in February.

The specter of communicable disease appeared twice in Danbury during this period. In 1916, the year before the war, a polio epidemic in New York threatened to spread to New England. Danbury officials responded quickly with extreme measures. Police stationed at the railroad depot and all major road connections banned visitors from entering the city. Local children were not allowed to leave Danbury or, if they were away, to return until the threat had passed. The restrictions worked. Danbury experienced only three cases of the disease, two of them in children from New Jersey who were already sick before they visited Danbury and who died shortly after arriving. Unlike many Connecticut border towns, Danbury avoided the full brunt of the epidemic.

When evidence of the Spanish influenza pandemic appeared in October 1918, just before the war's end, Danbury officials responded quickly and comprehensively as they had done two years earlier. The town health officer, Dr. George Lemmer, reported that only a few days after the disease made its appearance, he had recorded 340 active cases. The worldwide pandemic strained but did not overwhelm the city. In early October, schools, including the state normal school and the newly established state trade school, cancelled classes indefinitely. Churches curtailed Sunday services; theaters closed. Officials, worried that crowds jammed into trolley and train cars on the way to the Danbury Fair would spread disease, cancelled the annual event at the last minute. Railroad cars filled with prize livestock arriving at the fairgrounds had to turn back as did some motorists, mostly from New York, who were stunned at the sight of the empty fairgrounds. City physicians learned to get by on a few hours of sleep each night and had to abandon their office practices to attend the sick. One doctor told the Danbury News that he had made 42 house calls in a single day and still had to refuse many requests for care, while the tiny two-person staff of the Visiting Nurses Association labored constantly during the crisis, often making its rounds in borrowed automobiles. More seriously ill patients filled the hospital's 60 beds and additional space in the former Children's Home orphanage on Town Hill Avenue. These measures enabled Danbury to suffer less than half the number of fatalities of similarly sized Connecticut cities such as Meriden. Nevertheless, over 2,000 people – roughly one in every 11 of the city's residents – contracted Spanish flu during October 1918, and 89 of them died.

All the enthusiasm and sacrifice of the war effort could not disguise the reality that Danbury's economy was in serious trouble. A combination of lower demand and a shortage of raw materials plagued the local hat industry. Large numbers of men in military uniform were no longer customers for Danbury's main product, a medium-grade fur felt hat. No Danbury firms specialized in making hats for the military, and only a few were flexible enough to tap this market. D.E. Loewe, for example, had to add a rare night shift to fulfill a contract with the army. At the same time, the worldwide nature of the conflict cut the supply of essential raw materials for making Danbury's main product. The industry could no longer obtain aniline chemical dyes from Germany and was forced to revert to inferior dyes made from tropical logwood. Germany's aggressive submarine warfare interrupted shipping of rabbit fur from France and the European continent. And in early 1918, the British government made the situation worse when it decreed that rabbits raised in Australia had to be used as food for soldiers rather than as a source of fur for hat production.

Given the bleak picture, Danbury workers sought employment in the booming munitions plants in Bridgeport. However, without a trolley connection between the two cities, unemployed Danburians could not commute from home and were forced to move to the crowded and expensive Park City. This population shift deprived many hatters who owned two- and three-family houses of desperately needed rental income. In the summer of 1918, a group of investors led by Danbury postmaster James Cuff sought federal assistance for laying railroad tracks to Long Hill outside of Bridgeport and for running special trains from Danbury.

Courtesy of Danbury Museum & Historical Society Authority

In an effort to relieve home-front food shortages, workers at the Mallory Hat Company harvest potatoes in 1918 at a farm leased by the company in Miry Brook.

Remington Arms and other factories, hard-pressed for workers, welcomed the plan and even posted signs advertising the proposed service. Some eager Bridgeport residents traveled to Danbury to search for bargain rentals. Unfortunately, Washington authorities showed no interest in the project.

At this time, several of the city's biggest hat manufacturers decided to take advantage of unsettled wartime conditions to launch an aggressive assault on the hatting unions. The struggle finally accomplished some manufacturers' long-sought goal of transforming Danbury from a union stronghold to an open-shop town. The increase in the price of raw materials, especially scarce imported fur, put pressure on both sides as they tried to negotiate a new bill of prices during the spring of 1917. The United Hatters, fearful of a rise in living costs that usually accompanies a war, sought to tie the bill of prices to the selling price of hats. That way, if inflation drove up prices, both the selling price of a hat and the workman's wage would go up. This arrangement had been part of the 1916 union contract for soft hats, and had been in place for derbies since 1902. Given wartime conditions, though, manufacturers were wary about granting wage increases without knowing their exact costs. Nevertheless, several major firms, including Mallory, went along with the union and quickly signed a new contract.

Others in the Danbury Fur Hat Manufacturers' Association balked. Led by Frank Lee, they refused to sign a contract containing the new bill of prices and, in 1917, triggered the longest and most devastating strike in the city's history. Lee, along with his former partner Harry McLachlan, the John W. Green firm and a few others, took the position that linking the bill of prices to the selling price of hats was a departure from past practices that had to be subject to arbitration, as spelled out by the Father Kennedy Accords. The union locals responded predictably that wage policy, not local arbitration, was handled by the national organization. Lee, well aware that the locals did not have the power to contradict decisions of the national leadership, knew they would have to choose either to withdraw the union label from Lee's hats or leave the national union. In a dramatic move in May of 1917, Lee climbed atop a packing crate in his factory at the close of a workday to explain his position to 300 finishers in his employ, including some union officials. A few days later the union locals voted to go on strike against Lee and the other unsigned companies.

The real issue behind Lee's actions was his conversion to the open-shop creed advocated at this time by many other industrial leaders in Connecticut. As late as 1913, Lee was willing to abide by the Father Kennedy Accords and submit a dispute to arbitration, but by 1917 he had come to believe that unions were "undemocratic" and that the national hatters union leadership represented a harmful outside presence in local affairs. Business executives in other parts of the state, such as Clarence Whitney, a Hartford industrialist who spearheaded the anti-union drive of the Manufacturers Association of Connecticut, strengthened Lee's resolve to hold on to his adamant position.

After seeing his factory idle for five weeks, Lee resorted to a familiar manufacturers' tactic, leasing the small Beltaire factory on north Main Street, which he proposed to operate as an open shop, and announcing that his "Big Shop" on Leemac Avenue was for sale. Disconcerted by the prospect of losing the city's largest employer, his striking employees formed a committee to confer with the United Hatters officers on a suitable response. But the committee's deliberations revealed divisions in the union ranks, one member warning that the loss of Lee's factory "might kill Danbury." Following the meeting, Makers Union local president Jeremiah Scully spent hours trying to persuade a stubborn Martin Lawlor that Lee would never bend on this issue. "We can break Lee," Lawlor responded defiantly.

Lee's allies in the Hat Manufacturers' Association lined up behind him, voting to close their plants rather than accept the new contract and criticizing the strike as a "death blow for Danbury." But following their largest meeting ever, during which more than a thousand union hat makers jammed the City Hall courtroom, spilled out into the hallways and even sat on judges' benches, the locals voted overwhelmingly to support the national union leadership's position. True to his word, Lee reopened on

Women members of the Red Cross, clad in white and carrying a huge American flag, staged frequent parades like this one on May 18, 1918, to promote their many war-related activities.

north Main Street as an open shop, but maintained his offer to submit to arbitration but only with a local union.

The strike took a different course from almost all others in Danbury's past. For the first time since 1882, things got ugly. Even the local newspaper's sanitized coverage could not ignore incidents of violence between union members and scabs that resulted in a court injunction protecting those who crossed the picket line. Threats were painted on the side of the barn on Frank Lee's farm. He took them seriously enough to withdraw his children from St. Peter's School, where they were being taunted by their classmates. According to his daughter, Lee slept with a revolver under his pillow during this time, and one night took a shot at a prowler trespassing near the house. Unlike previous strikes, the unions now received minimal support from the public, and the forces within the community that usually pushed for settlement – the clergy and downtown merchants – played different roles. Important members of the clergy were hostile to the strikers. Reverend A.C. Coburn of St. James Episcopal Church denounced the strike as unpatriotic during a time of war and militantly advocated for the open shop. Rev. Walter Shanley of St. Peter's Roman Catholic Church, who never hesitated to speak out or write about such social issues as temperance and gambling, also expressed disapproval of the strike, particularly of the national union leadership. Shanley, who had begun his pastorate at St. Peter's on the same week that Father Kennedy had begun his at St. Joseph's, took a different stance toward the unions, sometimes exchanging volleys with Martin Lawlor in the form of letters to the editors of *The News*. His remarks in one sermon provoked Makers' Union local President Jeremiah Scully to the unheard-of act of protesting loudly from his pew before stalking out of church. The Mercantile Bureau of the Chamber of Commerce decided to remain neutral and, when individual merchants circulated a petition calling for an end to the strike, it was ignored. A citizens committee appointed by the mayor accomplished nothing.

In desperation, the unions hoped to counter this opposition by appealing to the federal government, then under the control of the seemingly more sympathetic administration of Democrat Woodrow Wilson. The U.S. Department of Labor twice sent investigators to Danbury. Both reached the same conclusion, that Lee and his associates had provoked the strike, were acting unfairly in trying to take advantage of the war emergency, and that their intransigence was prolonging the walkout. Despite these favorable findings, the National War Labor Board, which held hearings on the matter in Washington in October of 1918, concluded that the Danbury strike did not hamper the conduct of the war and so took no action.

The Lee strike had no definitive climax or dramatic final scene. In the popular mind, it merged with the discouraging 1917 settlement of the prolonged Loewe suit. With no help from Washington, the unions faced growing pressure from their members to lift the restriction against employment in the open-shop factories. In January 1922, more than three-and-a-half years after the strike began, both Danbury locals secured the approval of the national executive board of the United Hatters and voted to permit members to accept jobs in all local factories. Frank Lee had won; Danbury was "America's model union town" no more.

Danbury had suffered a series of blows during World War I that shook the city's confidence. A brutal winter, a terrifying pandemic, a major economic downturn and a divisive strike in its major industry had seemingly banished the earlier boomtown mentality permanently. Unlike Bridgeport, whose population jumped by 25 percent during the war, Danbury's rank among the state's largest cities fell to 10th place. Thanks to the widespread publicity about the Loewe v. Lawlor case, the city's image as a progressive place gave way to a reputation for "labor trouble." Apprehension about the condition of the hat industry was strong. A worried Charles Merritt voiced the anxiety of established factory owners when he candidly warned a town meeting in 1917, "We who have property here are highly concerned about Danbury's future."

At this critical point, Frank Lee and a few other businessmen again stepped forward to promote a new direction for Danbury. Even though he had made his fortune as the operator of the largest hat factory in the city, Lee argued that the only cure for Danbury's economic woes was to diversify its industrial base. The group led the drive to convince the state to establish its newest trade school in Danbury, where youths would be taught a variety of occupations. More significantly, using the newly organized Chamber of Commerce as a vehicle, Lee and his associates began a campaign to attract non-hatting firms to the city. The first limited successes had come in 1916, when a combination of Chamber salesmanship and generous financing persuaded the National Electric Utilities Corporation, a small New York manufacturing company, to move to Danbury. Shortly afterward, Bridgeport's giant Warner Corset Company agreed to set up a branch paper box factory in the city. When Lewis Heim, a skilled local machinist and inventor, decided in 1916 that the time was ripe for his company to mass produce his newly-invented centerless grinding machine that could fabricate ball bearings and other parts needed by the young automobile industry, the Chamber sprang into action. Excited by Heim's vision of a workforce of a thousand people, the organization helped him acquire land on Maple Avenue for a new factory and persuaded the New Haven Railroad to extend a rail spur to the facility. Unfortunately, lawsuits over his patents paralyzed the operation, which never had more than 125 employees, and ultimately forced the owner to sell his patent rights and leave Danbury, although his scaled-down firm remained in the city.

The chamber concluded from these mixed results that it needed a comprehensive plan if diversification was to become more than a slogan. To gather data to support these efforts the chamber hired a consulting firm to conduct an industrial survey of Danbury, which unexpectedly found much to be optimistic about. Three men worked full time for two months in early 1917 to produce a remarkable 445-page description of the city's economy that also made a number of recommendations. Some, like drafting a city plan and building a community center, were long-range. One of the economic recommendations was the "incubator idea," which urged Danbury to seek "varied industries of comparatively small size with endless possibilities for expansion." The visiting experts also outlined mechanisms used by cities around the country to attract new industries.

Armed with this information, an upbeat group of chamber members met at the banquet hall in the Odd Fellows Building on West Street in early July 1918 to make the "incubator idea" a reality by setting up the Danbury Industrial Corporation (DIC). Supported by the sale of stock, the organization had broad power to acquire land, build plants and lease industrial space that could coax new industries "with endless possibilities" to move to Danbury. Critics noted that half of the original directors of the corporation, as well as its first president, Frank Lee, were hatters involved in an anti-union drive, and suspected their motives.

But the broader public did not share this skepticism, and there was no evidence that bringing in nonunion firms was the organizers' sole intent. The first two fundraising campaigns, in August 1918 and September 1919, netted over a quarter of a million dollars. Hat manufacturers purchased the largest block of stock, but many investors were individuals who could afford only the $10 price of a single share. Large hat firms like Lee and Mallory made it possible for their employees to purchase stock on a time-payment plan.

By the end of the war, the new corporation had contacted 21 small companies, many of them in New York City. Despite its eagerness to lure firms with growth potential, the DIC followed strict selection standards, inspecting not only an interested firm's plant, but also its financial records. Only three prospects initially agreed to relocate to Danbury, all recruited without the promise of any financial subsidy. Lansden Electric Truck leased space in the Frank Lee factory. In 1919, Lee sold a three-acre segment of his company ball field on the corner of Triangle Street and Leemac Avenue so the DIC could erect two factory buildings (still standing) for Keystone Instant Foods. Another early client was the American Insulation Company, maker of molded insulation.

All of these initial ventures failed within a few years. A scarcity of labor became an unexpected problem for them as hatting made a temporary comeback in the 1920s. More seriously, while these young companies might have possessed "unlimited possibilities for expansion," they also carried substantial risk. The popularity of gas-powered vehicles in the '20s limited demands for Lansden's electric trucks. Instant food was a concept that didn't become familiar to Americans until the 1950s, nor did molded insulation in refrigerators until the 1940s. Public support of the DIC waned, and many stockholders tried unsuccessfully to sell back their shares. It is possible that the DIC itself might have folded without the backing of Frank Lee, who served as its president until his death in 1937. As the city's largest employer, Lee had the financial and physical resources to carry the endeavor through its infancy. His giant plant on Leemac Avenue was like a mother ship, nurturing recruited companies by offering them modern manufacturing space and an available source of electric power. Danbury continued to make enormous quantities of hats for decades but thanks to Lee, a new pattern had been set. Many of the firms that fed Danbury's economic renaissance after World War II were small, visionary startups and the DIC survived to assist many of those firms. Its continued existence was a signal that Danbury had embarked on a new direction and was setting out a welcome mat for change and innovation.♦

Hat production revived briefly after World War I. The Mallory Company, in 1919, constructed the tallest building in the city to be used for finishing hats. The building is visible to the left in this aerial view of the firm's Rose Street complex. The new facility was connected to the older sections by a tunnel that ran under the street.

"Prosperity, Peace and Progress"

To worried and slightly embarrassed Danburians, the 1920 Federal Census confirmed that their city was one of the few urban centers in the state to lose population during World War I. Hatting, the mainstay of the local economy, was not an essential wartime industry and therefore did not reap the economic benefits that armament production brought to nearby Bridgeport and other Connecticut industrial cities. In contrast, Danbury shared fully in the prosperity that swept the nation in the postwar decade, because hat manufacturing was a fashion-sensitive industry that catered to civilian consumer tastes. Once again, hatting became the life force of the community. Major hat companies expanded their factories in anticipation of growing demand. In 1919, the Mallory Company, which continued its policy of cooperating with the unions, modernized its operations on Rose Street by erecting a six-story concrete building for finishing hats. According to George Rafferty, a longtime Mallory employee and manager, a tunnel under the road connected the existing back-shop with the new building. That's where "there was an elevator that took the hat bodies up to the top floor," Rafferty remembered years later. "As each operation was done, it went down. By the time (the hat) got down to the bottom floor, it was done … Mallory had the perfect setup." Such efficiency paid off, as 1927 was the most profitable year in the firm's long history thanks to peak sales of both felt and straw hats. The company was also able to pioneer the city's first profit-sharing plan.

Frank Lee rebounded from the long wartime strike, re-established production in his "big shop" on Leemac Avenue, and continued to manufacture hats under his own brand. Lee was the primary supplier of men's hats for the J.C. Penney discount store chain. Continuing his civic involvement, in 1927 he started a daily newspaper, *The Danbury Times*, which merged with the rival *Evening News* in 1933. Lee pioneered, under pressure from insurance companies, a new formula for carroting fur that didn't contain mercury. He hired a Russian émigré chemist, Dr. Constantine Fabian, who developed the first non-mercuric carrot during the late 1920s.*

All segments of society shared the good times. By 1926, the Ridgewood Country Club, established on the site of the Rundle and White stock farm in 1921, already had a full membership and a long waiting list. As late as 1929, with segments of the national economy already beginning to falter, four costly private residences were under construction on prestigious Deer Hill Avenue. Members of the middle and working classes were equally well off. The amount of money deposited in local savings banks increased substantially each year, as did the number of homes built and new cars purchased. In 1924, for example, 16 homes, 500 automobiles, and 100 garages were added to the town Grand List (a register of taxable property.) Three years later, 85 new homes appeared for the first time on the tax roll. In 1926 an unprecedented 612 pieces of property were sold, more by 100 than had changed hands the previous year. Danbury's economy was so robust that it had attracted enough new residents to boost the city's population by almost 5,000 people by 1930.

* The hatting unions continued to campaign for legislation outlawing mercuric carroting solutions. When the federal government banned mercury in hatting on December 1, 1941, it marked the union's biggest single success after World War I. For decades thereafter the unions memorialized the date of passage of this law.

Surprisingly, the most persistent reservation about the health of the economy came from hat mogul Frank Lee who often used his annual report to the stockholders of the DIC to point out that little headway had been made in diversifying the city's single industry base. In 1927, at the peak of national prosperity, he candidly acknowledged that, despite the efforts of the DIC, no new manufacturing company had built a factory in Danbury in the past five years. He warned that the large amount of residential and commercial construction taking place in the city was deceptive because hatting, the traditional engine of the economy, was in permanent decline. Hat finishing, he reminded his audience, was already following the path of shoes and textiles out of New England to the South and Midwest.

But the predominant public and private mood was unquestioningly upbeat. *The Danbury Evening News* expressed the confidence felt by most residents in a special double-column message on New Year's Day, under the bold headline: "OUTLOOK FOR 1927 IS BRIGHT." "No cloud is discernible to-day [sic] upon the business, industrial or civic horizon," the paper insisted. At the start and again at the close of this glowing editorial, the writer used identical alliterative terms to emphasize that Danbury had reached a pinnacle of "prosperity, peace, and progress."

During this brief interlude of full employment and higher wages, the growing population of Danbury embraced new forms of technology that enabled most citizens to become enthusiastic participants in a national consumer society. Automobiles, electric lights, oil heat, telephones, electricity-powered home appliances such as refrigerators and vacuum cleaners, radios and phonographs – all available and used in a limited way before World War I – became popular, even essential, possessions in the postwar era. This energy revolution not only transformed individual lifestyles, it also altered the physical appearance and functioning of the city itself. At the same time, concentration on unprecedented personal abundance created an opportunity for a self-selected elite of industrial and business leaders operating outside the established political system to respond to what they saw as the collective needs of a changing community.

In this heady period, the community became dependent on electricity for lighting and operating a range of domestic, commercial and industrial machines. To meet this demand, power had to be brought from a distant hydroelectric source. In 1919, the Danbury and Bethel Gas and Electric Company completed a twenty-mile-long transmission line to supply the area with power generated by the Connecticut Light and Power Company's (CL&P's) recently built Stevenson Dam on the Housatonic River at Monroe. Boasting that consumption of electricity in Danbury had increased two hundred times in little more than a decade, the company launched a "Wire Your Home" campaign in 1923 to convince remaining holdouts to sign up. Customers could contract for this service on the installment plan by paying less than three dollars a month for eighteen months. In return, they would receive a gift of a lightweight electric iron as a bonus. Between 1926 and 1929, CL&P made electricity even more accessible by constructing the Rocky River complex on the Housatonic at New Milford, tapping the 11-mile-long, man-made Lake Candlewood reservoir for power. Candlewood was the largest body of water in the state, its southern tip reaching into Danbury.

Electricity made the radio a family friend. No longer was it necessary to jam into Wooster Square to get telegraphic reports of breaking events relayed by megaphone from the newspaper office as the crowd estimated at 2,000 people had done in 1923 to follow the Jack Dempsey-Luis Firpo championship-boxing bout. Instead, they could listen to immediate news reports from the comfort of their living rooms, and they did so to monitor results of the 1928 presidential election. Beginning in 1924, *The Danbury Evening News* facilitated radio use by listing the lineup of available stations and programs in the daily paper.

The radio and its frequent partner, the phonograph, changed the nature of home entertainment. In 1925 Heim's Music Store opened a stylish new facility on a busy section of Main Street near Wooster Square to display the latest model cabinet radios and radio-Victrola combinations. Eager customers marveled at the soundproof listening booths that made it possible to sample a wide selection of 10-inch records before buying.

Courtesy of the Danbury Museum & Historical Society Authority

By 1929, when this picture was taken, Main Street north of Keeler Street had strengthened its position as the retail and entertainment hub of the region. The Empress Theater had been modernized to keep up with its ornate new neighbor the Palace Theater, which was completed in 1928 and connected to the fashionable Martha Apartments (large building, mid-right).

Throughout this decade, many stopped at the store each Friday, when the latest Victor releases went on sale. Danbury households had become part of a national audience.

The automobile played a particularly influential role in altering life during these years. From fewer than 500 cars in town before World War I, Danbury's autos increased to 3,000 registered by 1923, and by 1927, more than 5,000 – one vehicle for every five residents.

The city's streets in the pre-war years had not been suited for automobile use. The major thoroughfares were surfaced with Belgian blocks, fine for horses hooves but rough on car tires. Other streets remained unpaved dirt that turned too often to mud. In 1919, the city approved a bond issue to macadamize* the principal streets, using the stone blocks discarded in the process to improve secondary roads. Under pressure from automobile

---

*The process of applying a smooth crushed stone and tar mixture over a concrete base.

clubs and other business and civic organizations, Connecticut did its part to open up the entire state to automobile travel. The General Assembly approved a trunk highway plan as early as 1907 that envisioned a spine of 14 major highways augmented by a grid of feeder roads that would link all sections of the state. With the help of federal money after 1921, state government provided an efficient highway system, paying for at least 75 percent of state road construction and maintenance costs. By the end of the 1920s, Danbury was the center of a network of concrete roads that stretched in all directions.

Danbury's relatively remote position in this expanding highway system led to one unexpected consequence. After the passage of the 18th Amendment in 1920 initiating Prohibition, the city became an attractive depot for criminal bootlegging operations. Federal agents regularly ambushed trucks conveying illegal whiskey on Sugar Hollow Road. In 1925, state police confiscated 35,000 quarts of liquor worth a quarter million dollars (today an amount that would be in the multi-millions) when they raided a still disguised as a chicken farm in the Beaver Brook district. As late as 1933, just before Prohibition ended, state police stopped a caravan of autos traveling from Canada to New York through Danbury with a cargo of hundreds of bottles of banned liquor.

At the same time, the rise of the automobile marked the end of the fixed rail era. The Danbury and Bethel Street Railway, the smallest system in the state as it had only 21 miles of track, became the first trolley line in Connecticut to cease operation. The company, which had not shown a profit for years, had plunged into bankruptcy in 1914. The court-appointed administrator, J. Moss Ives, did his best to reinvigorate the operation. He eliminated routes, sought a state subsidy and fought, in court, the competing jitneys, the large vans that carried passengers for a fee, Finally, in 1926, Ives joined the automobile revolution by reorganizing the utility as the Danbury and Bethel Transportation Company and began to operate a small fleet of buses.

Cars and trucks, in addition to eliminating fixed-rail competition, began to change the physical appearance of the city. Large older homes on both

ends of Main Street and on White Street were torn down to make room for
automobile dealers and gas stations. State routes 6, 7, and 202 channeled
traffic through the center of the city, causing constant gridlock. Vehicle
parking and grade-level railroad crossings added to the congestion in the
downtown. The Hotel Green's owners had the foresight to double the
capacity of the building in 1914. Now it was ready to take advantage of
the boom in tourist traffic created in part by the opening in 1924 of the
Bear Mountain Bridge, the first bridge to span the Hudson River below
Albany. A sign at the New York-Connecticut state line on what locals
called the Danbury-Brewster Road welcomed travelers to "THE GATE-
WAY TO NEW ENGLAND." They came in droves. Business was so brisk,
particularly on weekends, that in 1928 the hotel added 35 more rooms
in the adjacent Pershing Building, built a year earlier to replace the 19th
century Taylor Opera House that had been destroyed by fire in 1922. Few
cities the size of Danbury could boast of a hotel with 185 guest rooms.

The automobile and the pattern of roads reinforced the role of the center
of Danbury, despite parking and traffic frustrations, as the entertainment
and retail hub of the region. Three theaters on Main Street were either
constructed or extensively renovated during the 1920s. The Empress – the
oldest and smallest facility – reopened in 1927, decorated in a fashionable
Spanish motif and featuring an expensive organ. Not to be outdone, the
manager of the Capitol, located at Wooster Square, called attention in
unconventional fashion to the modernization of his 1,500-seat movie
theater by scattering free passes over downtown from a rented airplane.
Both theaters, however, paled in comparison to the elegant Palace on Main
Street opposite City Hall. It was built in 1928 by the Griffing brothers,
enterprising real-estate tycoons who at the same time constructed the
adjacent five-story, Colonial Revival style Martha apartment building.*
According to a full-page pictorial spread in *The Evening News*, "thousands
were turned away" from a three-and-a-half-hour gala opening that featured
a nine-piece orchestra and a welcoming oration by the mayor. The art

---

* In reality the two buildings are connected. The entrance to the Palace is through a ground floor storefront
in the then fashionable apartment. Shortly after it opened Mayor Anthony Sunderland took up residence in
the Martha.

Courtesy of the Danbury Museum & Historical Society Authority

Although a trolley is visible and full of passengers in this photograph, it is clear from the large "Automobile Station" banner that the Hotel Green on Main Street was eager in the 1920s to take advantage of the heavy tourist traffic coming from New York. The hotel was the social center of the community during this period.

objects in the lobby stunned the audience, as did the ornate theater itself that could accommodate 2,000 patrons for talking movies or vaudeville productions – nearly double the combined capacity of the two smaller theaters. In a centralizing trend that affected other local ventures, Warner Brothers, a national firm already in control of forty film outlets in New England, took over the operation of both the Palace and the nearby Empress in 1929.

The rapid expansion and subsequent surprise sale of the McLean Brothers dry goods store, a modest fixture on Main Street since the 1870s, illustrates the powerful economic forces at work in the decade. In 1924, C. Stuart McLean, the shrewd third-generation family member to operate the store, sensed that the time was right to move his company to a new level. He purchased and then demolished the adjacent Bacon Family homestead, one of three century-old residences left on this portion of Main Street. McLean then commissioned Philip Sunderland, Danbury's most prominent architect, to design an impressive addition to his store to occupy this now vacant space. When Sunderland was finished, the proud owner felt justified in designating the two-story, 14,000-square-foot structure, which stretched 400 feet back from McLean's property's 70-foot frontage on Main Street, as "THE GREAT STORE." The building's limestone facade, arched glass and ornamental bronze entrance doors dazzled shoppers who, once inside, realized that Danbury now had a handsome, comprehensive department store with services ranging from a bargain basement to cold storage for fur coats. The newspaper reporter who attended the September 1924 grand opening of the new facility observed that the "most frequently expressed comment on the part of visitors to the store last evening was perhaps upon the metropolitan appearance of the establishment."

Clearly McLean had made a shrewd business decision. In each of the next three years the store earned a healthy profit that reached a peak of $23,000 in 1927. Such success generated interest from out-of-town investors. In August 1927, explaining that soaring sales required operating on a larger scale than he could manage, McLean sold the store for close to $750,000 to the Genung Company, a firm that owned five retail outlets in Westchester County. The sale was the largest commercial transaction recorded in Danbury up to that time. Although Genung executives insisted they did not run a chain-store business and guaranteed that the Danbury facility would continue to exist as an independent entity, control had passed out of local hands. But who it was that actually owned the business did not seem to bother customers. The first major event sponsored by the new management in September 1927 was an elaborate fashion show that drew a crowd of more than 1,000 shoppers, most of them women. They blocked the sidewalk and spilled into the street as they eagerly sought admittance.

National chain stores also discovered Danbury in the 1920s. The city welcomed its first modern food market in 1925 when the Mohican Company headquartered in New York City but with stores scattered from Maine to Ohio, opened in the Hull block of Main Street. In 1927, the J. C. Penney Company, owner of more than 800 branches and located in all parts of the nation, established a two-story retail outlet at the corner of

Main and Liberty Streets. After a careful market survey alerted Sears and Roebuck, in the process of making a transition from an exclusively mail-order operation, to the potential of the Danbury area, the Chicago company rushed to complete construction of a handsome, block-long facility on lower Main Street where it could offer ample parking. When it opened its doors in 1929, the store employed a staff of more than 70 clerks.

In contrast to the energy of private investors, local government was passive during the 1920s. Elected officials in both the city and the town were content to satisfy the minimal basic needs of police and fire protection, an adequate water supply, and paved streets. Political parties did not challenge the status quo. The post of mayor was part time and mostly ceremonial. There was not much difference between the Republican administrations of William Gilbert (1919-1923) and A. Homer Fillow (1923-1927) or that of Democrat Anthony Sunderland (1927-1931). No other political parties sought influence.

But public policy was not ignored during this placid period of self-satisfaction. While women participated in large numbers in national, state, and city elections after the passage of the 19th Amendment in 1920, they did not challenge male direction of local affairs. An elite group of business leaders and key hat factory owners dealt with important urban problems informally through a private organization known simply as the Booster Club. From its founding in 1919 until it accepted an invitation to affiliate with the Rotary International in 1926, the Booster Club exercised quasi-governmental power in Danbury. A small episode conveys a sense of the influence of the club. In 1923, Reverend John Deyo, a local minister, hesitated to invite the journalist Hamilton Holt to speak in Danbury until he had received assurance from the Boosters that the passionate advocate of the League of Nations would be well received.

The Boosters weekly luncheon at the Hotel Green was a forum where members discussed a range of contemporary issues: the Americanization of recent immigrants; the consolidation of town and city government; the frequency of train service from New York City; and the scarcity of automobile parking spots downtown. When faced with particularly critical problems, the Boosters moved from debate to action. In 1920, in an attempt to remedy an acute local labor shortage that they attributed to a lack of affordable housing, the club entered the real estate market by forming the Danbury Housing Corporation that would finance home construction. Following the pattern of the DIC, the Housing Corporation sold stock that was eagerly subscribed, at least at first, by the city's elite businessmen led by Frank Lee who invested almost $9,000. However, enthusiasm for this approach faded before any house plans were drawn or loans made. In early 1921, the Boosters shifted strategy and backed a more conventional building and loan association.

In the same year, the Boosters expressed alarm that no playground existed in the city. Danbury was "no longer a rural New England village where children are safe to run wild," warned Judge J. Moss Ives. "We are an industrial city and need to keep children off the streets." Under Ives' leadership, the Boosters commissioned the National Recreation Association to survey the city's needs and to make recommendations for improvement. Despite the Boosters enthusiastic backing of the plan drawn up by the visiting professional inspection team, the frugal City Council refused to appropriate the estimated $5,000 required to implement it.

Though frustrated, the Boosters needed to address an even more pressing challenge involving the city's youth. The high school on Main Street was desperately inadequate, operating on double sessions without space for music and physical education or even for student assemblies. Yet at a town meeting held in early 1922, voters rejected by a wide margin a proposal to build a new high school. In response, the state supervisor of secondary education threatened to ban further use of the old facility. Here civic leaders, with the Boosters an aroused nucleus, mounted a campaign to convince voters that Danbury needed to face reality and build a modern high school on property already owned by the city on White Street. Voters reversed their position at a second town meeting, and construction began in 1925. As he surveyed the work progressing on the new school, Mayor Fillow paid tribute to the Boosters. He insisted that the controversial bond issue that financed the building would never have been approved without the effort of the club members. The high school – now White Hall on the Midtown campus of Western Connecticut State University – opened in 1927.

By the time of its opening, the new high school had a neighbor: Fairfield Hall, the first dormitory and only the second building on the Danbury Normal School campus. Almost from the time the normal school began operation in 1903, Principal John Perkins had urged the General Assembly to provide boarding facilities for out-of-town students, arguing that this was the only way the tiny teacher-training institution could grow in size and influence. Now the Booster Club took charge of applying political pressure. In 1923, members had journeyed to Hartford to support a bill that authorized $300,000 to finance construction of a dormitory on White Street. When the education committee of the legislature traveled to Danbury for a campus tour and lunch at the Hotel Green, Theodore Bowen of the Boosters presented the city's case. These tactics convinced the lawmakers to approve the appropriation, though reduced in size, only to have Governor George Templeton, an economy-minded acolyte of Republican Party boss J. Henry Roraback, veto the bill.

Undaunted, the Boosters set up a special committee headed by Judge Samuel Davis to guide an identical bill through the legislature in 1925. When the education and appropriations committees held a joint hearing on the Danbury bill on March 25, 1925, the Boosters sprang into action. Banker Martin Griffing, the group's president, canceled the club's regular meeting that day so members could travel to Hartford to attend the hearing. A convoy of automobiles left the Hotel Green at 10:30 a.m. to transport thirty luminaries, including Judge Martin Cunningham and Frank Lee, to the hearing room in the capitol. There, these determined dignitaries testified on behalf of a bill again requesting $300,000 for dormitory construction. This time, after being reduced by one-third, the appropriation passed the General Assembly and the governor grudgingly signed the authorization. By the end of the decade, two modern school buildings, in good part monuments to the civic commitment of the Booster Club, stood side by side on White Street.

The climax of the Booster's involvement in shaping public policy came close to blurring the line between government and private organizations. The potential of aviation in the 1920s captivated the imagination of Club members, who believed that Danbury's future depended on turning the portion of Tucker Farm on Miry Brook Road used by pilots as a primitive landing site called Tucker Field into a first class commercial airport. Unfortunately, city and town government officials had little interest in this goal. To counter this resistance, Governor John Trumbull, an enthusiastic pilot, flew to Danbury and urged the Boosters to force government's hand by acquiring the crucially located 72-acre property. In 1926, a special aviation committee of the Boosters headed by Ira Wildman raised $15,000 to buy the land and finance grading of a runway. Convincing local government to accept ownership and financial responsibility for the airfield proved more difficult. The members of the city common council felt that because the facility would benefit the entire area, it should be the responsibility of the town. Pleading that they had no available cash for this purpose, the town selectmen agreed to ask voters for a future appropriation. With this shaky understanding, the Boosters turned ownership of the airport land over to the town on November 1, 1927. Shortly afterwards, a special town meeting decided to entrust the operation of Tucker Field for the next 20 years to the Danbury Airport Corporation, a private entity whose directors were Frank Lee, A.E. Tweedy and J. Edgar Pike, all influential Boosters. The mingling of public and private was complete. During the 1920s, a prosperous public was willing to cede political power to a confident business elite.♦

Courtesy of Danbury Museum & Historical Society Authority

Connecticut Light & Power Company employed more than 1,000 workers to complete, in just three years (1926-29), the monumental task of creating the largest lake in the state. This rare photo shows laborers using hand tools and horse-drawn equipment to prepare an unidentified area of what will become the lake bed..

Spotlight Chapter Six

Candlewood Lake

J. Henry Roraback, the boss of the Republican Party in Connecticut from 1912 until his death in 1937, enhanced the Danbury area's physical environment not by his political power, but by his entrepreneurial vision that turned the Housatonic River into a major source of hydroelectric power. This achievement was begun in 1917, when existing power franchises merged into the Connecticut Light and Power Company (CL&P), and advanced in 1919 by the construction of the Stevenson Dam. But the influential Roraback realized that he had to find a way to regulate the Housatonic's rate of water flow. His ingenious solution, accomplished between 1926 and 1929, was to dam the basin of its Rocky River tributary, then pump water from the Housatonic in New Milford up 252 feet to flood the basin, creating a reservoir that could be tapped when the volume of water in the Housatonic was low. The aptly described water "storage battery" created by this bold and expensive engineering feat was the meandering, 11-mile-long Candlewood Lake, the largest body of water in Connecticut. The lake touched Danbury and five neighboring towns, giving the region a unique and precious resource.

The creation of what for a short time was called Lake Danbury was a strictly corporate initiative requiring no public discussion or approval. In fact, the Danbury newspaper, while enthusiastic about the project, did not cover the progress of construction in any detail. Some locals were even skeptical that the effort would produce anything more than "a stinking mudflat." But beginning in 1926, surveyors left their rented North Street offices in Danbury each morning in a fleet of automobiles to plot all the land in the Rocky River valley up to 440 feet above sea level. Most of the 35 families that owned small tobacco or dairy farms in the basin sold their property willingly at the price the company offered. Even though Connecticut Light and Power possessed the authority of eminent domain, it had to resort to this tactic in only five cases. Clearing began once the 5,420 acres, including four natural ponds, had been acquired to contain the reservoir. Five hundred lumberjacks from as far away as Maine and Canada cut and burned all the trees, brush, and buildings on the site. Witnesses commented on the acrid smoke that blanketed the area for weeks. Six small cemeteries also had to be relocated.

While the lake bed was being prepared, an army of workers built a containment dam almost 1,000 feet long, 700 feet wide, and 100 feet high, along with a power plant. Both were located in New Milford, as were five smaller dikes at spots around what would be the water's edge. Roraback hired the United Gas and Improvement Company (UGI) of Philadelphia, a firm that had provided financial backing for previous CL&P projects, to do the construction. The main work camp, known locally as "UGI-ville," and four smaller satellite villages housed as many as 1,000 laborers. Pumping began in February 1928, and by September 1929, the lake had reached the proper elevation of 429 feet so that the Rocky River power plant could go into operation. However, it would take time for western Connecticut to recognize and take full advantage of the recreational potential of this five-million-dollar rearrangement of nature.

Two Danbury physicians, Dr. Frederick Pickett and Dr. William Bronson, were among the first to sense that the lake would increase the value of nearby property. As early as 1926, even before CL&P had acquired all the necessary acreage for the lake, the two men began to buy land that would border the future shoreline. During the 1930s they sold 50-by-50-ft parcels of land in a planned development they named "Aqua Vista" to purchasers primarily from New York City who built small log cabins, many without foundations, for summer use. Other alert investors established similar settlements of summer cottages in the pre-war years with bucolic names like Candlewood Isle, Point Driftwood, and Candlewood Knolls. These seasonal communities shared one negative characteristic: they were openly anti-Semitic, refusing to accept Jews. After World War II, the nature of settlements around Candlewood Lake changed. Restrictive covenants ultimately disappeared. Large-scale developments of year-round housing attracted a more affluent population. Recreational use of the lake soared. Candlewood Lake became a major engine driving regional growth.◆

Danbury's Main Street shared three major state highway routes. Even in this mid-Depression (1936) view looking south from White Street, the challenge of heavy automobile use is evident. Note the angled parking and the installation of a manually operated traffic signal at the busy Wooster Square intersection. Both were required to accommodate the increase of traffic in this area.

Depression Decade

Few in Danbury paid much attention when the Associated Charities society closed its doors in August 1939. After all, the Great Depression was fading, and the attention of the public focused on the darkening war clouds in Europe. Associated Charities had been established by prominent hat manufacturer Edmund Tweedy and other philanthropic citizens in 1879 as a voluntary, grass-roots organization, and it had gone on to provide financial relief to the needy in Danbury for more than fifty years. In large part, its demise stemmed from natural causes such as the aging of dedicated veteran leaders. But even more significant was the fact that the federal government, in responding to the national depression, had assumed primary responsibility for addressing poverty and unemployment in Danbury. Thanks to the New Deal, the Associated Charities had become obsolete.

The passing of this venerable, public-spirited body was more than a minor footnote to history because it symbolized a comprehensive shift in attitude during the Depression decade in Danbury. During these troubled years, confidence in the community's ability to solve serious social problems on a local voluntary basis gave way to acceptance of, even dependence on, federal help to cope with economic dislocation. As a result, public works projects financed by Washington enabled Danbury to meet civic infrastructure needs that had long been ignored.

Evidence of hard times in Danbury first appeared during the winter of 1930-31. The annual report of Associated Charities issued in October 1930 could not be ignored. Long-time Associated Charities President Charles Mallory warned that the caseload of the agency had doubled in the past year. In response, the Common Council authorized the establishment of a committee on unemployment to investigate local conditions. It took this step despite the jaunty optimism of Mayor Anthony Sunderland who judged, "Personally I think that Danbury is not so badly off as other places." Heavy snowfall during that winter enabled the public works department to hire some men from the crowds eagerly looking for work that lined up at its City Hall office and Rose Street yard after each storm.

Danbury's first formal response to the Depression was a private one. In July 1931, the Rotary Club (formerly the Booster Club), the Lions Club and the Businessmen's Association joined forces to set up a free employment service in City Hall. In the first two weeks of operation, the volunteers, despite the lack of town or city financial support, registered almost 150 people and found jobs for 20 of them.

Then, suddenly, prosperity returned to the hatting industry. Milliners who had delayed placing new orders for women's felt hats because of concern about the economy began to demand large quantities of the latest movie-inspired fad, the Empress Eugenie hat. During June, July, and August of 1931, Danbury factories turned out 120,000 hat bodies a day. Some factories worked three shifts; others put in a full day on Saturday. As veteran hatter George Rafferty remembered years later, "When that Princess [sic] Eugenie rush was on, those trucks would come up in the afternoon, and they'd wait for the day's production. When that last hat was out the door, the truck would go to New York." This spurt, which had faded by September, brought the city unwanted publicity as a haven for those searching for work. In an interview with *The New York Times*, First Selectman Elijah Sturdevant, who would be defeated in October as the Democrats swept the town election for the first time since 1919, urged desperate people seeking jobs to stay away. He then gave the reporter a perceptive analysis of the state of the local economy: "Danbury for the most part is a community of home owners and skilled workers. Toward the end of last winter, people of that class began to apply to us for relief, having used up their savings. So this sudden prosperity was badly needed. It has already passed its peak, however, for hatting is a seasonal industry and the period of part-time work will soon be here."

Sturdevant was correct, the boom was short-lived. By the fall of 1931, the Danbury unemployment commission, under the leadership of businessman Frank Hanson, had geared up to raise $20,000 in private donations so that the unemployed could be hired to carry out a variety of public improvement projects. The response was generous. The Mallory Hat Company contributed $1,000; Frank Lee sent a personal check for $500. Hatters who were working assigned a portion of their wages to the cause. Hoyt-Messinger employees, for example, pledged $300 a week over a six-week period.

During 1932, the unemployment commission kept some men busy on a variety of tasks. The Balmforth School grounds were graded; more than 16,000 trees were planted at the West Lake Reservoir; An American Legion-sponsored undertaking for veterans installed cinder sidewalks in outlying areas; and preliminary steps were taken to create a public park on land bordering the tip of Lake Candlewood and leased from the CL&P. The most dramatic project was a cleanup of the Still River, where teams of men in high rubber boots trudged through the river channel with forked sticks and rakes, picking up debris. Though well intentioned, Hanson and his commission were constantly short of funds and therefore could place only a fraction of those who applied, even by reducing hours for each individual from three to two days a week. In late January 1932, the commission admitted it had only enough cash to hire 50 men at a time, about 10 percent of the needy. When almost 250 idle men gathered outside City Hall on a blustery day in mid-March, the commission could afford to put fewer than 20 men to work.

The Depression exposed the financial shortcomings of city government. The city's Grand List shrank by close to $250,000, due primarily to a sharp decline in car purchases. By the start of 1932, Danburians owed almost $500,000 in back taxes. A large floating debt, accumulated to finance road improvements in rosier times, increased the burden, and a dysfunctional tax collection schedule that did not coincide with the city's fiscal year complicated the situation. Taxes were due on November 1, while the fiscal year began on July 1, requiring the city to borrow in anticipation of taxes. This wasteful system was more inconvenient than devastating until the four local banks refused to advance any money for this purpose in August 1932. Then panic set in. An audit of city books demanded by the banks revealed that Danbury was operating in the red. When the first snow fell in December 1932, the city of Danbury had no funds to pay to plow it.

City government, now controlled by the Democrats, struggled to put its house in order. Increased assessments on automobiles prompted more than two hundred angry citizens to storm City Hall in protest. In March 1932, the Board of Finance cut $92,000 from the budget, mainly by deferring payment of the bill for paving West Street. But still more extreme measures were required. At the start of classes in September 1932, teachers' wages were slashed by 10 percent, a cut that a month earlier had affected firemen, policemen and other city employees. All those on the city payroll went from July to November in 1932 without any salary, the longest of several pay interruptions they suffered during the early years of the Depression.

Such painful measures were mere stopgaps. In the opinion of many residents, a total restructuring of city finances was necessary. On July 3, 1932, about 70 representatives of civic groups recruited by the Rotary Club met at St. James Church and took matters into their own hands by appointing a 25-person committee, headed by the president of the City National Bank, silk manufacturer A.E. Tweedy, to scrutinize Danbury's financial affairs. A few months later this aroused group, calling themselves

Courtesy of Stephen Flanagan

Danbury received a grant from the Federal Emergency Relief Administration in 1934 to refurbish the interior of its classic library on Main Street. The opportunity prompted Charles Federer, a Bethel artist and book illustrator, to volunteer to paint an appropriate mural on the wall of the Children's Reading Room. Working without remuneration for more than a year, he utilized local children as models for his large mural depicting a story-telling bard and his rapt audience. Finished in 1935 and still in remarkable condition, the historic painting is proudly preserved by the Danbury Music Centre, present occupant of the building.

the Danbury Civic Association, became the spearhead for tax reform and the most insistent advocate of government consolidation. The "Depression has been a good thing" one leading member, Probate Judge Martin Cunningham, assured a meeting of the Rotary Club, because it would force Danbury to put its financial house in order.

The Depression might tidy up the banks' balance sheets, but as the winter of 1932-33 approached, the number of unemployed individuals skyrocketed. This year there would be no fashion boom to help the hatting industry. Frank Lee found it harder to live up to his pledge, made the previous season, to hire all laid-off Danbury hatters by stretching out the available work. Inadequate work to share stymied the "Share the Work Plan" advocated so confidently by hatting officials. In this emergency, Jeremiah Scully, President of the Danbury Hat Makers Association, set up a soup kitchen on Crosby Street in January 1933. Supported by private donations of money and staffed by volunteer labor, the Danbury

Unemployment Restaurant provided breakfast and supper to a daily average of more than 200 men, women and children until May 1. In February the soup kitchen began to serve lunch to more than 100 students from the Balmforth and New Street schools, a practice that continued throughout the summer.

When Connecticut Tax Commissioner William H. Blodgett revealed that Danbury led the state in percentage of long-term debt, the Common Council, stung by criticism of the city's financial mess, hired New York City consultant Herbert Swan to draw up a financial reform bill to be submitted to the General Assembly. Swan, who in the 1920s had prepared the city's first zoning regulations, startled the council by insisting that a 21-mill tax rate was necessary to wipe out the debt accumulated over the past 40 years. In addition, he recommended that the Danbury charter be revised to facilitate more cooperation between the city and the town. The April 1933 crisis, when the city could no longer borrow money and municipal employees again went without pay, underscored the urgency of the consultant's advice. In desperation, the city issued taxpayers anticipation notes, which gave a six-percent discount to property owners who paid their taxes immediately rather than waiting until the November deadline. While this device did take care of the city payroll, the disappointingly small sum collected made no dent in the combined city and town debt that Swan predicted would hit almost two million dollars by 1934.

Supported by the Civic Association, consultant Swan, an engineer who respected the values of efficiency and rationality, presented to the Common Council a bill with sweeping changes in the city charter. In order to minimize partisan politics, Swan advocated setting up a unicameral City Council whose seven members would be elected at-large every four years, with the daily operation of the city placed in the hands of a professional city manager. This radical proposal touched off a heated debate. An overflow meeting of the Civic Association enthusiastically endorsed the changes and voted to send representatives to Hartford to testify for the bill. On the other hand, political leaders were adamantly opposed. Tom Keating, long time Democratic Party chairman, termed it too abrupt, too expensive, and not reflective of the will of the citizens. Whether this was true or not, the Common Council refused to submit the controversial bill to a referendum and instead voted to back a more modest substitute bill. The battle was joined in Hartford on May 12, 1933, in a three-hour meeting of the General Assembly's cities and boroughs committee. Attendance was so large that the proceedings had to be shifted from a hearing room to the House Chamber. Thomas Bowen, who had earlier told a Civic Association rally that this was a fight between the politicians and the "people," joined with Judge Cunningham and Lynn Wilson, the editorial writer of *The Danbury News-Times*, in testifying for the Swan bill. Aldermen, councilmen, and Corporation Counsel Keating were among the more than one hundred – twice the number in favor – who spoke for a less drastic bill. Its major provision was to make taxes due at the start of the fiscal year. The legislature ultimately approved this mild measure that constituted the city's bow to fiscal responsibility. The October 1933 sweep of town elections by the Taxpayers League and the March 1935 ouster of the Democrats from the mayor's office by Republican Adam Roth may have been a judgment on politics as usual.

While politicians bickered, the Depression worsened. Against the backdrop of rising unemployment, labor unrest surfaced. In July 1933, angry hatters picketed George McLachlan's factory on Rowan Street to challenge the discharge of union workers. State police had to be called when a crowd of protesters slashed the tires and hurled stones at the cars of workers who crossed the picket lines. Despite the bitter opposition of the Hat Makers Union, the resolute McLachlan maintained an open shop throughout the decade. Even in May 1935, when a rock with a note warning McLachlan to "Close shop or we will get you" shattered a window of his Farview Avenue home, he did not back down.

In September 1933, a thousand mostly Lebanese members of the United Fur Workers of Danbury, a local union organized and led by Reverend Nicholas Wehby of St. George Antiochian Orthodox Church on Elm Street, walked out of 16 fur shops in Danbury and Bethel in a disagreement over wages. Less than a year later, in June 1934, the distress of fur workers erupted into violence that shocked Danburians. On June 5, strikers stoned and wrecked three taxis carrying non-union employees away from the American Hatters and Furriers factory on River Street. Crowds of aroused fur workers clashed with police, sending several, including the chief, to the hospital. Eleven strikers, including several women, were arrested and lectured by Judge Henry Wilson who warned them that "We do not want this type of disturbance in Danbury." As Mark Asmer, the head of the United Fur Workers, complained in broken English, "This money earned by sweating of the brow is denied them, yet they are not even allowed to yell and complain." In an open letter addressed to the Danbury Businessmen's Association, Asmer insisted that his members could not support their families on the current meager wage. In all, the fur workers spent 14 weeks on strike during 1934 but failed to get recognition of their union.

The Depression reached its lowest point as the winter of 1933-34 approached. The Danbury unemployment committee once again

Courtesy of Janice Howard

As part of the New Deal, the federal government set up two Civilian Conservation Corps camps in the Danbury area. Camp Hook existed for only a year at Squantz Pond in New Fairfield, while Camp Fechner, on Wooster Mountain in Danbury's Sugar Hollow district, operated for five years. The young men pictured here, all between the ages of 18 and 25, engaged in forestry work – particularly in an effort to combat elm blight. They were paid $30 a month and had to send a portion of this amount home to their families.

began to solicit funds for its relief operation. The Salvation Army began feeding 75 persons a day in November. At the start of 1934, Associated Charities had to add more families to their overburdened caseload. At this critical juncture, the federal government appeared on the local scene, soon becoming the almost exclusive source of unemployment relief and the eagerly sought font of funds for badly needed public works projects. A succession of New Deal agencies, usually designated by their initials rather than their full bureaucratic name – CWA for the Civil Works Administration, FERA for the Federal Emergency Relief Administration, and WPA for the Works Progress Administration – provided jobs for thousands of men on a wide range of smaller projects. The Public Works Administration (PWA), under the control of the Interior Department, financed major construction including modernization of Danbury's antiquated sewer treatment system. In 1938, the eagerly sought building of the Federal Correctional Institution in Danbury brought more jobs to the area.

The first workers on the federal payroll were hired in December 1933. Frank Hanson, recently appointed head of the Danbury CWA office, assigned 500 men to improve the filtration beds at the sewage treatment plant in Beaver Brook, in response to a lawsuit from enraged residents of Beaver Brook and Brookfield. Later the same month, another 200 began to raise the grade of the airport runways so they would be level with adjoining highways. All federal agencies whose primary purpose was to subsidize jobs followed the same rules. Workers had to be taken from the roster of the unemployed (1,500 had registered in Danbury by January 1934.) Federal funds would cover wages, while the local sponsor needed to supply equipment and supplies. By the time the CWA ended its brief Danbury existence in April 1934 it had spent over $125,000, with more than 75 percent of the total expenditure coming from Washington.

Although the winter emergency was over, unemployment remained stubbornly high, persuading New Deal officials not to abandon its relief role. That Danbury depended on this help is clear. The FERA, established in April 1934, continued to fund the airport and sewage plant projects, and assigned 250 more out-of-work men to do needed painting at the fire-house, Broadview Farm, and the normal school. In the summer of 1934, Mayor Walter Morgan traveled to Hartford in an effort to persuade Eleanor Little, the Connecticut head of the FERA, to allocate more money for his community.

Thanks to an FERA grant, a longstanding Danbury traffic problem received attention, if not a solution. The Main Street link between West and White streets – the funnel for two major federal and four important state highways – suffered from chronic automobile traffic congestion. Many unprofessional estimates had been made of the volume of traffic, including one done by a *Danbury News-Times* reporter in August 1934, who asserted that 50,000 cars traveled that stretch of road on a summer weekend. In the fall of 1934, the FERA conducted a six-week traffic study utilizing 50 people to record around-the-clock counts at six critical points. The summary report, presented to a joint meeting of the Rotary Club, Lions Club and the Businessmen's Association at the Hotel Green in February 1935, documented that 15,000 cars passed through the city on a normal weekday and recommended such improvements as widening Main Street in several spots and eliminating diagonal parking in the critical area. In response, an indecisive city government first abolished angle parking, then reinstated it to placate angry merchants, and finally banned it again.

When the FERA ended its one-year life span in 1935, the WPA, an organization intended to be a more permanent federal agency, took its place. From 1935 through 1940, the WPA funded numerous local projects including the construction of Beaver Brook School and finishing the town park on Lake Candlewood. It was WPA money that enabled Danbury to establish its first inner-city park, although the route to the dedication of Rogers Park in 1940 was convoluted. It began in November 1935 with a complaint from Reverend A. C. Coburn, the founder and headmaster of the Wooster School, about the noise from the nearby airport that received heavy use from private pilots. The educator coupled his criticism with a suggestion that the airport would make an ideal "athletic park." *The News-Times*, sympathetic to Coburn's plight, praised his solution. What followed, according to the newspaper, was a heavily attended, but "disgraceful and confused," town meeting where speakers jeered and hissed at each other for more than three hours before agreeing to hold a referendum to decide the fate of the airport. The voters on December 6, 1935, on the strength of the strong opposition by the Fourth Ward that overcame narrow favorable margins in the other three wards, rejected turning the airport into a park.

However, this heated dispute focused community attention on the lack of playgrounds and parks in the city. The Lions Club funded and operated the only functioning playground, which was located at the corner of Osborne Street and Locust Avenue. The club resurrected the previously rejected proposal of Cephas Rogers, a local industrialist hard hit by the depression. Rogers had offered to give the city, in lieu of his $6,000 tax debt, a piece of property of about 20 acres that he owned at the intersection of Main and South streets. This time the service club persuaded the Common Council to accept Rogers' offer and to apply to the WPA for funds to drain the swampy land, construct access roads and build athletic facilities. With the city providing only $15,000 for equipment, 200 laborers began to reclaim the crucial spot in 1937. Despite cutbacks in WPA funding at the end of the 1930s, work on Rogers Park moved ahead steadily. When finished in mid-1940, the project cost about $175,000, of which the city paid a little over $30,000.

Not all New Deal alphabet agencies provided direct assistance to the unemployed. The PWA, set up by the National Recovery Act in 1933 and administered by the Interior Department, sought to boost the economy by helping to finance large-scale, carefully planned physical improvements that were carried out by private contractors. Danbury's sewer system was a major beneficiary of Washington aid. At the start of the Depression, the city's disposal system, which combined storm water with industrial and residential waste, was dangerously outmoded. In 1930, the Connecticut State Water Commission reminded city leaders that the present filtration process had been installed 30 years before to serve a smaller city. The commission strongly urged that it be brought up to minimum standards. Built to accommodate an annual flow of 750,000 gallons, the filtration system groaned under a load of more than double that amount. However, by the end of the decade, thanks to PWA assistance, Danbury boasted an improved water system with modern filter beds and a more efficient new sewer treatment plant in Beaver Brook. About half of the million-dollar cost for this upgrade was borne by the federal government.

A more controversial PWA-backed undertaking, the expansion of the South Street School, brought out the lingering tension between welcoming federal support and resentment of federal control. In September 1936, the PWA approved a grant of $52,600 for new classrooms and the board of finance quickly authorized the city's share of $64,500. Acting on the advice of the Connecticut State Board of Education, PWA officials recommended that the new building be erected not adjacent to the present structure on South Street, but a short distance away on less costly Triangle Street land. Area residents balked, claiming that the new location exposed students to dangerous traffic and unhealthy fumes from a nearby fur factory. The Board of Education dispatched Judge J. Moss Ives to Washington to deal with the impasse. When he returned, his message was blunt: If you want government money, build on Triangle Street. Ignoring this edict, an acrimonious town meeting on January 26, 1937, voted to locate the school addition on the original South Street plot, an expensive decision requiring purchase of privately owned property and higher foundation costs due to the swampy nature of the site. Only the intervention of Connecticut Democratic senators Francis Maloney and Augustine Lonergan overruled PWA objections and enabled Danbury to retain federal financial aid. The whole affair sparked local grumbling, highlighted by a Rotary Club-sponsored debate on the hidden pitfalls of federal generosity.

The surprise economic decline that began in late 1937 and continued until mid-1938 rocked Danbury along with the rest of the nation. The emergency overwhelmed local resources. By January 1938, town government needed to provide support for over 500 families, a record high, on a budget that had been reduced to $70,000 in anticipation of better times. Free food staples were distributed to the unemployed from a storage room in the basement of City Hall. Less than five months into the fiscal

In the summer of 1938, Danburians were surprised but pleased at the news that a $2 million prison would be built by the federal government on a 150-acre tract overlooking Candlewood Lake (visible at the top of this aerial photo). The Federal Correctional Institution, then a minimum-security facility, opened in 1940.

year, the entire budget for outdoor relief had been spent and the town had to borrow from a local bank. When First Selectman Marcus Schlitter proposed levying a special property tax to repay this loan, another animated town meeting rejected the plan. One resident was quoted as saying that this was the "stormiest" town meeting he had witnessed in thirty-five years of regular attendance. As a substitute, the town undertook an aggressive campaign to collect the more than half-million dollars that was owed in back taxes. Danbury even had difficulty paying its small share of WPA projects.

It was now automatic to look to the federal government for help in this crisis. Mayor Martin Cunningham and Selectman Schlitter conferred with Congressman Albert Phillips to seek ways to pump more federal money into the city. The WPA increased funding for existing projects such as work at Rogers Park. The PWA agreed to finance expansion of the high school as well as construction of a new state trade school building on land behind the Teachers College. The decision of U.S. Attorney General Homer Cummings, a former Connecticut senator and Stamford resident, to locate the first federal prison in New England in Danbury promised major benefits to the community. Some initial apprehension quickly gave way to expectation of increased employment and business expansion that would be generated by this $2 million facility. In addition, special PWA grants and a Department of Justice loan enabled the city to extend water and sewer lines to the Federal Correctional Institution that opened in 1940. *The Danbury News-Times* was never in doubt about the significance of this gift from Washington. A bold headline celebrated the new relationship between Danbury and the national government that had developed in the Great Depression decade. "FEDERAL FUNDS ARE POURING IN," proclaimed the newspaper joyously.♦

Courtesy of Danbury Museum & Historical Society Authority

The 1936 Danbury Trojan semi-professional football squad. Jack Thompson (no. 11, back row) was the organizer, manager, coach and quarterback of a team that attracted large crowds to Lee Field for games during the late 1930s.

Chapter Seven Spotlight

Danbury Trojans

The Danbury Trojans, the dominant semi-professional football team in Connecticut during the 1930s, brought excitement and pride to a city struggling with economic woes. With a roster studded with well-known former college players, the team attracted crowds of up to 3,000 spectators to Lee Field on Triangle Street to witness games with state rivals and teams from the established National Football League (NFL). However, before the decade ended, the financial burden of maintaining a top-notch team along with falling ticket sales forced the team to disband. The Danbury Trojans themselves were victims of the Depression they had helped the community endure.

Jack Thompson, the first Danbury High School graduate to earn a college athletic scholarship, organized the team in 1931, shortly after returning home from Lafayette College in Pennsylvania, where he had earned letters in three sports and then rejected a professional baseball contract from the New York Yankees. For the next nine years, Thompson, a gifted promoter as well as a superb athlete, served as the coach and star quarterback of the Trojans. Success came quickly. In the first few seasons this team of former high-school players, members of local club teams, and an increasingly large sprinkling of stars from area colleges, attracted crowds of over 3,000 fans to

Sunday afternoon games at Lee Field. A converted baseball facility, the field was located in the shadow of the huge Lee Hat Company factory. Heated rivalries developed with squads from other Connecticut cities, particularly Bristol and Torrington; but in 1933, Danbury's Trojans claimed the first of three consecutive state championships.

With fan interest at a high level, the Trojans' ambition grew. More prestigious college players, some from distant schools, were imported. Beginning in 1935, teams from the powerful NFL, such as the New York Giants, played hotly contested, early September exhibition games in Danbury. A year later, the Trojans invested in modernizing Lee Field, described by Thompson as "woefully inadequate" for football. The gridiron was graded and reseeded; the grandstand was doubled in size so that it could accommodate 3,000 spectators – "comfortably," Thompson assured the public – and floodlights for night games were added. As the sports editor for *The Danbury Evening News* enthused on the eve of the 1936 season's opening game against the Brooklyn Dodgers, "Big time football comes to Lee Stadium tonight!"

For a few years, public response remained strong. For example, a crowd of close to 2,000 fans stood five deep around the practice field to watch the team scrimmage prior to the start of the 1937 season. In 1938, the Trojans for the only time defeated a major power, upsetting the Brooklyn Dodgers 13-0 on the strength of two long passes by the indefatigable Thompson. The team confidently joined the American Professional Football Association, a new league made up of larger and more distant cities like Jersey City and Providence.

At the same time, the plunge in the national economy in 1937 worked against the Trojans. Travel costs and visiting-team guarantees in the new circuit soared, while paid-attendance per game declined to less than 2,000, a figure far below the financial break-even point. Thompson did all that he could to increase patronage. He cut ticket prices to 75 cents from the normal one dollar and released costly players. He threatened to move the team to another city unless support improved. A hastily arranged tussle with the Bristol West Enders, Danbury's traditional foe, designed to demonstrate community backing in 1939, produced the team's first victory of the season but drew only a small crowd. The harried coach was desperate enough to offer future Supreme Court Justice Byron "Whizzer" White, an All-American back at the University of Colorado, a chance to continue to play football for the Trojans on weekends in the hope that his presence would attract more customers. White, who had entered Yale Law School in 1939, declined. Such measures were in vain. The Trojans, a central element of Depression life in Danbury, ceased existence after the dismal 1939 season.

Despite the disappointing final years, contemporaries did not forget the accomplishments of the Trojans and their player-coach. When a group of now-elderly athletes formed the Old Timers Athletic Association in 1964, they unanimously agreed that Jack Thompson would be the first – and in their inaugural year, the only – person to be honored. A generation of Danburians remembered and appreciated the exciting play of the Trojans that helped the community cope with the trials of the Great Depression.♦

Draftees headed for military training during World War II depart before a large crowd gathered in front of the Fairfield County Courthouse on south Main Street. Approximately 4,000 men and women from Danbury served in active duty during the conflict.

Home-Front Sacrifice

The outbreak of war in Europe in 1939 stimulated the American economy. The nation responded with enthusiasm to President Franklin Roosevelt's plea that we become "the arsenal of democracy." Cities with defense plants became instant boomtowns. In Connecticut, workers from all over the country poured into places like Hartford, Bridgeport and New London in search of jobs in armament production. However, Danbury, as in World War I, did not share in this economic bonanza.

Signs that the Depression – usually associated only with the 1930s – continued in Danbury well into the next decade are abundant. In January 1941, the savings banks in the city held $60,000 less in personal accounts than in 1939. Even before wartime restrictions and shortages, there had been little residential construction. Most of the 31 homes built in the city in 1941 were in the Crescent Park development where tiny Cape Cod cottages on the western end of Park Avenue offered a low purchase price of $4,000 that could be guaranteed by the Federal Housing Authority (FHA).

Once the war began, Danbury was still not in the economic mainstream. The Connecticut Department of Labor indicated in August 1942 that Danbury was the only city in the state not to benefit from war work. To underscore this situation, the state agency pointed out that fewer people were currently employed than in 1939. Six months after Pearl Harbor, the unemployment rate in Danbury of close to 7 percent remained the highest of any Connecticut city.

In several crucial ways, the conflict hurt rather than helped the hatting industry, the backbone of the local economy. Most damaging was the interruption in the normal supply of fur from the European continent, and a 50 percent decrease in fur imports from England. Hat companies were forced to rely on Australian rabbit fur, an uncertain source subject to shipping risks in the Pacific war zone. Hatting, not considered an industry essential to the war effort, could not protect highly skilled workers from compulsory military service. Conversion of hat factories to war-related production was difficult because the wooden frame buildings that housed most local factories were not substantial enough to tolerate the installation of heavy machinery. There is also some indication that hatters, jealous of their artisan status, were not eager to be retrained.

The Danbury economy remained in the grip of the Depression until mid 1943. By this time a combination of the draft, which began taking young men out of the job market in 1941, and the employment of Danbury residents in booming war industries in other cities such as Waterbury, Stratford, Norwalk, New Haven, Hartford, and especially Bridgeport, had erased the labor surplus in the city. Two additional internal factors helped boost the local economy to a more healthy, if not robust, condition: the quick changeover of several established machine shops to producing items for war use, and the settlement of several out-of-town manufacturing companies in the city, the result of the "missionary" work of the Chamber of Commerce and its energetic President Edwin V. Haigh.

Danbury shared in war production primarily as a "feeder" city exporting labor to other parts of the state. Migration of large numbers of workers to Bridgeport began long before Pearl Harbor. Worried that Danbury would become what one citizen who to wrote him termed a "ghost city," and urged by harried Bridgeport officials to prevent Danburians from moving to the overcrowded Park City (Bridgeport), First Selectman Marcus Schlitter took steps in early 1941 to provide convenient bus transportation between the two cities so that Danbury residents could commute to work. From 1941 until the end of the war, buses departed from the front of the Pershing Building at 5:20 a.m. each day to transport local citizens to jobs at Remington Arms and other factories in Bridgeport. Demand for workers was so intense that the state Labor Department had no trouble placing 200 applicants from Danbury in Bridgeport munitions plants in the single month of October 1942. Local people took advantage of labor shortages in other Connecticut industrial cities, as well. Carpools, taxis, and jitneys transported hundreds of workers to Waterbury, Stratford, Norwalk, New Haven, and even as far as the Pratt and Whitney complex in the Hartford area. The pool of available Danbury war workers willing to travel did not dry up until the end of 1943.

Some Danbury firms connected to the hat industry adapted to the new situation by becoming subcontractors supplying components for armament manufacturers. The employees of the machine department of the Lee Company, the city's largest hat maker, put in 60 hours per week turning out parts for Remington Arms. Doran Brothers, a firm that specialized in fabricating machinery for the hat industry before the war, shifted to filling the needs of war industries and, in the process, doubled the size of its work force. Smaller companies like Turner Machine and Boesch Machine made similar conversions.

Thanks to the aggressive promotion by the Chamber of Commerce, a few businesses engaged in war work were lured to Danbury. When the inability to import silk from Japan forced the Tweedy Silk mill to go out of business in 1942, the Chamber convinced Bridgeport Fabrics, operator of five other plants in the United States and Canada, to purchase the Tweedy machinery and move it to the vacant Asher Papish fur factory, where it would be used to turn out parachutes for military use. Shortly after this coup, in March 1942, the H. Wibling Tool Company, supplier of parts for such industrial giants as Pratt and Whitney and Bendix, left New York City to come and settle in the former Hannon Fur factory on Taylor Street. Other wartime newcomers were the General Electric Company, which set up temporary quarters for a branch of its small-apparatus division in a building on Triangle Street owned by the Lee Company, and the Risdon Company, a producer of small metal items such as lipstick containers, which moved from Naugatuck to space in Danbury's Amerigo Vespucci Lodge in 1943. The Bard Parker Company, a comparative newcomer to the city, was the first local recipient of the Army-Navy "E" Award for its work in turning out parts for anti-aircraft guns.

The most significant recruiting triumph of the Chamber of Commerce was in bringing the Barden Corporation to Danbury. After a careful survey of potential host towns in New England and New York State, the partnership between the United States Naval Bureau of Ordinance and the Norden Corporation chose Danbury in August 1942 as the location for a facility that was desperately needed. Here, the high-precision ball bearings required by the sophisticated bombsight developed by the Norwalk firm would be made and inspected. Within just nine months, the recently formed Barden Corporation subsidiary of Norden* began production in the extensively renovated, former Tweedy Silk mill on East Franklin Street that had recently closed its doors. Two hundred young women, after completing an intensive three-week training course taught by state trade-school staff in an unused Main Street store, inspected delicate bombsight bearings that the company insisted "can't be good enough" but "must be perfect." By the end of the war, 70 percent of the workforce was female.

If the war in Europe did not boost the Danbury economy, it aroused people's emotions. Sympathy for victims of international aggression was pervasive. It took the Rotary Club's Finnish Relief Committee only a few weeks to raise $1,000 for aid to citizens of the beleaguered tiny nation. And during the summer of 1940, volunteers solicited funds for a program called "Bundles for Britain," organizing a chapter of the Committee to

---

* The two owners of the Norden Corporation were Carl Norden and Theodore Barth. The name "Barden is made up of the first three letters of Barth's name and the last three of Norden's."

Defend America by Aiding the Allies. At the same time, every grocery and drugstore in the city collected money to purchase food and medicine for French refugees. The Danbury Trade School operated around the clock to train machinists for vital Connecticut industries. In late 1940, the Selective Service, after registering more than 4,000 Danbury residents, tapped 12 young men in its first call for one year of military training. Until the attack on Pearl Harbor, when quotas would more than double, an average of 50 to 60 young men from Danbury were drafted each month.

The pace of preparedness picked up in 1941. Battery D, the Danbury -based unit of the National Guard, reported for active duty. Army and Navy recruiting stations remained open from 8 a.m. until midnight in order to process recruits. Residents became accustomed to military truck convoys rumbling through the city en route to Fort Devens in Massachusetts. The 1941 Danbury Fair, the last to be held for the duration of the war, exhibited a model air-raid shelter complete with background sounds of exploding bombs. Representatives of civic groups formed the Committee for the Defense of Danbury, headed by George Howell, to be the local clearinghouse for war-related activities. One of the organization's first undertakings was to sponsor a 13-week series of lectures on such topics as "Fundamentals of Fighting Incendiary Bombs." Donald Tweedy, a professional musician and founder of the Danbury Music Center, was chairman of the Civil Defense Institute that put together preparedness classes. In explaining the need for what might be seen as extreme measures for a nation not yet at war, Tweedy presented to fellow Danbury citizens a rationale for the personal sacrifice which would be demanded in the years ahead:

> Systematic and complete organization of civilian defense is the surest way to arm our people morally. To bring our people together in common action, to instill in them patterns of behavior looking toward the good of the entire community, to call on them to sacrifice their own private concerns occasionally for the sake of public safety, for the sake of being prepared in a public emergency, this is moral armament.

Once the United States had entered the conflict, Danbury donned its full

Courtesy of Danbury Museum & Historical Society Authority

These serious-faced men standing in a lookout built atop the Mallory finishing building (the tallest building in the city) were part of a large contingent of volunteers who kept watch for enemy aircraft from this perch until the round-the-clock surveillance ended in October 1943.

moral armament. Sacrifices were real. Draft quotas increased dramatically. Up to 150 men, including previously exempt husbands and fathers, were called each month. For the first time, a large number of women served in the Army and Navy. Others gave of their time and energy to assist those in the military. The volunteers who made up the Committee of One-Hundred Women mailed over 5,000 birthday packages to Danbury service personnel stationed around the world during the three years of the group's existence.

Most Danbury citizens willingly altered their normal schedules to protect the community from possible enemy air raids – a patriotic activity that could be justified primarily as a symbolic way to discharge their felt obligation to contribute to the common good. Until October 1943, when the effort was discontinued, more than 200 volunteers scanned the sky 24 hours a day to detect any hostile aircraft. Started by the American Legion, the program set up six lookout points in different parts of the city, anchored by a tower built on the King Street farm of William Waterbury. Officials eventually determined that this location had a blind spot that prevented full coverage, so the observation tower was moved to the roof of the Mallory factory on Rose Street, the tallest structure in the city. Through all types of weather, a seven-passenger limousine donated by the Fillow Automobile Company transported trained civilian observers to their three-hour shifts as airplane spotters. To be ready in case an enemy plane appeared, the so-called "black-out drill" became an accepted part of wartime life. Another cadre of neighborhood volunteers, armed in Danbury's case with a city ordinance requiring cooperation, made sure the city went dark within minutes whenever a warning siren sounded.*

Other public-spirited actions were morally satisfying and more directly connected to military needs. The Salvage for Victory Committee, administered by E. Paul McKenney, mobilized everyone from Boy Scouts to corporate executives in a series of collections of valuable scrap items such as metal (including the trolley rails still embedded in White Street and an historic cannon from Putnam Park), rags, fat, rubber, and even old phonograph records. The four red-white-and-blue salvage bins became familiar landmarks in the city. A highly publicized drive in October 1942 collected 140 million pounds of scrap metal – an average of more than 50 pounds for each resident! Neighborhoods competed to erect mountains of discarded metal. The largest pile, topped with an effigy of Hitler, was located at the corner of Beaver and Elm Streets.

The most irritating home-front sacrifice was the complicated system of rationing and price controls set up by the U.S. Office of Price Administration (OPA). Limits on gasoline, tires, fuel oil, meat, sugar, coffee and other staples affected daily life and eventually produced some resentment, especially as the war grew in duration. Black-market violations of federal regulations became more common. Given public sensitivity, the government was unable to enforce rationing rigidly. In the summer of 1943, for example, the OPA attempted to police a ban on pleasure driving. During the summer months, three inspectors patrolled country-club parking lots and resort areas near Lake Candlewood looking for violators.

---

* The siren, also located at the Mallory factory, was the same instrument used to alert citizens during World War 1 that a troop train was passing through the city.

The results were minimal. On a June weekend, 13 drivers were issued tickets for motoring to Lake Zoar for a swim, some paying for the junket by having their gas ration books suspended for one month. In reality, sacrifice was a negotiated concept.

Wartime social problems did not skip Danbury although they were less serious than in many communities. Superintendent of Schools Walter Sweet decried the rise in truancy, which he attributed to parents who were working long hours and therefore failing to supervise their children. The Danbury Defense Committee responded to a 1942 survey that revealed a pressing need for daycare for preschool children by establishing this service in a building donated by the Lee Company. Worries about juvenile delinquency led to renewed calls for the creation of a facility that would offer wholesome recreational opportunities for young people. As a step toward this goal, the newly established Community Chest pledged in 1940 to set aside the surplus from its annual fund drives to help finance a community center. In late 1945, the Community Chest handed over $12,000 that it had accumulated for this purpose to George McLachlan, the head of the War Memorial Committee. The money represented the first contribution to a major campaign conducted, in May 1946, which raised funds to build a community center as a "living memorial" to the 103 Danbury citizens who died in World War II.

"Danbury Looks Ahead," the upbeat title given to the series of community forums held in April 1944, marked the psychological transition from war to peace. Attention now shifted to the postwar economy with a heavy emphasis on the need to shed the "hat town" image. A month after V-J day, the DIC showed a renewed commitment to make this happen by announcing that it would erect a number of modern industrial buildings in an effort to attract diverse firms to the city. Shrewd investors had already taken steps to tap the recreational potential of Lake Candlewood, recognized as an important pillar of a more balanced economy. The boldest idea was promoted by Fred Carley, sales manager of the Danbury and Bethel Gas and Electric Company, along with a group of eager sportsmen who wanted to turn the lake into a Mecca for vacationers, especially fishermen.

Courtesy of Danbury Museum & Historical Society Authority

McCrory's department store on Main Street promoted the fourth War Bond Drive in February 1944 by filling a display window with pictures of local men in military service.

"There is no reason we can't make Lake Candlewood the sports center of eastern America," Carley enthused to a *New York Herald Tribune* columnist in July 1944. The Connecticut Postwar Planning Board evidently agreed and gave the project a high priority. Even before the war ended, the state began to stock the lake with thousands of small-mouth bass. In late 1944, real-estate developers Ralph and Raymond Reynolds purchased almost 200 acres of prime lakefront land in New Fairfield from CL&P. Immediately after the war, the two brothers would build Candlewood Shores, a large residential community with both summer and year-round dwellings.

Many in the business community hoped that an expanded Danbury Airport, a beneficiary of federal attention during the conflict, could contribute to postwar economic development. Before the war, the tiny airport was little more than a rough airstrip. Situated in the rural countryside next to the Danbury Fairgrounds, it had only one runway, no terminal, no control tower and no landing lights. Pilots had to navigate the wind currents in the narrow slot between Moses and Spruce mountains then land by sight relying on their own skill. Daredevils on occasion attempted risky night landings using automobile headlights as a guide. Soon after the attack on Pearl Harbor, the Army designated the airport as an emergency fighter base. As a consequence, WPA crews upgraded the facility by enlarging the single existing north-south runway, constructing a hard-surface, east-to-west runway and installing a drainage system. Although the airport never became an active fighter base – the Army preferred the larger field at Westchester County Airport in White Plains – the WPA's improvements increased the postwar potential of the airport. Because the federal government insisted on complete municipal ownership of the facility, the Town of Danbury assumed all the stock of the old Danbury Airport commission and the field acquired its present name, Danbury Municipal Airport.

As the end of the military conflict approached, one divisive issue surfaced indicating that postwar planning would not go smoothly. Looking ahead to the expected rapid settlement of the suburban areas of the town, the town's selectmen, in September 1944, appointed a commission to devise zoning regulations that would balance the needs of industry with those of homeowners. Trouble began when the commission hired Herbert Swan, the New York engineer who had drafted the city zoning ordinance in the 1920s but was remembered negatively as an advocate of consolidation when he was retained by the city during the fiscal crisis of the 1930s. Packed public hearings on the proposed zoning rules during the summer of 1945 were explosive. Mere mention of Swan's name evoked shouts of "Throw him out!" and "Tar and feather him!" from the audience. The Independent Citizens Committee led by perennial gadfly Mrs. P. J. LaCava and novelist Rose Wilder Lane, led the opposition to zoning. The flamboyant Lane bluntly asserted that she did "not intend to have her 'American Way of Life' regimented by rules which would prohibit" her from doing what she wanted with her home on her three acres of land. At a town meeting on August 8, a raucous crowd estimated by *The News-Times* at 1,200 angry citizens, overwhelmingly rejected the zoning proposals and, for good measure, abolished the zoning commission. "Tonight we are fighting the same issue as our Americans of Danbury fought in 1776, and that is, shall we be free," proclaimed Lane. It was clear that the spirit of wartime sacrifice, a willingness to defer personal goals to a greater civic need, had expired. ♦

?lans For Community Center Approved By Bo

ARTIST'S CONCEPTION OF WAR MEMORIAL-COMMUNITY CENTER

CLOSEUP OF WAR MEMORIAL AND CENOTAPH

Large Cenotaph Will Be Cent. al Figure Of

Courtesy of The News-Times

Inflation and a shortage of building materials forced delay in the construction – and ultimately a severe reduction in the size – of architect William Webb Sunderland's original "living war memorial," pictured in this November 1947 artist's sketch.

Chapter Eight Spotlight

War Memorial

On Armistice Day, November 11, 1951, Danbury finally opened the World War II War Memorial building. Despite beautiful autumn weather and a crowd of 3,500 people, the dedication was anti-climatic and a bit apologetic. *The News-Times* prefaced an architectural evaluation of the structure with the admission that many would call the building "plain." The newspaper insisted, however, that it demonstrated the "beauty of strong fundamental form." Speakers at the day's event minimized attention to the Spartan look and the reduced size that constituted less than half of the originally projected memorial, focusing instead on celebrating the valor of the 103 Danbury men who had died in the conflict.

182

The unsettled nature of the postwar world was responsible for the long delay in building the War Memorial. Planning for a community center for Danbury had predated World War II. In 1940, the first Community Chest campaign set aside $5,000 for this purpose with the promise that the surplus from each subsequent year's drive would be added to the fund. In the last months of the war, a well-attended public meeting, called to determine an appropriate memorial to the war dead, decided to adopt the community center concept rather than erect a traditional statue. Capitalizing on the momentum of war-bond drives, the officials of the Danbury War Memorial Association conducted a two-week campaign to raise $250,000. The drive was keynoted by the slogan "To Honor the Dead; To Serve the Living." Danburians responded enthusiastically. Businesses and organizations pledged large sums. High-school students, for example, donated $5,000. Many individuals assigned two days' pay for the monument. Popular support was so great that the drive collected $382,000, well in excess of the target amount.

The next step in the process came in November 1947, when local architect William Webb Sunderland presented his design for the structure that would be built near the Main Street entrance to Rogers Park. The plan called for two identical buildings, an auditorium and a gymnasium, joined by a cenotaph, or empty tomb, of polished granite. An artist's sketch in color of the proposed complex, displayed in the window of the Danbury & Bethel Gas and Electric Company on Main Street, evoked many compliments.

Unfortunately, the shortage of essential building materials and the soaring interest rates forced a delay in completing the building. As time passed and inflation remained high, officers of the Community Center Association decided to seek bids for the gymnasium portion only. When these estimates totaled far more than the organization had in the bank, the architect was ordered to scale down further his already shrinking design. The memorial structure that was finally completed in 1951 was a trade-off between wartime idealism and the reality of postwar economic adjustment. J. Harry White, master of ceremonies at the dedication, captured the compromise nature of the living memorial when he referred to the gymnasium that still serves the recreational needs of Danbury residents as a "dream come partly true." ♦

1945 to 1985
A Fresh Energy

Frustrated by traffic congestion on Route 7 in the Norwalk-Wilton area, the Perkin-Elmer Corporation in 1967 moved its Optical Division to this modern factory (pictured under construction) on Wooster Heights overlooking the airport. By 1970, the company had more than 1000 employees in Danbury.

Economic Renaissance

A few days after Thanksgiving in 1968, eight prominent Danbury citizens flew to New Orleans to attend the 74th annual Conference of the National Municipal League. This trip was far from routine. The delegation was on a mission to convince a prestigious jury that Danbury, already selected as one of the 22 finalists in the All-American City competition co-sponsored by the League and *Look* magazine, deserved the year's highest award. Three men were chosen to present the city's credentials for All-American distinction. Steve Collins, veteran editor of *The Danbury News-Times*, who was responsible for preparing the detailed nominating package, spoke about the city's economic transformation. He also promoted hometown enthusiasm for the quest with detailed newspaper coverage of the trip. Sam Hyman, youthful North Carolina native and head of the active Danbury branch of the National Association for the Advancement of Colored People (NAACP), detailed the way the local community had begun to come together across class and racial lines to air, and then to address, pressing social problems. Forty-five-year-old Democratic Mayor Gino Arconti, elected by a landslide a year earlier, downplayed traditional measures of urban health in his closing comments and instead emphasized the crucial role of motivated volunteers in finding solutions to his city's problems. "The growth of the volunteer movement in Danbury has been fantastic," he boasted.

The ultimate decision of the judges to award Danbury honorable-mention status rather than the coveted All-American prize disappointed but did not lessen the pride of the Danbury boosters who realized that 20 years earlier, in the bleak years immediately following World War II, most Danburians would have scoffed at the possibility that the fading industrial city would ever be a candidate for national praise. At that time, Danbury seemed to be yet another New England mill town destined to collapse when the dominant industry failed or moved away, leaving behind vacant factories, stranded workers and a ruined economy. Fortunately, Danbury escaped this outcome. The decline of the hatting industry that had buttressed the local economy and shaped its culture for more than a century was a traumatic – but not terminal – event.

The fate of the two largest Danbury hat firms tells the story of the demise of that core industry. As late as 1927, the Mallory Company, one of the largest hat factories in the city, proudly reported that it had its best sales year in its more than one-hundred-year history. Fewer than two decades later, in 1946, the company sold its massive brick, concrete and steel Rose Hill plant to the John D. Stetson Company of Philadelphia, marking the first time that a Danbury hat company would not be locally owned. The shock of Stetson's decision in 1957 to shut down the Mallory front shop, throwing 300 skilled hat finishers out of work, produced howls of protest from the hatters union as well as Danbury elected officials and members of the Connecticut Congressional delegation. However, the Philadelphia company, with its eyes fixed on a shaky bottom line, refused to reconsider its action and instead closed the entire plant in 1960.

The simultaneous disappearance of the Frank H. Lee Company, owned but no longer run by its founding family, was even more ominous. In the same year that Stetson shuttered the Mallory facility, the Philadelphia firm bought the Lee operation that had once been the largest hat factory in the nation, providing jobs for 1500 Danbury workers in peak pre-war times. Four years later, Stetson closed Lee's nine-building Leemac Avenue complex where the work force had shrunk to less than 300 aging employees. By 1960, not a single Danbury company manufactured complete hats and only three small firms continued to make rough hat bodies that were shipped to markets distant from the once proud Hat City for final assembly. Hatting no longer played a significant role in the Danbury economy.

Contrary to the dreary scenario that was repeated in countless New England industrial centers, the death of Danbury's basic industry did not bring economic disaster. Instead, many young and bold manufacturers of technologically sophisticated products established their small and medium-size firms in the city, thereby sparking an economic boom. Between 1945 and 1970, more than 60 firms – most fabricating items used in the fields of precision metal products, communications, and electronics – began operation in the city. Danbury retained its identity as a factory town, but in little more than 20 years completed a painless transition from clinging to an obsolete hatting past to embracing a high-tech future.

Economists were the first to put numbers on the shift. In 1951, the Connecticut Employment Service expressed surprise at the changes in employment patterns taking place in Danbury. The state agency pointed out that in 1940, two-thirds of the 6,700 factory workers employed in the city – a total of 4,200 people – were engaged in hatting. Ten years later, while almost the same number, about 4,100, were still hatters, this figure represented less than half of the 9,410 individuals then working in Danbury factories. The growth in non-hatting factory jobs in Danbury continued to increase so rapidly that the head of the Connecticut Development Commission temporarily dropped his statistical reserve to exclaim that the city, by 1957, had become the "hottest spot in the state for new industries." Three years later, in 1960, another stunned state employment service official reported that Danbury now ranked as one of the six most active areas of the state in generating factory jobs, despite the fact that it

Courtesy of The News Times

A Unimate industrial robot turns the first shovelful of earth at the expansion of the Unimation plant on Shelter Rock Road in 1976. Corporation President Joseph Engelberger, at center wearing his trademark bowtie, became a minor celebrity, at one point appearing on the *Tonight Show* with Johnny Carson, where a Unimate, the world's first line of industrial robots, conducted the band and putted a golf ball.

was not located in a heavily populated part of Connecticut. By the end of the 1950s, the dread of unemployment had been replaced by a frantic search for skilled workers with which to staff booming Danbury factories. In 1959, the research director of the Connecticut Department of Labor told worried personnel directors of area companies, who had gathered to discuss the crisis over lunch at Brookfield's White Turkey Inn, that they would need to find 2,800 skilled employees over the next five years. He suggested recruiting more married women.

The Danbury Chamber of Commerce tried a more dramatic alternative in the frantic search for qualified employees for local factories when it leased billboards at 14 key points in the state's industrial heartland advertising the availability of jobs in Danbury.* The chief executives of many firms,

---

* Ironically, in light of the eagerness of Danburians to fill jobs in distant war plants during World War II, some of the target communities (Bridgeport, for example) resented the message on these billboards and forced the removal of the offensive second part of the Chamber's "Work and Live in Danbury" message.

including the outspoken Edward Baruch of Heli-Coil, a precision metal connector fabricator who had moved his business from a rented two-car garage in Long Island City to a new factory on Shelter Rock Road in 1951, urged the state to expand the training program at Henry Abbot Tech and the city to incorporate a job-training facility as part of a badly needed new high school. His firm was a pioneer in setting up a prisoner work-release program with the Danbury Federal Correctional Institution.

The reinvigorated economic base accelerated the pace of population growth. Danbury's 1950 population of about 30,000 individuals, a modest nine-percent increase over the 1940 total, surged ahead in the next decade. Laurence Moore, a consultant with Technical Planning Associates, a New Haven firm that specialized in providing professional guidance for smaller Connecticut cities, put this growth in perspective in his first report to the recently appointed city planning commission. Moore pointed out that Danbury had added 8,000 people in the 30 years between 1920 and 1950, while in just seven years from 1950 to 1957, the city's population expanded by 9,000 people. This robust growth rate did not slow in the following decade. By 1970, Danbury's population topped 50,000.

This economic renaissance was not a miracle or even an accident; it was the product of the same economic forces that had made Danbury a thriving hat manufacturing center: a prime location, a plentiful and experienced labor force, and eager community support. Economic growth rather than stagnation took place because the area offered many advantages to fledgling businesses. The location of the city fewer than 65 miles from New York was attractive to companies seeking to relocate from the metropolis. Unlike most other Connecticut cities, Danbury offered ample land within its municipal borders – land that lent itself to the construction of sprawling, one-story horizontal factories favored by postwar industry. Reasonably priced vacant land on the southeastern flank of the city was tied into the still-important national railway network. Automobile and truck traffic on the emerging interstate highway system made Danbury an affordable alternative for companies stymied by the high cost of real estate closer to New York City. Even though the Yankee Expressway by-pass around

Danbury was not completed and folded into I-84 until the early 1960s, plans had been far enough along a decade earlier to stimulate industrial development on the northeastern fringe of the city. Alert developer Seymour Powers established his Danbury Industrial Park adjacent to the projected route of the Interstate as early as 1953. In addition to the appeal of affordable industrial space, the prospect of a rural lifestyle in still-bucolic western Connecticut, and especially the lure of nearby Lake Candlewood, pleased executives fleeing urban problems.

With hatting floundering, Danbury offered a large pool of experienced workers who were accustomed to, and content with, a factory regimen. They were stable and most were non-union. Best of all they needed jobs. Many of them were women who had been a key component of the hat-making process. By 1962, women held over 40% of all Danbury's jobs, a figure far higher than the national average. They were favored for pre-cision work that required dexterity; in some factories like Davis & Geck, Risdon and American Radionics, most of the workforce was female. John Douglas, the founder of Republic Foil, one of the first firms to settle in Danbury after World War II, assured his fellow industrialists at a get-ac-quainted dinner sponsored by the Chamber of Commerce in 1958, that they had come to the right place. "Danburians are steeped in tradition," he concluded. " … they may learn a bit slower than people in large industrial areas but you can't beat our local people for loyalty and cooperation."

Hatting left behind other prime assets: Abandoned mostly modest-sized factories located in the center of the city provided low-cost startup quarters for fledgling firms. A well-developed reservoir system that had provided the abundant water supply required for hat making would be a welcome bonus for prospective companies. The continued success of machine shops that had served the hat industry as well as the presence of Henry Abbott Technical School helped guarantee a pool of skilled operatives.

As in the past, Danbury officials welcomed industry. Long before hatting had begun to ebb, city leaders had taken steps to diversify its economy. Although the privately financed, non-profit Danbury Industrial Corporation (DIC), organized in 1917, had been able to woo only six small, non-hatting firms to the city during the 1920s and 30s, it did accumulate large tracts of land served by the railroad and zoned for industrial use. After World War II, the corporation made this attractive property on the south side of the city bordering Bethel available to outside companies on flexible terms as an inducement to settle in Danbury. At the same time, the local Chamber of Commerce was particularly aggressive in searching for companies looking to relocate. In addition, private developers played an important role in bringing industry to Danbury. Once the segment of I-84 that circled the city opened in 1960, Seymour Powers tripled the size of his planned industrial complex adjacent to the superhighway. Renamed Commerce Park, by 1970 it provided customized space for several dozen small companies in such fields as aerospace and computer technology. Although city government did not grant tax concessions to relocating firms, it willingly extended water and sewer lines and access roads to accommodate new factories.

The interplay of these forces and their impact on the decisions of new businesses to move to and expand in Danbury during the 1950s and 60s, which transformed the economy and raised the morale of the community, can best be understood by following the specific paths to Danbury that were taken by some of the most important companies. Two tiny firms, attracted to the area by the DIC long before World War II, grew in similar ways to become significant players in the emerging postwar high-tech economy.

In 1919, Knud Knudsen, a Danish immigrant whose skills as a toolmaker had been perfected in the Detroit automobile plants he pioneered, as well as in the wartime munitions industry, searched for an opportunity to start his own company. Attracted to Danbury by Frank Lee's offer of cheap leased industrial space on the third floor of his hat factory, Knudsen began fabricating electrical connectors and signal devices. The firm, then named the Danbury Electrical Manufacturing Company, survived and ultimately shifted to rented quarters on the first floor of the recently closed Tweedy Silk Mill on East Franklin Street, where it remained from 1933 to 1942. A series of modest mergers followed that pushed the still-small company into the emerging field of electronics. There it attracted notice of the worldwide Amphenol Corporation, a firm eager to become part of the Danbury economic renaissance. In 1957, this Chicago-based conglomerate absorbed the Knudsen operation, purchased the former Tweedy mill from the Barden Corporation, revamped it, and significantly expanded production of electronic devices. Pleased with life in Danbury, Amphenol closed its Long Island City plant in 1963 and tripled the number of its employees in Danbury to over 600, making it one of the largest industrial operations in the city.

Another early success of the DIC blossomed into a major element of the new economy. Founded in 1916, the Bard-Parker Company was a maker of hospital and medical equipment, especially surgical scalpels. The company had moved its manufacturing operation from New York City to Croton Falls in 1929; then, four years later, it moved to nearby Danbury, where its approximately 70 employees had settled into space provided by the DIC on Triangle Street.

The postwar economic boom made Bard-Parker an attractive takeover target. In 1956 Becton, Dickinson and Company, a corporate behemoth with headquarters in New Jersey, acquired the Danbury firm and immediately expanded production. By the mid 1960s, Bard-Parker's five plants scattered around the city bulged with 650 employees.

The unusual history of the Barden Corporation, the prime exception to the pattern that Danbury did not profit directly from military production during World War II, epitomizes the rapid transformation of Danbury's economy. In 1942, Barden, a new firm highly subsidized by the U.S. Navy, began to fabricate precision ball bearings in the vacant Tweedy Silk Mill for use in the bombsite manufactured by its parent company, Norwalk-based Norden Company. By the end of the war, the firm employed 400 workers.

But Barden was not a temporary wartime operation. The company's president, F. E. Erickson, speaking in 1944 at a forum on Danbury's future, insisted that the firm had been located in Danbury primarily to benefit from "people who are eager and willing workers with the Connecticut heritage of craftsmanship and brains." After the conflict ended and the Navy withdrew its supervision, the company retooled and expanded the old factory in order to supply high-quality bearings for civilian uses. By the early 1960s, Barden had become the largest industrial firm in the city, employing more than 1300 people (three quarters of them women), as many as were still employed in the entire declining hat industry. After the twin 1955 floods inundated the East Franklin Street plant, Barden executives resisted the temptation to abandon Danbury. Instead, the company constructed a modern facility on the high ground it still occupies, overlooking the airport on the western edge of the city where it offered convenience to I-84 and Route 7.

John Douglas, a wealthy 1929 Yale graduate and executive with several large corporations, was eager to take advantage of the innovations in the metals industry. Douglas had observed these changes while serving as a dollar-a-year man with the Office of Production Management in Washington, D.C., during World War II. In 1945, with borrowed money, he formed a company to manufacture heavy-duty aluminum foil primarily for electronic applications. Steered by the New Haven Railroad to Danbury where he was welcomed by an eager Chamber of Commerce, he purchased a half-built factory from the DIC and the Republic Foil Corporation began production in 1947 as one of the first postwar start-ups to settle in Danbury. Stimulated by military needs during the Korean War along with sales of consumer packaging and decorative items, the company flourished during the 1950s. By the end of the decade, several additions to the original factory on Triangle Street had been built to accommodate a research lab, engineering department, and state-of-the-art rolling mill. Speaking about the firm's expansion during a Danbury Chamber of Commerce meeting in 1961, Douglas asked the audience to realize that when the company started in the city in 1946, he was the sole employee. Fifteen years later, he asserted with pride, the annual payroll for his 175 employees topped one million dollars.

"If Danbury wanted us, we wanted Danbury," the vice president for marketing of the Eagle Pencil Company told an overflow crowd of

Rotarians having lunch at the Hotel Green on May 15, 1957. Owners of the nation's leading maker of pencils and stationary items had decided in 1955 that the accelerating cost of doing business in New York City, where Eagle had been operating for more than 100 years, forced them to find a more affordable home. After an exhaustive exploration of potential host communities all over the country, Eagle concluded that it wanted to come to Danbury for the same reasons that influenced most newcomers: a deep labor pool and ample water supply; good highway and railroad freight access; reasonably priced land for expansion; and attractive living conditions for employees. But most persuasive to management was the fact that no other community within reasonable distance of New York City displayed more eagerness to attract new business.

Danbury communicated that it wanted the Eagle Pencil Company in dramatic fashion. Five hundred citizens attended a steamy midsummer town meeting in 1956, where they unanimously authorized the purchase of land and the construction of a lengthy road and bridge needed to reach the factory site chosen by Eagle on former farmland east of Federal Road. In an effusive gesture of support, the gathering rose to its feet to applaud the company representative who had made the expensive request. His optimistic promise of "one hundred successful years in Danbury" seemed to cement the community partnership. In 1958, Eagle was one of five major factories to open in Danbury. Barden, Reeves Soundcraft, Chayes Dental, and the Mosler Corporation also moved into new facilities in that boom year.

Increasingly, the companies that started up in Danbury or relocated there in the 1960s tended to be based on research and advanced technology and sometimes on unique inventions. Their employees included not only traditional industrial workers like assemblers and machinists, but also college-educated research scientists and engineers – most of them new to the city.

In 1970, the Optical Technology Division of the Perkin-Elmer Corporation was one of the city's largest industrial employers with a workforce of more than 1000, a figure that grew to 1700 in the mid-80s. Three years

Engineers at Perkin-Elmer's Danbury plant had to invent much of the technology, including the "null corrector" that guided the device pictured here, to produce the mirror for the Hubble Space Telescope, one of the major scientific advances of the 20th century that allowed scientists to observe light from the distant past of deep space. When delays and cost overruns drew the scrutiny of Congress, NASA forced the company to ship the mirror in Sept. 1983 before full testing was completed. This resulted in flawed images when the mirror went into orbit, which had to be corrected in a special space mission in 1990.

earlier, exasperated by the chronic congestion on lower Route 7, the company left the Norwalk-Wilton area and relocated in Danbury after building a modern facility atop Wooster Heights that was designed to avoid the flight paths of the nearby Danbury Airport. The new arrival quickly made Danbury a major player in the sophisticated field of aerospace research. The astronauts on the 1969 Apollo moon-landing flight wore coated visors and used carbon-dioxide sensors in their space suits developed by Perkin-Elmer, and their rocket featured precision instruments designed by the company. The firm's crowning achievement was initiated in 1977, when NASA entrusted it with the responsibility for grinding and polishing the Hubble Space Telescope's mirror and developing fine guidance sensors and other key components.

Joseph Engleberger, a young physicist out of Columbia University, was working for a Danbury defense contractor in 1956 when he met George

Devol, an inventor, who told Engleberger about his patent on a mechanical arm that could be programmed to do regular tasks. Recognizing the potential of this concept, Engleberger in 1962 formed a company in Danbury named Unimation Inc. to develop and manufacture industrial robots called Unimates. These quickly became fixtures on automobile assembly lines in the United States and Japan, where they performed heavy and dangerous jobs previously done by highly paid human labor. By the mid 1970s, Unimation produced Unimates at the rate of two dozen a month, had 700 people on its payroll, and had expanded its plant. Engleberger, born in New York City, found Danbury to be a hospitable base for an innovative business. "I wanted to make the business go," he remembered, "and all I can say is there wasn't a single thing about Danbury that would have led me to say I should be somewhere else. It was a very open-opportunity place. I found Danbury always helpful. The people who supplied me from small businesses around were always conscientious. No one ever tried to take advantage of me."

The stream of companies that poured into Danbury in the 1950s and 1960s did more than rejuvenate the city's sagging economy. Sudden prosperity and rapid population growth forced the community to face problems that it had long deferred. Needs that had been slighted by a dormant town of 30,000 could not be ignored by a booming city of 50,000. City Hall, the public library, and the headquarters of the police and fire departments were woefully inadequate. Soaring school enrollment taxed existing facilities. The few elementary schools built during the 1950s merely replaced outmoded structures described by a member of the school building committee in 1948 as "probably the most decayed public buildings I ever went into." The city's sole high school, built in 1927 to service 1,100 students, regularly had to resort to double sessions to accommodate almost twice that number. As late as 1960, those attending the Service Bureau for Women's Organizations conference in Danbury characterized the educational situation in the host city in such harsh terms as "appalling," "shocking" and "almost incredible." Industrial, commercial and residential land development on the fringe of the city at a distance from the downtown area exposed the inefficiency of Danbury's dual form of government. The political system that divided power between the inner city and the surrounding town proved to be a relic of the 19th century. Clogged traffic on an internal road system established by early settlers, limited inner-city parking, and an aversion to comprehensive planning and zoning threatened the traditional dominance of the central business district.

A gradual change in attitude toward public policy accompanied the economic renaissance of the postwar years. It became increasingly apparent that Danbury could sustain and fully benefit from its economic good fortune only by a willingness on the part of its citizens to tackle problems previously thought to be intractable. During the 1950s and '60s a younger generation of men and women – some native Danburians, but many of them executives of recently arrived high-tech companies – assumed positions of influence in the community. Educated, energetic, optimistic and possessing organizational savvy, the new power elite mobilized the community in a campaign to make Danbury a more progressive place. They saw no reason why the former provincial hat town could not become an All-American city.♦

June Goodman and E. John Larsen, key figures in the Committee of 1000, distribute information kits to 600 volunteers who pledged to contact friends and neighbors about the importance of supporting the school-building referendum held on Valentine's Day, February 14, 1962.

For a Better Danbury

Like most American communities, Danbury began to look ahead to postwar problems and priorities long before fighting stopped in World War II. In November 1944, the Danbury Board of Education, worried about the impact the more than 700 babies born in the city during each of the wartime years would soon have on the city's long neglected school system, authorized the standing "Committee on School Houses" to survey existing educational facilities and to make recommendations for improvements. The all-male group visited the 12 schools in the system, interviewed staff and issued a comprehensive report the following November. Only three schools were rated in satisfactory condition. However, the committee made clear that this designation did not imply an ability to meet all present needs or those that would arise in the future. For example, although the high-school building that opened in 1929 was clearly not dilapidated, the report conceded that faculty members were "seriously handicapped in carrying out its program" because of a lack of modern facilities. The remaining schools – three of them more than 50 years old, including the New Street School built shortly after the Civil War and still without indoor toilets – were categorized in scathing terms as outmoded and inadequate. Whenever the subcommittee chair, John J. Stone, spoke to community groups about the survey, he summed up local school conditions with a single blunt adjective: "deplorable."

The lack of public response to this critical report disappointed the board of education. Even though *The News-Times* published the full text of the survey, readers evidently paid little attention to its content because it did not generate any demand for reform. Reverend Harry Adams Hersey, a school board member and former chair of the board, was not surprised by this apathy. "The populace has not as yet arisen," explained the feisty Unitarian minister.

Twenty years later, a dramatically different account of the Danbury school situation appeared in a prestigious national publication. A lengthy article, entitled "How to Win the Fight For a New School," in the January 1964 issue of *Redbook* magazine, portrayed Danbury as a textbook model of an activist community that had relied on "hard work and inventiveness" to mobilize voters in 1962 to approve an unprecedented school-building program costing $9 million by an overwhelming 3-to-1 margin. The article quoted with approval the elated verdict of *News-Times* editor Steve Collins, who described the victory as due to motivated citizens acting as the "most continuously effective organization I've seen here, and I've been here all my life." Danbury citizens had emphatically "arisen."

The Danbury school system's modernization in the 1950s and '60s was the earliest and most vivid evidence of a shift in civic attitudes away from tolerance of the fading hatting era's narrow status quo. Instead, there was now a willingness to expend funds in order to improve the quality of life in this larger, more prosperous city. During this period of economic and population growth, a coalition emerged. Its nucleus featured executives of recently arrived manufacturing companies who demanded better-trained employees and college-educated men and especially college-educated women, both native to Danbury and newcomers, who were unwilling to accept a sub-par education for their children. The energy supplied by this committed core generated a fresh, more assertive mood in the city.

It is difficult to understand the struggle over the fate of Danbury schools in the two decades after World War II without an awareness of the built-in conflict between the two elected bodies that shaped educational policy in the community. The Danbury Town Board of Education, set up in 1903 as a non-partisan, 12-person body with six Republican and six Democratic representatives, was charged with enforcing state-mandated laws governing education. Ultimately the elected members, eager to improve school performance, answered to state educational officials who shared the same goal. However, the town's board of finance, responsible solely to the Danbury voters, provided the necessary funds to build and operate the schools. Traditionally, the finance board was more receptive to the arguments of those forces eager to keep spending and taxes low.

The advocates for better schools were fortunate that Rabbi Jerome Malino was the most persuasive voice on the board of education during these transition years. Coming to Danbury in 1935 to minister to a tiny Jewish congregation in what he then regarded as a provincial mill town, the scholarly Malino spent the rest of his long life – he died in 2002 – striving to raise the cultural horizons of his adopted home. None of his many contributions were more valuable than his 18 years of leadership of the board of education.* From 1947 to 1969, Malino served either as the president or vice president of that body for eight terms.**

As area children born in the wartime baby boom began to enter Danbury's elementary schools, the board realized that, enthusiastic public support or not, it had to attempt to remedy two deficiencies. Not only were the older school buildings outmoded and in some cases unsafe, most had been located near the center of the city in order to serve the bulk of the

---

* In a 1987 interview, the articulate Rabbi explained that he saw his role in this key post as a passionate defender of human values nourished by education in opposition to the more material values advocated by the Finance Board. To fulfill this ideal, he prodded other members of the school board diplomatically, welcomed sympathetic community groups to the cause, and eloquently defended Board positions at town meetings.

** In an effort to emphasize its non-partisan nature the Board instituted a policy of alternating the chairmanship each term between a Democratic and a Republican member. Whenever the important position went to the Republicans during his period of service, the party chose Malino as chair.

population that, in the 19th century, lived close to the main source of employment – the hat factories. In 1949, the board convinced the town to support a building program that would provide modern schools in areas outside the city limits, where the majority of new homes were being built. Between 1952 and 1958, three new elementary schools opened that were more accessible to young families drawn to the suburbs. Despite complaints that the designated farmland location on the eastern flank of the city would expose young pupils to a dangerously long walk, the Park Avenue School, tastefully designed by local architect Philip Sunderland, was the first school built in Danbury in the postwar years. It relieved pressure on the ancient New Street School. In 1955, the Hayestown School, also a Sunderland project, welcomed students who lived in the growing northern fringe near Lake Candlewood. Three years later, the 16-room Mill Ridge School began to serve residents of the distant Lake Avenue area. Each of the three schools was financed by a bond issue of approximately $700,000.

During the early 1950s, the State of Connecticut carried some of the burden of building schools in Danbury. Henry Abbot Technical School, in 1953, moved into a modern facility that was financed and operated by the state. However, the Connecticut General Assembly balked at funding a new "lab" school for Danbury Teachers College. A bill introduced in 1949 by Senator Alice Rowland of Ridgefield, which proposed that the state share costs with the city for an up-to-date elementary school to replace the decrepit Balmforth Avenue School as a training facility for student teachers, was defeated. The legislature agreed only to transfer the state-owned land on Roberts Avenue, which was adjacent to the college campus, to the city. Undeterred, Danbury voters approved another bond issue in 1951 covering the entire cost of a new practice school on this site. The Roberts Avenue School, staffed by college faculty, greeted 450 students for the first time in September 1953. It would continue to be run by the college until 1968.

Financing four new elementary schools within a five-year span was a momentous accomplishment for a city that had previously built only two elementary schools in the 20th century – both constructed and paid for by federal Depression relief agencies. The board of education could not have persuaded voters to accept this task without help from dedicated volunteers like June Goodman. A New York City native and graduate of Oberlin College, Goodman came to Danbury in 1946 with her husband, William, a Dartmouth College alumnus and World War II veteran, who took over management of his father's struggling Bieber-Goodman hat factory. The couple joined with other young liberals to organize the Fair City Foundation as a forum for discussion of key national and local issues. With this as a power base, and further motivated by the educational needs of her five children, June invigorated the Parent Teachers Association (PTA). As president she transformed what had been primarily a sedate social group into an active lobby for quality schools.

When author Norman Cousins, a member of Governor Chester Bowles' Committee on Education, pointed out to the PTA in 1950 that Danbury was one of only 20 towns in the state that had not made a recent comprehensive study of their school systems, Goodman and her mostly female allies decided to form the Citizens Committee on Education in order to undertake this task. What they described as a "non-professional, non-profit, non-partisan organization" was definitely not a passive group. With tireless energy its members carried out a classroom-by-classroom survey of existing public schools; campaigned for increased teachers salaries they claimed were the lowest in the state; protested to the board of finance about unwarranted cuts in the school budget; distributed a primer entitled "Know Your Schools" on the organization of the Danbury school system; and spoke to any service club or community organization that would tender an invitation. Goodman, who set the tireless pace, could be abrasive; but she was also persistent and effective. Looking back at this era, her longtime friend and associate Christine Rotello praised her tenacity. "She kept at it no matter how discouraging things would get," Rotello marveled.

Despite building four elementary schools in five years, Danbury could not keep up with the swelling number of students who showed up at school doors each September. In 1952, total enrollment in the public schools topped 4,000 for the first time. By 1955, the number had ballooned to

5,000. Even more distressing, the bulge in student enrollment extended to the already-crowded high school in 1956. A year later, high school students began a schedule of half-day double sessions that would last almost four years.

The finance board, badgered by economy advocates, many of them members of the vocal taxpayers association organized by spirited gadflies Sarah Rothkopf and Madeline LaCava, responded to each higher enrollment plateau by slashing the school budget by $50,000 in 1952, and by $80,000 in 1955. Wealthy real-estate developer Perry Katz, backer and prime spokesman for the tiny budget-study committee, expressed the rationale for these cuts succinctly. Unlike the "millionaire towns of West Hartford and Greenwich, Danbury can't afford more," he asserted, without qualification. The finance board encouraged this resistance by warning that any plan to build a new high school would require a massive five-mill tax increase.

The members of the board of education were also under mounting pressure to address escalating school needs. The Citizens Committee on Education reminded the board that delay would only make the situation worse, projecting that the current 30-year-old high-school building would, by 1959, face the impossible task of accommodating 2,000 students, almost double the facility's intended capacity of 1,100. Building an up-to-date high-school facility, group spokesperson June Goodman insisted, was "Danbury's greatest challenge since the early 1920s." Executives of important local industries such as Barden, Sperry, and Davis and Geck agreed and, identifying their companies as major taxpayers, wrote letters stressing their dependence on scientifically trained employees. Technical Planning Associates, a firm hired as a consultant by the town planning commission, heightened the sense of urgency by forecasting that the pace of population growth, particularly to the north, would force the city to erect two high schools by 1975.

Rabbi Malino, then the chair of the school board, responded with a public guarantee that a new high school would be in operation by 1962. To support this promise, the school board, with the backing of a special fact-finding committee consisting of representatives of the finance board, the board of education, the town selectman and the planning commission headed by Bill Goodman, put forward in 1959 a plan for a school accommodating 2,200 students that could be built on city-owned land formerly known as the Broadview Farm for a cost of $4.5 million. Instead of leaving this costly program to the judgment of a town meeting, as recommended by the board of education, a petition instigated by the taxpayers association forced its submission to a full referendum. Board members were stunned when, on July 14, 1959, voters soundly rejected the proposal by a 2-to-1 margin.

Shock quickly gave way to renewed action. In a rare front-page editorial, *News-Times* editor Steve Collins suggested the proper response. Under the bold headline, "State the Facts Adequately," he criticized the result of the referendum as an unrealistic decision to avoid a solution to a persistent problem, and faulted the board of education for a feeble effort at educating the voters. A diverse collection of Danbury citizens mounted an intensive campaign in the months that followed, determined to sell the school building program. A group calling itself "The Committee of Ten," led by Eagle Pencil executive Rolf Thal, took the first step by convincing the board to hire a New York-based professional educational consulting firm headed by Dr. Nicholaus L. Englehardt, a resident of nearby South Salem, to analyze the town's educational needs. During the six months that Englehardt spent researching this situation in Danbury, June Goodman and her allies, sure that the consultant's final report would buttress their position, were busy recruiting and training an army of volunteers. Around a large table in the "Garden Room" of Goodman's residence, they first carved up the map of Danbury into clusters of 10 homes each. Then, calling on their contacts with people already involved in a variety of community activities ranging from the Girl Scouts to Rotary, they enlisted representatives who would be responsible for contacting each of the 10-family segments and informing them of the plight of the Danbury schools. Gradually the original Committee of Ten grew to what for dramatic effect was labeled the Committee of 1000, although in actuality there were closer to 2,500 persons ultimately mobilized in this grassroots campaign.

YOUR **YES** MEANS

NO DOUBLE SESSIONS
IN ANY SCHOOL

THE END OF OVERCROWDING
IN ALL SCHOOLS

VOTE **YES** FEB. 14
TO GIVE <u>ALL</u> DANBURY CHILDREN
FULL-TIME SCHOOLS

Courtesy of Western Connecticut State University Archives

The Committee of 1000 bombarded voters with graphic advertisements such as this one that helped win support for two referenda in 1961 and 1962. The referenda financed an unprecedented school-building program.

Englehardt's findings, made public in April 1961, painted a grim picture. They confirmed that town schools were 38 percent over capacity and warned they would be almost twice as crowded within four years. The consultant prescribed strong medicine. In order to guarantee that "all children … receive a full education in the years immediately ahead," the Englehardt report declared, the town would need to spend a staggering $9.5 million to build a 2,500-student high school on Clapboard Ridge, rather than on the too-small Broadview property. In addition, three new elementary schools would be needed, one each in the Great Plain, Clapboard Ridge and Shelter Rock areas, along with an extensive addition to the Morris Street School. Even though the steep cost was double the amount of money that had been decisively rejected just two years earlier, the board of education embraced the full recommendation in May 1961, and prepared to face the voters. The crucial first step, a referendum on a $600,000-bond issue covering the expense of acquiring sites for the new schools and underwriting the required architectural design, would take place on June 4, 1961.

This time the Committee of 1000 was ready. Volunteers painstakingly recruited during the previous six months prepared to meet with their assigned 10 families. Each volunteer was given a kit of pertinent information along with printed tips on how to persuade their targets. "Don't high pressure people," they were admonished. Dr. Englehardt met with volunteers and personally answered their questions. Workers were urged to make two visits to each family and report the result of face-to-face meetings to campaign headquarters in the Goodman home via special phone lines. Emphasis was also put on publicity. A speakers' bureau headed by Francis Stephens, a Bard-Parker executive, spread the message. Bumper stickers proclaiming "SOS Save our Schools, Vote Yes!" appeared on thousands of automobiles. Local industries defrayed the cost of printing and mailing information packets. Advertisements warning voters not to be fooled "by a few selfish men" appeared in the daily newspaper whose pages were filled with orchestrated letters to the editor supporting the pro-school position. Even students were encouraged to use this medium to express their frustrations. One high school junior, identified by the paper as a "Short-Changed Student," put the impact of double sessions in personal terms when he wrote, "When I graduate next year and go to college I will have had three years of high school rather than four." Finally, on the day of the referendum, volunteers operating from an apartment on Fifth Avenue, across the street from the polling station in the White Street High School, used eight recently installed phone lines to get out the vote. This intense effort changed minds as the first hurdle was cleared by a 2-to-1 vote.

Eight months later the Committee of 1000 repeated this performance in order to win backing for the $8.9 million bond issue necessary to pay for construction of the cluster of new schools. The school building committee headed by former Mayor John Previdi kicked off an elaborate information campaign by unveiling models of the proposed schools at a January 1962 town meeting. Rabbi Malino, once again chairman of the Danbury Board of Education, acknowledged that building so many schools at once was "a monumental undertaking" but urged citizens to realize that "fulfillment of the maximum potential in human beings is the purpose of education." Dr. Englehardt, engaged as a consultant by the building committee, answered questions from the overflow crowd. Convinced of the effectiveness of the person-to-person approach, the Committee of 1000, under the chairmanship of American Cyanamid executive E. John Larsen, then unleashed 640 volunteers who, armed with slick, 26-page information kits, were tasked with contacting at least 10,000 voters before the referendum scheduled for Valentine's Day, February 14, 1962. Despite a surprise 14-inch snowfall that buried the area on that day, Danbury voters approved of the largest bond issue they had ever been asked to consider, and by a wide margin. Dr. Ruth Haas, President of Danbury Teachers College, put the accomplishment of the citizen-volunteers in perspective when she wrote to Goodman the following day. "You and all your ardent workers ... have done for Danbury, that which was considered almost impossible," she said.

But even though it was clear that the people had spoken decisively, the resourceful taxpayers association was not finished. Taking advantage of a provision in the original Danbury town charter that permitted a petition signed by a mere 200 voters to force yet another referendum, this one reduced the school bond issue to $2 million – in effect scuttling the entire building program. Irritated as much by the outmoded character of the town charter as the tactics of the die-hard opposition, the Committee of 1000 geared up to rebuff this challenge. "This time nobody goofed; the law itself is at fault," the exasperated committee chairman, E. John Larsen, explained to volunteers before urging them to get out the message that "a small group of selfish, disgruntled people wants to upset the judgment of

Danbury citizens in providing for the future of Danbury's children." A spirited phone campaign in response alerted voters who rejected the substitute bond issue on June 5, 1962, by a 2-to-1 margin. Work on the desperately needed school construction could finally begin.

The full modernization program was completed with the dedication in 1965 of the Great Plain, Shelter Rock, and King Street schools, as well as the two-story addition to the Morris Street School, and one of the largest high schools in Connecticut on Clapboard Ridge. Before those projects were realized, however, pressure had mounted to erect the city's first junior high school. In response, the board of education and Dr. Haas proposed a solution that would benefit both the city and the fast-growing teacher's college. The city would sell the vacant high school located next to the teachers college campus on White Street, to the state. The state could then convert the school's interior into desperately needed college classrooms. With the money from the sale of the high school, the city would finance construction of a junior high school on the city-owned Broadview Farm, aided by a state subsidy that would defray one-third of the cost.* Another appealing feature of this deal, from the city's point of view, was that no property would be removed from the tax rolls as occurred when the college bought privately owned land for expansion.

The General Assembly and Danbury voters saw the wisdom of this scenario. In 1961, the legislature added $1 million to the original $1.5 million approved by the 1959 legislature for the purchase and renovation of the building. In 1963, the Connecticut State Bonding Commission bestowed its blessings. In June 1964, a special Danbury town meeting accepted $1.9 million as the sale price of the 35-year-old high school, and approved spending the money for construction of Broadview Junior High School, which would open in 1967.

The school building surge of the early 1960s, while crucial, did not ease the pressure on the Danbury school system permanently. By the end of

---

* The Englehardt firm had judged that Broadview Farm, originally favored by the Board of Education as the site for the senior high school, was too small and contained too much below-ground ledge for this purpose.

the decade, continued population growth again overtaxed existing schools, forcing the board of education to plan for three additional elementary schools and a second junior high school. The successful effort to convince a majority of Danbury citizens to accept a huge bond issue and tax hike to pay for an important public purpose was of lasting significance. It was the first sustained evidence that postwar prosperity and the entrance of a more cosmopolitan leadership were in the process of making Danbury a more forward-looking place.◆

IF... you want modern, efficient government_

IF... you want better control of public expenditures_

IF... you want better road maintenance_

IF... you want a better tax break_

IF... you want a better central business center_

VOTE YES FOR CONSOLIDATION ON TUESDAY, SEPT 24

YOUR YES VOTE IS NEEDED!

The Committee of 1000 used the same type of publicity and volunteer effort in 1963 to convince voters to unify city government that had worked earlier in winning approval of education reform. This direct-mail piece answers the question of how consolidation would benefit city residents.

A Stone-Age Government

The Committee of 1000 did not disband after the three successful school referenda of 1961 and 1962. The exhausted volunteers paused to savor the accomplishment and the official recognition of their key role in bringing it about. John Previdi, the chair of the school building committee, acknowledged this debt in a letter to June Goodman. "The success of the campaign was in a very great measure due to your efforts and those of your many associates," wrote the grateful former mayor. However, rather than fading into self-satisfied retirement, the organization decided to join the mounting effort to dislodge an even more entrenched obstacle in the path of a better Danbury: the town's antiquated form of government.

Danbury's governmental system was a product of historical evolution rather than logic. For more than 250 years, the entire town – 42.7 square miles in size – had operated under political rules set down in 1702 by the state legislature, which stipulated that key decisions had to be made by a general town meeting open to all citizens and then carried out by an elected three-person board of selectmen. In an effort to manage the population and commercial growth that took place in the center of the town during and immediately after the American Revolution, the Connecticut General Assembly in 1822 created an overlapping level of jurisdiction by establishing a borough government that could provide vital services such as police and fire protection to this congested core. When the borough mechanism proved unable to cope with the problems that accompanied the rise of hatting, the legislature in 1889 replaced the borough with a city charter. A bicameral legislature, made up of an elected four-member board of aldermen and an eight-person board of councilmen, wielded power through a set of joint standing committees in the populous but physically compact – less than five square miles – city portion of the town. The mayor was primarily a ceremonial figure. All residents paid taxes to the town, but city dwellers also paid taxes to the city. A popular image used to illustrate this cumbersome system of dual government for the benefit of baffled observers was that the town was the saucer holding the cup that was the city.

Almost from the start, periodic efforts, usually stimulated by national reform campaigns, attempted to unify town and city. In 1905, at the height of the Progressive Era, leaders of the local Good Government Club pushed a bill through the legislature that would consolidate Danbury's governing bodies into a single entity, albeit with a provision attached requiring approval of a majority of voters before it could go into effect. After a spirited exchange of pro and con letters in the Danbury newspaper, written by citizens identifying themselves only with colorful pseudonyms like "Fair Play," "Parson," and "Ulysses," the consolidation ordinance suffered a narrow referendum defeat. Critics attributed the rejection to rural suspicion that the new arrangement would slight their interests.

Another attempt to streamline Danbury government came during the early years of the New Deal. In 1933 the Danbury Civic Association, led by Judge Martin Cunningham and other respected town leaders, engaged Herbert Swan, an urban planner from New York City, to draft a charter revision and consolidation ordinance for submission to the Cities and Boroughs Committee of the General Assembly. The bill featured a professional city manager; but despite its enthusiastic support by several hundred Danburians who traveled to Hartford to testify at the most animated hearing of the legislative session, it was reported unfavorably by the committee and ultimately was rejected by both houses of the legislature. Republicans and Democrats alike paid attention to the fierce opposition of Danbury politicians who were content with the status quo. Nevertheless, in recognition of the clear need for a more businesslike arrangement, the General Assembly did take a step toward unified government by establishing a joint tax board to coordinate tax assessment and collection in both the city and the surrounding town.

For the next 20 years, political expediency blocked any further serious move to modernize Danbury's government. Both parties had learned to live with, and profit from, dual government. The Democrats normally controlled the City Council, where the entrenched standing committees gave them access to patronage. Thomas Keating, the longtime chairman of the Danbury Democratic Party and an influential Democratic state committeeman, regularly engineered huge majorities for his handpicked candidates, including three terms as mayor in the late 1950s for pliant John Define. Given Keating's hold on city politics, it is not surprising that he resisted any tinkering with the existing system. Change could come only after his death in 1962. Meanwhile, the Republican Party dominated town offices and jobs. Joseph Sauer, who served as first selectman from 1949 to 1965, though not openly hostile to consolidation, provided no leadership for any movement towards amalgamation.

Demographic reality ultimately forced politicians to confront the glaring weaknesses of divided government. Almost all of the substantial residential and industrial expansion that took place in Danbury during the 1950s and 1960s occurred outside the city limits. When World War II ended, Danbury's total population had barely budged from its 1930 level of 27,000. But by 1960, close to 40,000 people resided in the same geographic space. A more detailed breakdown of this 30-year growth pattern reveals that, while the number of people living within the city limits remained static at about 22,000, the population residing outside the city had exploded from less than 5,000 to over 16,000. As a result, some of the areas of the town bordering the city became just as densely populated as the city itself. Because few parcels of land suitable for industrial use remained within the compact city, most of the new manufacturing companies that moved into Danbury during this boom period built facilities outside the city limits.

The gap between the services available in the city and those offered in the town was immense. The city alone maintained paid professional police and fire departments while the town depended on volunteer fire companies and a few state police officers stationed in the distant Ridgefield barracks – the same arrangement relied on by small, rural towns. Because hat factories, which were clustered in the heart of the city, had required abundant water and a modern sewage-treatment plant, only city residents enjoyed plentiful water piped in from an extensive set of reservoirs, and benefitted from a well-developed network of sewers. Where possible, the city, for a modest fee, extended its water pipes and sewers to town neighborhoods that spilled over the border – the so called "extra-city" areas – if recipients were willing to pay the cost of linking to city water lines and sewer mains. One study estimates that more than 2,000 connections were made to the city water supply in town neighborhoods by the mid 1960s. Some industrial plants, like Eagle Pencil, which used large quantities of water in its production process, were willing to absorb the significant expense of tying into the city system. Given this migration, it became increasingly obvious that if Danbury was to continue to grow and prosper, all areas of the town needed access to a full array of urban services.

As residential, commercial, and industrial expansion mushroomed in parts of Danbury distant from the city center, more city dwellers complained that divided government imposed an unfair tax burden on them. Like all town citizens, urban residents paid the general town tax. In addition, however, those who owned property inside the city limits absorbed the full escalating cost of municipal services available in the center city that also indirectly benefited those living outside city boundaries. A detailed examination of the operation of the tax system in 1963 and 1964, the last

Courtesy of Danbury Museum and Historical Society Authority.

Judge T. Clark Hull administers the oath of office to J. Thayer Bowman, the first mayor of a consolidated Danbury, after town and city were joined in 1965. Hull went on to a distinguished career that included service as state lieutenant governor and state Supreme Court justice.

years before dual government was abandoned, removed all doubt that city residents paid "considerably more that their fair share of taxes." The study documented that "the city taxpayer was paying 100 percent of the cost of city government and more than 50 percent of the cost of town government." The clear inequity of this arrangement fueled escalating demands for reform.

More than any other irritant, the confusing duplication of town and city offices and programs annoyed businessmen, especially those new to Danbury. In addition to paying two sets of taxes, executives of local companies expressed frustration at having to deal with two highway departments, two health departments, two engineering departments and two legal departments, as well as both a city and town clerk whose jurisdictions were, some suspected, deliberately confusing. After wrestling with what he termed Danbury's "stone-age government" for a little over a year, Robert Jeffries, the CEO of Data Control Systems, warned the Rotary Club in 1960 that the town would have difficulty in attracting and retaining additional industry until local government regulations became more rational and transparent. Established business leaders felt the same way. Robert Tomlinson, the President of the Barden Corporation, a mainstay of the city's high-tech economy, minced no words when he castigated dual government as "outmoded, inefficient, expensive, and frustrating."

Until 1957, the difficulty of persuading the General Assembly to legislate appropriate changes – the only route available to Connecticut towns wishing to alter their charter – discouraged efforts to make Danbury's government more efficient and equitable. In that year, however, the legislature passed the Home Rule Act, which enabled communities to revise their own government simply by following clearly stipulated rules, thereby eliminating political obstruction and the need for special pleading in Hartford. Danbury ultimately became the first municipality in the state to take advantage of these provisions to blend town and city government.

Despite the opening provided by the state legislature, change came slowly. Both political parties talked about the need for consolidation but took no steps to begin the process. Two-term Republican Mayor John Previdi named a commission to study unification but was so disappointed with the group's report that he never released it. When he left office in 1955, he warned that abolishing dual government was an absolute necessity. Two years later in 1957, Democratic leader and future mayor Gino Arconti resigned from the board of alderman, echoing the call for consolidation and blasting the framework of local government as "obsolete." Many in both parties, like prominent Republican lawyer T. Clark Hull and Democratic activist June Goodman, impatient for change, threw their energies behind an effort to substitute a representative town meeting for the unwieldy general town meeting, which, in the hands of special interest groups like the taxpayers association, had become an instrument to block progress. Although voters approved this less radical step by a substantial margin in 1960, indicating widespread support for legislative modernization, a minor procedural error prevented it from becoming a reality.*

A shift in the political winds in 1961 was the catalyst that finally brought action on consolidation. John Define had been tapped by Democratic boss Tom Keating for a 4th term as mayor in 1961, despite grumbling within the party about his lackluster performance. When Define suddenly withdrew from the race, his surprise exit created an opportunity for proponents of consolidation. The Republican mayoral candidate, J. Thayer Bowman, a member of an established Danbury family who operated a thriving insurance and real-estate firm, pledged in his campaign to end divided government. After his election, Bowman backed up his promise and, with measured steps, began the process set down in the Home Rule Act to revise the 1889 city charter. In 1961, he appointed five prominent attorneys, including Hull and H. LeRoy Jackson, a recognized expert on the historical background of local government, to provide guidance on consolidation issues. Following state regulations carefully, Bowman orchestrated a simultaneous town meeting and session of the City Council on October 15, 1962 (the town meeting was in the high school auditorium; the City Council met on the auditorium stage), that appointed a 15-member commission, representing all political, geographic, and ideological interests, to draft a consolidation ordinance. On September 24, 1963, after almost a full year of study, meetings, and community outreach, the Consolidation Commission placed its handiwork before the voters.

The unified government proposed by the Consolidation Commission corrected many of the evils of the past. Wasteful duplication was eliminated and the tax burden was more equitably distributed. In

---

* The faulty wording of the official election notice could have been corrected by a simple action of the state legislature. Yet a bill seeking this clarification never got out of the Cities and Boroughs Committee, where Tom Keating still wielded considerable influence.

proposing a new structure of government that would meet the challenges of the future, the Commission had to abide by the stringent regulations of the Home Rule Act that required all charter changes be limited to revisions of the existing 1889 city charter. Consequently, in the new format, the mayor and Common Council remained in existence, but with a reallocation of their responsibilities. A strong mayor assumed complete executive power. The standing committees of the Common Council that in the past had exercised executive authority were abolished. Instead, a unicameral Common Council, enlarged to 21 members representing seven wards rather than four, would function as an exclusively legislative body. In order to facilitate a smooth transition, these changes would not go into effect until two years after a successful referendum.

Even before the final text of the consolidation ordinance was approved by the Commission on August 27, 1963, supporters began a campaign to convince voters that they should vote for it. Despite the prospect of increased taxes, leaders of large corporations backed consolidation enthusiastically. John Hoffer, the president of Viking Wire, one of the first companies to start up in Danbury after the war, spoke for his colleagues when he declared, "I feel it is something that must come if this community is to prosper." He added a dire warning: "I don't think this community can survive in fifteen years under dual government." The Committee of 1000 was also in the vanguard. Using a variation of the strategy that had helped win approval of the school building program less than two years earlier, volunteers working from photocopied pages of the city directory telephoned their neighbors to urge their support. Those deemed favorably disposed received a second phone call on the day of the referendum. Bulk mailings highlighting the advantages of consolidation in personalized terms and with graphic illustrations poured out of campaign headquarters on West Street. The bold headline of one handbill succinctly captured this theme, proclaiming, "How CONSOLIDATION will benefit YOU!"

The Danbury News-Times, invigorated by a change in ownership, played the dominant role in explaining and advocating consolidation to all segments of the population. In 1956, James Ottaway, the publisher of a handful of small town newspapers in upstate New York and Pennsylvania, had purchased the Danbury newspaper, becoming the first owner living outside the community. A hard-driving businessman, Ottaway vowed to make Danbury the flagship publication of his expanding chain. "We have come to Danbury to make a good newspaper a better newspaper," he promised. To accomplish this he spent money on modern equipment and added experienced personnel. In 1962, he shortened the newspaper's name to "*The News-Times*" to emphasize its regional ambitions. No innovation was more important than Ottaway's willingness to allow the staff freedom to take strong stands on controversial local issues.

Steve Collins took full advantage of this opportunity. Returning to his hometown newspaper after wartime service in the Navy, Collins in 1949 became the youngest editor in the state. Fiercely proud of Danbury and its history, he was eager to use the press to champion causes that he believed would improve the quality of life in the city. Blunt editorials written by Collins supplemented exhaustive news coverage backing zoning and planning reforms in the late 1950s, and the costly school building program of the early 1960s. But the newspaper pulled out all the stops to convince voters that they should finally end dual government. It was, Collins contended, "certainly the most important matter of the 20th century." In an unusual move for a small newspaper, the editor released Don Fraser, the newspaper's veteran city-hall reporter, from other duties so that he could concentrate exclusively on this subject. The climax of this news blitz came in the months immediately preceding the referendum. Beginning in late June 1963 and extending for twelve consecutive weeks, each Saturday's issue of *The News-Times* carried a near full-page article exploring a single aspect of consolidation. A hard-hitting supportive editorial by Collins accompanied Fraser's in-depth reporting.

Even with all this effort, the more than 11,000 Danbury voters who participated in the referendum on September 24, 1963, backed consolidation by a mere 89-vote margin. The narrow victory surprised many. Collins, for example, admitted that he was "startled" by the slim margin. He attributed it to the implacable, and probably inevitable, resistance many residents who lived outside the city limits had to any tax increase. In his opinion, the educational assault of *The News-Times* turned the tide in favor of consolidation. Writing in 1983, Collins, then the editorial-page editor of the paper, asserted that the support of small homeowners in the city's Fourth Ward, "who believed what their newspaper had told them," was decisive.

The amalgamation of town and city government, which went into effect on New Year's Day of 1965, marked the most significant accomplishment of the progressive coalition that emerged in Danbury during the postwar years. This alliance of emboldened, organized citizens, influential industrialists committed to their adopted community, and a crusading public-spirited press, overturned an archaic form of government that had lasted for 250 years. Civic energy stimulated by economic prosperity had freed Danbury from the shackles of "Stone Age Government."♦

In August and October of 1955, torrential rains caused the Still River to inundate large parts of Danbury including the Wooster Square area of Main Street (foreground) and badly damaged White Street (to the east). The need for flood protection led Danbury to seek federal assistance.

The Lure of Federal Money

In 1955, Danbury was in the process of shedding its past as a single-industry mill town and moving into a more promising future as the home of many sophisticated high-tech industries. The Still River was barely noticed in the euphoria of the mid-1950s. Those who paid any attention to it considered the wispy stream that meandered through the center of Danbury to be a polluted, multi-colored health hazard, devoid of all but the hardiest aquatic life. After a rain, the river's sulfurous smell permeated the atmosphere. Tires, old household appliances and other discarded items were dumped into the river routinely to wash downstream, finally collecting behind bridges and abandoned milldams. In the downtown area, the growing city encroached on the river by extending building foundations and sewer and water lines into the riverbed.

On August 18 and 19, 1955, the Still River reminded Danbury of its power. In a 24-hour period spanning those two days, Hurricane Diane dropped more than five inches of rain on the city, bringing the total for that month to more than 15 inches. Belying its name, the Still River surged over its banks and inundated the bowl-shaped downtown causing an estimated $3 million in damages. The water flooded stores, factories, and homes along the river from North Street to Beaver Brook. Retail stores on White Street between Main and Maple, many with apartments on upper floors, were the hardest hit. Twenty-five families had to be evacuated by boat from City Hamlet, a low area on North Main Street.

The floodwater receded quickly, but for the merchants recovery was slow and costly. The experience of Ben Doto, the owner of Ben's Workingmen's Store at 42 White Street, was typical. He had received a large shipment of winter clothing, valued at between $25,000 and $30,000, shortly before the flood struck. Mud and water ruined about 10 percent of his inventory and so badly damaged the balance that he was forced to dispose of it at special sale prices that netted only 40 cents on the dollar. His neighbor Lou Ginsberg, the owner of Ace Industrial Hardware, had to discount his merchandise up to 75 percent after water filled the cellar and rose several feet on the ground floor of his store at 47 White Street. The basement of Feinson's Men's Store, on the corner of White and Main, was also flooded, forcing the company to sell $10,000 worth of merchandise at similar deep discounts.

These losses were dwarfed by the loss suffered by the Barden Corporation. The rampaging water of the river where it flowed along the back of the leased plant on East Franklin Street smashed windows in the process of inundating such vital areas as the tool-making department, grinding room, storage area for precision gauges, and plant cafeteria. Approximately 300 machines and 1,000 electric motors had to be rebuilt. Fifty thousand dollars worth of gauges were taken by boat to Henry Abbott Technical School, where employees worked around the clock to clean and dry them. It required five fire engines to pump out the building before a squadron of male employees could begin scrubbing floors and walls. For three weeks the plant could not operate.

Little wonder the community was jittery on October 13, when heavy rains began again. By Saturday morning, October 15, almost 4.5 inches had fallen – close to the amount that had triggered the August disaster. Instead of subsiding, the storm grew worse on Saturday night, forcing the Still River over its banks for the second time. When the rain finally ceased on Monday morning more than 12 inches of rain had soaked Danbury in four days and the city had suffered the worst flood in its history.

This time floodwater cut the city in two. All bridges over the river were damaged. For several days the only way for essential traffic to get from one side of the city to another was via the battered Cross Street Bridge. Sections of the city that had not been touched by the August flood felt the river's rage. Railroad freight cars marooned on tracks in the Mill Plain area were almost covered by water. The nearby Fairgrounds resembled a lake. On the other side of Danbury, water spilled into factories in the Leemac and Shelter Rock area, keeping parts of the large Frank H. Lee Company out of operation for a week. The entire city was without power at the height of the flood, when the Housatonic Electric Power Company abandoned its sandbagging precautions and shut down the Triangle Street Substation.

Even though the October flood harmed more of Danbury, the most vulnerable sections were the same ones that had suffered in August. Main Street on either side of Wooster Square, Elm Street and River Street to the west, Franklin and Patch Street to the north, Delay Street and Chestnut Street to the east – all were re-flooded. Once again White Street was devastated. Carrara's Fruit Market, a 100-ft-long metal structure, was lifted from its foundations by the rampaging waters and slammed against a neighboring building 20 feet away. Harry Harris, whose auto-parts store escaped harm in August, estimated that water flowed through his store to a depth of four feet and was as high as seven feet in an adjacent storage building. Ralph Urban measured 69 inches of water in his White Street appliance store, compared to 24 inches in August. A stunned reporter from *The Danbury News-Times*, getting his first look at the flood damage after the waters had gone down, declared that White Street should be renamed "Black Street" because everything was covered with dark, sticky mud.

The same factories were ravaged. The Barden Corporation had to repeat the process of rescue and rehabilitation of delicate machinery and cleanup of their leased quarters for a second time within as many months. Aging hat factories in the Beaver-Rose Street area were badly damaged. Portions of the wall of both the American Hatters and Furriers factory and the Mallory backshop were turned into rubble by the surging waters. The October flood caused an estimated $6 million in damage.

For three days, downtown Danbury resembled a war zone. Large dump trucks, the only vehicles that could navigate the inundated streets, evacuated those marooned in apartments. Other individuals, such as 13-year-old Eugene Ward, were snatched off the roof of a Main Street building by a U.S. Army helicopter from Sikorsky Field. The displaced residents were cared for in an emergency shelter set up in the War Memorial in Rogers Park. On Sunday night, a fleet of 22 fire trucks from the New York City Fire Department rolled into Danbury to assist in the cleanup.

This flood did not spare human life. Robert J. Keating, a 40-year-old Danbury policeman, died of a heart attack while attempting to rescue a family on Thorpe Street extension. After the floodwaters subsided, the body of Christopher Wheeler, who lived on Rowan Street, was found partially buried by mud and debris near the Chestnut Street bridge.

The twin floods left behind badly damaged roads, buildings, and confidence. Looking back, citizens realized that, at least since the minor flood brought on by the 1938 hurricane, they had been courting trouble. It was apparent that the Corps of Engineers had been correct in a 1940 report that warned about the danger of building too close to the river and permitting obstructions to block the river bed. Before the last basement had been pumped dry, shaken Danbury residents reached a conclusion about the flood and the menace of the unpredictable stream that would change the face of the downtown forever.

Angry business and industrial leaders spearheaded by John McCann, an executive with Sperry Products, were the first to respond. Along with officials of both political parties, they formed the Citizens Committee for Flood Control Action to make sure that the river would never again be allowed to cause trouble. Some companies, like Davis and Geck, threatened to abandon expansion plans without a guarantee of effective flood control. Herbert Everett, the head of the Chamber of Commerce, warned that fear of the rampaging river had already convinced two firms once eager to move to Danbury to question this decision. But the stark ultimatum delivered by F.E. Erickson, the founder and president of the Barden Corporation, whose converted hatting silk factory headquarters had been battered twice by the Still River, drove home the message that the unchecked river menaced the community's economic health. "If we get another flood, we're through," the respected businessman declared. "We can't spend $300,000 on cleanup every two months. We can't stay in Danbury."

In search of security, the Citizens Committee turned first to the United States Army with a request that the Army Corps of Engineers (ACE) assume responsibility for designing, building, and paying for the rechanneling of the Still River. Despite initial skepticism that the project qualified for federal attention, the ACE agreed to undertake a detailed engineering study of the local situation. In March 1957, after a 15-month investigation, the ACE disappointed Danbury officials by recommending an elaborate solution that would provide the highest (500-year) level of flood protection at a staggering cost of $16 million. Even more discouraging, the ACE ruled that the Flood Control Act of 1938, which allowed federal funds to be used only when the monetary benefit to a community exceeded the cost of a flood-control project, prohibited assistance to Danbury. To ACE accountants, the math was simple: the estimated $9 million in damages caused by the two 1955 floods in Danbury fell far short of justifying federal underwriting of the expense for future protection.

Not all federal agencies responded the same way to Danbury's plight. On March 13, 1956, while ACE engineers were painstakingly surveying the still-fresh flood damage, two representatives of the U.S. Urban Renewal and Redevelopment Commission traveled by train to Danbury from their New York City office to present an attractive proposition to a worried community. The visitors explained that the Housing Acts of 1949 and 1954 provided substantial financial support for rejuvenation of decaying

Courtesy of The News-Times

This cartoon by staff artist Robert Donovan appeared in *The Danbury News-Times* a few days before the April 1956 bond-issue vote. At stake were monies needed to pay for the city's share of the urban renewal package, and the cartoon urged the public not to pass up a bargain.

urban centers, even those in smaller cities. Originally focused on slum clearance, Congress now permitted using government tax money to replace substandard buildings with modern income-producing structures, improve traffic circulation, and provide convenient parking in blighted urban zones. These experts expressed confidence that the Housing and Home Finance Agency (HHFA) would fund a project that combined harnessing the Still River with rejuvenation of the inundated portions of the city.

The details of such a program were relatively uncomplicated and incredibly generous. HHFA was willing to pay two-thirds of the cost of buying all the structures in each blighted area, bulldozing the run-down buildings, and then selling the cleared land to developers anxious to finance high-end commercial projects on the site. The willingness of state government to pay half of the remaining one-third share of the cost of this partnership made the arrangement even more appealing. Danburians had no difficulty imagining that the approximately 25 acres of the most severely flooded land flanking the course of the Still River on both sides of Main along White and Elm streets, while not primarily a residential slum, could easily qualify for this assistance. This was a badly damaged area filled with obsolete buildings, including some shabby hat factories. The prospect of transforming it into a prosperous commercial enclave served by an efficient road system and offering ample parking was irresistible. Such a magnet, supporters believed, would help preserve downtown Danbury's historical position as the economic core of the surrounding region, which was already threatened by suburban sprawl.

In order to make this vision a reality, Danbury willingly took steps to comply with required federal guidelines. The upgrading of a blighted area had to be a component of a well-thought-out urban master plan; in 1957, the city established a planning commission to draft such a document. Shortly afterward, the fledgling planning commission engaged Technical Planning Associates (TPA) of New Haven to provide professional assistance for this task – another federal stipulation. On June 2, 1956, Mayor John Define appointed George O'Brien, a businessman and veteran Democratic politician, to chair a nine-member redevelopment agency that would apply for federal support and manage the redevelopment process. Joseph Canale, the longtime head of the Danbury Housing Authority, became the part-time executive director of this key agency primarily because he was the only local official who had extensive experience dealing with Washington.

Even though the urban renewal program focused on transforming down-town land, it did not ignore the Still River. The Urban Renewal Agency agreed to regard any money spent by the local community in rechanneling and relocating the river – including the construction of bridges and roads – as fulfilling Danbury's one-sixth share of the overall redevelopment cost. As early as April 13, 1956, the public, urged on by the Danbury Committee for Flood Control Action and the ebullient *News-Times*, responded to the lure of federal money by approving a $1.5 million bond issue for flood control by a huge 6-to-1 margin.

Over the next 20 years, following a scaled-down, four-phase, flood-control blueprint devised by the Connecticut State Water Resources Commission, the bed of the Still River in the center of the city was straightened, deepened, contained by concrete walls, and covered over in a few places. The first segment, between Triangle and Cross Streets, was completed in 1957. Danbury taxpayers paid for and carried out most of these changes – although in the latter stages of the work, relaxed federal rules allowed the Corps of Engineers to contribute funds and expertise.

Danbury soon learned that while urban renewal funds were tempting, they were also slow in coming. Despite the encouragement and example of Mayor Richard Lee, who had turned New Haven into a model city with cash from the federal government, it took several years before the Danbury Redevelopment Agency was ready to make a formal request for federal assistance.* On July 16, 1958, the agency finally submitted an application to Washington for a $5.4 million urban-renewal grant that would cover the expense of razing 123 major buildings and relocating 104 families in order to prepare the targeted land for development. Of the total amount, the federal government would contribute $3.6 million and the state would give $900,000, leaving Danbury to come up with $900,000 in the form of in-kind contributions. No wonder George O'Brien, the local Redevelopment Agency chair could exclaim almost incredulously, "Here is a case where we will be getting an outright gift of $4.5 million." *The Danbury News-Times* agreed. In an editorial entitled "Danbury's Golden Opportunity," editor Stephen Collins guaranteed readers that "Danbury can't go wrong in approving this plan." In February 1959, the Urban Renewal

* The charismatic Lee extolled the benefits of urban renewal to the Chamber of Commerce on several occasions. At a Chamber luncheon in February 1958, he assured members, "What New Haven has done on a grand scale, Danbury ... can do on a scale befitting the community's needs.".

Courtesy of Danbury Preservation Trust

A mid-1960s ground-level view of the cleared redevelopment land between Crosby Street looking toward White Street with Main Street to the right. The city permitted shoppers to park temporarily in the muddy area during the Christmas season.

Administration accepted Danbury's application. More than three years after the 1955 floods, urban renewal could get underway. Not surprisingly considerable delay still lay ahead. Tearing down close to 125 major buildings; constructing channel work on the Still River in the redevelopment area; and building bridges over Main and White streets occupied two more years. It took considerable time to relocate the families made homeless by the demolition, as was required by federal rules. Fortunately, two-thirds of this uprooted group were eligible for federally subsidized, low-income housing in buildings like Laurel Gardens, which the Danbury Housing Authority had built on the site of the shabby City Hamlet neighborhood, an area hard hit by the floods. Even the efforts of newly elected Mayor Thayer Bowman to speed up the glacial process by naming Thomas Stevens as the new head of the Redevelopment Agency in 1962, and replacing five agency members, had minimal effect.

It was not until early 1964 that Danbury officials could begin the crucial search for an investor who would rejuvenate the downtown by filling the now cleared and leveled landscape with income-producing buildings. With startling speed, the Redevelopment Agency accepted the proposal of Leonard Farber, a retail shopping center developer from Hartsdale, New York. Farber promised to transform the key segment of empty redevelopment land – the 23.6-acre area west of Main Street that was designated as Parcel A on planning maps – into a consumer destination by constructing an enclosed shopping complex with parking for 750 cars, and a nearby 10-story circular apartment tower. No city the size of Danbury, Farber promised, would have such an elegant facility at its core.

It did not take long for Danburians to realize that further delay was still an unavoidable component of the redevelopment process. Farber had difficulty finding high-quality stores willing to lease space in the proposed mall. Major retailers such as Macy's, Gimbels, Read's and Sears showed no interest. As a result of an unexpected downturn in the economy, the apartment tower was eliminated from the plan. The now cautious Farber refused to identify his prospective tenants publicly. Instead, he requested and received several extensions of the commitment deadline from the concerned Redevelopment Agency. Not until November 1966 did the once confident developer actually take title to Parcel A for the stipulated $435,000 purchase price so that construction could finally get underway. In early March 1968, almost 13 years after the Still River surged over its banks, the opening of the 60,000-square-foot, two-story Danbury Mall, anchored by the little-known Grand Way Department store, marked the culmination of Danbury's first experience with federally sponsored urban renewal.

The balance sheet on this long and complicated project was mixed. There were positive outcomes: The Still River was permanently tamed; segments of a more functional road system were put in place; and more downtown parking was added. However, it was clear that the Danbury Mall and the First National Market that had been persuaded by Farber to move a few doors south on Main Street to occupy the second largest renewal parcel located between Crosby and White streets, would not solve the growing

Courtesy of Danbury Preservation Trust

This aerial view, taken in the mid-1960s, shows the cleared redevelopment land east of Main Street (right side of photo) looking south from Crosby Street (foreground) toward what is left of buildings on White Street. The Still River, encased in a concrete channel, snakes through the bleak landscape.

economic problems of downtown Danbury. To address what the Chamber of Commerce termed the "deteriorating conditions" faced by merchants in the central business district, Danbury once again turned to Washington and a strategy of enticing federal funds for assistance.

In 1962, long before the city had located a developer willing to build new buildings on the land cleared in the first phase of urban renewal, Mayor Thayer Bowman urged the Redevelopment Agency to expand its vision and take advantage of more flexible federal regulations in order to revitalize the established core of Danbury's downtown business district.* Bolstered by a generous planning grant from the Housing and Urban Development Agency (HUD), the Redevelopment Agency in 1964 unveiled the General Neighborhood Renewal Plan, soon renamed the Mid-Town East Renewal Plan. Its purpose was to transform more than 200 acres of downtown land

---

* Under altered HUD regulations, participating cities did not have to demolish all structures in a renewal area, a change that earned editorial approval from *The News-Times* because it was no longer necessary to turn "large sections of downtown into a waste land."

located behind the commercial buildings on the east side of Main Street, and extending along White Street to the east. In addition to acquiring property in this area bordering the Still River, which was needed to close the final gap in flood control, the objective was to improve circulation and parking in the heart of the city. To accomplish this, a pair of multilane, limited-access highways were proposed that would bisect the downtown from South Street to North Street and from West Street to Federal Road. These would tie the central business district to the Yankee Expressway, which was soon to be incorporated into the Interstate system. The projected six-lane, east-west Crosstown Expressway would pass over the New Haven Railroad's tracks via a bridge near White Street. On the planners' drawing board, the ubiquitous railroad would no longer snarl Danbury traffic.

The ambitious renewal plan shrank in scope, but grew in duration and cost as it evolved during the 1960s and early 1970s. Ultimately, its cost soared as high as $16 million and completion stretched over a projected 15- year period. However, the one crucial feature that never varied was the understanding that HUD would pay 75 percent of the bill with the state and local community splitting the balance. As in the first, still incomplete, phase of urban renewal, Danbury could count on the fact that in-kind contributions, such as the $2 million earned by the sale of the old high school to the state for the use of Western Connecticut State College, would ease or possibly eliminate any financial burden to the local community. Few challenged the head of the Danbury Redevelopment Agency, Thomas Stevens, when he predicted in 1968 that this second phase of urban renewal, like the first one, would cost Danbury "probably nothing."

Danbury again realized that dependence on a distant decision maker to accomplish complex and expensive objectives such as flood control and rehabilitation of the downtown – tasks deemed beyond the reach of local initiative and funding – had hidden pitfalls. For one thing, the balance of national political power was always subject to unpredictable electoral change. The Republican administration of Richard Nixon, who came to power in 1969, unlike its Democratic predecessors, did not favor generous assistance to beleaguered cities. Consequently, the flow of federal money for urban renewal projects slowed to a trickle. Washington refused to allocate the entire cost of projects in advance and instead funded only segments that could be completed in a single year. Regional HUD offices in Boston and New York continually delayed responding to the annual re-applications required by this cumbersome process. In addition, the community block-grant approach adopted by the Republicans forced the Redevelopment Agency to compete with other local programs for a portion of reduced federal support. A frustrated Stevens, the prime mover of Mid-Town East Renewal Plan, stepped down as head of the Redevelopment Agency in 1972. As a result of these obstacles, the opening in 1976 of Patriot Drive, the truncated, four-lane Main Street bypass that ran from Liberty Street to White Street through a landscape of recently cleared land, marked the major accomplishment of the second stage of urban renewal in Danbury.

By 1975, 20 years after the most devastating natural disaster in Danbury's history, the Still River, thanks in good part to federal assistance, no longer menaced the downtown. However, the expectation that the $26 million subsidy provided by Washington during these two decades would reinvigorate the central business district was not realized. The Danbury Mall quickly failed. The closing of the Grand Way anchor store in 1974 precipitated the flight of smaller, marginal tenants until, by 1978, just 10 years after it opened, the already rundown shopping plaza was vacant. When Wilton-based General DataComm purchased the facility for use as its headquarters, it spared the city the embarrassment of a prominent eyesore. Even the usually optimistic Mayor Gino Arconti, in a 1973 speech delivered near the end of his administration, showed his distress over the situation, lamenting, " … the downtown is deteriorating." It was evident that the 20-year partnership had failed to alter the powerful economic and social forces that had inexorably determined the nature of Danbury's downtown. ♦

On October 21, 1979, a crowd of about 400 people of mixed races marched down Main Street in silence to protest Klu Klux Klan activity in Danbury. Note the presence of soon-to-be elected Mayor James Dyer in a prominent position behind the banner.

"This too is Danbury"

Although hardly a bastion of activism, the campus of the burgeoning Danbury State Teachers College did not escape the reform fervor that swept the nation in the 1960s. The school's most ambitious social initiative of that era came in 1966. Fortified with funds provided by the federal government under the Higher Education Act, the college administration that year commissioned Columbia University's Bureau of Applied Social Research to study the Danbury area in order to identify the pressing problems of the region and to suggest ways in which the college could contribute to improving the quality of life in its home community. Columbia sociologist David Wilder, assisted by Robert Hill, an African-American graduate student at Columbia, started with a core list of contacts provided by the college and ultimately interviewed 180 prominent citizens between July and September of 1966. There was remarkable consensus among those consulted. As Wilder phrased it in dispassionate social-science language at the start of his lengthy 70-page summary document, "Virtually all respondents spoke about the poor, the growing Negro population of Danbury, or some aspect of human relations as being a serious problem in Danbury," he said. He then added for emphasis, "No other problem area received such unanimous recognition." The report made clear that the sizable migration of African-Americans to Danbury in the two decades after World War II had created a set of interlocking challenges for both the white and non-white populations of the city.

The increase of African-American settlement in Danbury was a smaller and tardier segment of the great migration of African-Americans to Connecticut that had taken place in the three decades after Pearl Harbor. In 1940, the 33,000 African-Americans living in the state represented less than 2 percent of the state's population. Drawn by wartime employment opportunities in booming Connecticut factories, however, African-Americans from New York City, the South, and even from the Caribbean flocked to the tiny state. By 1950, their numbers totaled almost 54,000. Connecticut's vigorous Cold War economy continued to attract non-white newcomers in the next decade. According to the 1960 census, the 107,450 African-Americans who resided in the state constituted 4.4 percent of the overall population. The great majority of these newcomers settled in large cities with an industrial base. Hartford, the center of aircraft engine production, is a case in point. By 1960, 15.5 percent of the population of the capital city was non-white.

African-American emigration to Danbury resembled this pattern but with some significant differences. A small African-American population of about 250 resided in Danbury at the start of World War II. Most were members of families who had lived in the city for many years. With hat production locked in a downward spiral and lacking significant war-related industries, Danbury attracted few immigrants in the 1940s. The number of Afri-can-Americans remained small – 496 persons, according to the census of 1950. However, during the next 20 years, the transformation of the local economy produced a dramatic spurt in the total population of the city, from slightly more than 30,000 – a size first reached in the 1920s – to over 50,000 by 1970. At the same time, the number of African-Americans living in Danbury grew at an even faster rate. A door-to-door canvas conducted by the local branch of the NAACP in 1963 found that the African-American population totaled 2,800 people. By 1970, the Census Bureau documented that African-Americans constituted 5.6 percent of the city's population.

Most of the newcomers came originally from the states of Virginia and North Carolina, with the neighboring North Carolina towns of Bethel and Greenfield sending especially large numbers. While the migration began in the border states, it often advanced in stages, with migrants first heading to New Jersey and New York. Once there, according to one person interviewed by a *News-Times* investigative reporter in 1968, " … they get discouraged, don't want to go back to the South and then look for places like Danbury." Most were young. The State Civil Rights Commission estimated that 75 percent of the new residents were less than 40 years of age. From a predominately rural background, they were handicapped by faulty educational preparation and lacked skills needed by the high-tech companies that had energized the local economy.

Even though Connecticut was a path-breaker in promoting equal treatment of all its citizens, non-white minorities were still subject to de-facto discrimination.* In Danbury, a chronic shortage of affordable housing for all citizens made finding suitable living accommodations a daunting challenge for newly arrived African-Americans. The State Civil Rights Commission in 1966 termed it the "overriding concern of most Danbury Negroes." However, unlike the settlement pattern in many Connecticut cities, blacks were not confined to one large ghetto but were scattered in smaller, restricted sites near downtown – a situation, as the state Civil Rights Commission pointed out, that tended to increase, not lessen, the frequency of discrimination. In fact, the commission claimed that the absence of a dominant ghetto was responsible for the false impression among many African-American immigrants that "Danbury is the worst city they have ever lived in." Danbury native Lionel Bascom,

---

* In 1943, Connecticut became the first state to set up a government agency, the Connecticut Interracial Commission, to address this problem. It was replaced in 1951 by the Commission on Civil Rights, which in turn was succeeded by the Commission on Human Rights and Opportunities in 1967. In 1947, Connecticut was the fourth state to enact a Fair Employment Practices Act. Two years later, at the same time that Governor Chester Bowles desegregated the Connecticut National Guard, the state banned discrimination in public housing.

currently a journalist and faculty member at Western Connecticut State University, recounted in a 2009 interview how, as a young boy in the 1950s, he was forced to take a round-about route from his home on Beaver Street to the New Hope Baptist church on Rowan Street in order to avoid going through the potentially hostile City Hamlet neighborhood. With that remembrance, he illustrated one of the hazards of Danbury's patch-work-quilt pattern of African-American neighborhoods.

In 1968, when *The News-Times* for the first time devoted significant space to a comprehensive examination of the situation of African-American residents, the paper identified seven neighborhoods where African-Americans lived. Some of these areas were no larger than a portion of a single street. The greatest number of these residents crowded into the district that included Beaver, River, Rose and Elm streets. Here older, sub-standard homes shared space with decaying hat factories. Most residents of this run-down section were forced to pay exorbitant rents to absentee land-lords. The Danbury Human Relations Commission, a group of dedicated volunteers from both races, came away from a 1961 visit to apartments in the Elm Street area occupied by African-Americans stunned by the crowded nature of the rooms that forced occupants to spend much of their time out-side on the sidewalk. Elizabeth Krom, a veteran state Commission on Civil Rights field representative assisting the local commission, told *The News-Times* that it was a "revelation" for her to discover that "there were beds in the kitchens and living rooms" of these cramped accommodations. "There was just no place to sit down," she complained. William Ratchford, who went on to serve as an influential Connecticut legislator and United States Congressman, gave an even more graphic description of this neighborhood at a public hearing in 1963, characterizing it as "an appalling slum ghetto ... within which a majority of our Negro citizens are forced to live." He confessed that he experienced "a sinking feeling in my stomach" whenever he entered the "unheated, sometimes vermin-infested rooms which too often lack toilet and plumbing facilities." Then, in an effort to dissolve the complacency of his listeners, the young attorney concluded, "Yes, this too is Danbury, and we have tolerated these conditions for a decade or longer."

Several factors complicated efforts to provide more adequate housing for African-Americans. First, the fact that the Elm Street district was the focal point of post-flood urban renewal forced the city to relocate the displaced residents, including one hundred African-American families who lived there. The Redevelopment Agency took this responsibility seriously but was hampered by a shortage of affordable replacement housing. Available space in low-income public housing was already at a premium. The Danbury Housing Authority, since its establishment in the early 1940s, had been able to provide subsidized housing for veterans, for the elderly, and for moderate-income tenants, but did not tackle low-income public housing until the 1955 floods generated an opportunity to clear squalid City Hamlet and build Laurel Gardens. In 1959, High Ridge, the second affordable public housing project, was completed. Both were quickly filled to capacity. By the early 1960s, only 14 African-American families uprooted by the flood could be accommodated in existing public housing. In 1968, just 15 percent, or 47 out of 315, of the families residing in low-income public housing units were African-Americans.

Faced with the obvious inadequacy of public housing, Republican Mayor Thayer Bowman in 1962 proposed the building of a 60-unit complex on Hager Street in the Beaver Brook district. His proposal touched off a six-year legal battle. Neighbors organized the Beaver Brook Association that blocked construction with time consuming and expensive court challenges, a tactic that *The News-Times* asserted was "in part" racially motivated. Finally, in 1968, even though the Connecticut Supreme Court had several times ruled that the project could proceed, the city abandoned the effort because of the heavy cost of continued litigation.

Efforts to expand African-American settlement into privately owned housing beyond the confines of the existing ghetto districts proved to be even more difficult. White property owners were resistant. One extreme reaction shocked most Danburians. In 1964, rumors that African-Americans intended to purchase two houses on Lake Avenue prompted an arson attack on both buildings, an action that *The News-Times*, in a stinging editorial, interpreted as a "revelation of the extent to which prejudice and bigotry exist in Danbury."

In the mid 1960s, several highly publicized episodes of animosity between white and black teenagers exposed another source of racial friction. The most serious incident occurred on July 24, 1965, when Danbury police resorted to tear gas to break up a mob of more than 500 teenagers who clashed on Main Street at 11 p.m., after dances at the Universalist Church and nearby Elks Hall ended. When clusters of black and white youth then drove to local drive-in restaurants to continue the altercation, police again were forced to intervene. A skirmish at the Lark Drive-In, located on Pembroke Road, resulted in the arrest of a 19-year old African-American who assaulted a policeman.

What was characterized as a "riot with racial overtones," prompted alarmed front-page coverage and multiple stories in the local press and even attracted the attention of national media. *The New York Times* disseminated the incendiary comments of the Danbury police chief. "Some of Danbury's Negroes have a chip on their shoulders," he snapped. "They should be knocked down and knocked down hard." The sober 1966 Civil Rights Commission report identified police attitudes and actions as a major cause of racial tension in Danbury. Rev. Leslie Lawson, pastor of Mt. Pleasant A.M.E. Zion Baptist Church and a former president of the Danbury branch of the NAACP, reached a more unnerving conclusion when he warned, "Danbury is on the brink of violence."

Opinions on the proper response to these disturbing events divided the African-American community. Older native Danburians, while offended by the existence of discrimination, tended to be willing to avoid animosity and to politely seek gradual incremental progress. In contrast, impatient younger newcomers believed that only assertive confrontation could budge the rigid social system. Two prominent Danbury African-American leaders with contrasting life stories and attitudes epitomized the division in the local minority community.

William Cruse, whose father had moved from Virginia to Danbury in 1888, graduated from Danbury High School in 1929 with accolades as a

Courtesy of the Danbury Museum and Historical Society Authority

Mayor Gino Arconti in discussion with Bill Cruse, the first African-American to serve on the City Council.

star athlete. Despite earning an accounting degree in 1931 from Baypath Business Institute in Springfield, Massachusetts, the only job open to him when he returned to Danbury was as a janitor with the Danbury and Bethel Gas and Electric Company. It would be a position he would hold with the company and its successors for 21 years. "They gave me the mop and the broom," Cruse told startled Western Connecticut State University students who interviewed him in 1979. His tolerance of this treatment was belatedly rewarded with a modest promotion when Northeast Utilities acquired the utility. By that time, his pride was also assuaged by the financial success of his real estate investments. Respected by the entire community, he was a deacon at New Hope Baptist Church, served on numerous civic boards and, in 1963, became the first African-American elected to the Danbury City Council. His rare public comments on such sensitive issues as housing and employment were not accusatory. In fact, he defended police actions to control teenage violence. At age 70, in a nostalgic interview with Ken Hanna, a lifelong white friend, Cruse reflected on the mixture of honor and discrimination that marked his life in Danbury. He justified his controlled moderation when recounting the details of his first experience of job discrimination by saying, "It was just one of the things a Black had to get used to in the first half of the 20th century." He then added with resignation, "You learned to accept it but you never got to like it."

Dr. Franklin Adams, a 32-year-old graduate of both Ohio State University and the University's Dental School, came to Danbury in 1960 with different ideas. After establishing a dental practice on West Street, the gregarious, personable and energetic young man plunged into Danbury affairs. He organized a dental clinic for the public school system, served on the boards of directors of the YMCA and the Camp Fire Girls, was a member of the Social Action Committee of the First Congregational Church, and helped organize the Young Democrats Club. "My feeling is that a man's maximum contribution must be to his own community," he told the members of the Jaycees, who in 1964 selected him the "Outstanding Young Man of the Year."

Adams' most important civic contribution came in revitalizing the Danbury chapter of the National Association for the Advancement of Colored People. As the impatient and inspirational head of the NAACP from 1962 to 1966, he pushed the organization to be more aggressive in challenging local instances of discrimination. Picketing became the favorite weapon of protest. Members of the respected Exchange Club were shocked, on a cold April day in 1964, when 40 angry NAACP pickets carrying signs demanding "Democracy not Hypocrisy" marched in the rain outside a restaurant that hosted a luncheon meeting of the club. The picketers were protesting the organization's discriminatory membership policy. Although the president of the service club insisted that this bold action amounted to "unnecessary harassment," it did get the attention of the community. On another frigid day in March 1965, pickets targeted City Hall to protest what the NAACP charged was the failure of officials to provide adequate public housing. With an implied criticism of the performance of the redevelopment agency, the signs carried by the protesters asked, "Urban Renewal or Negro Removal?" Adams was particularly harsh in criticizing police handling of teenage challenges; nor did he spare Mayor Bowman for "dodging the issue" of racial strife in Danbury.

Adams' stay in Danbury was brief. In 1966, when he was named the chairman of the State Commission on Human Rights and Opportunities, he relocated to Hartford. In the years that followed he had a distinguished career that included earning a master's degree in public health at Yale University, service as the dean of the University of Connecticut School of Allied Health Programs and, in 1997, appointment by Governor William O'Neill as the state commissioner of health. He left behind in Danbury a cadre of young followers such as Sam Hyman, his successor as head of the local NAACP, who were committed to his policy of demanding, not requesting, equal treatment.

Danbury politicians responded slowly to these movements. Even though the attention of Republican Mayor Thayer Bowman was necessarily focused on the transition to consolidated government and the prolonged timetable for urban renewal, he was clearly worried about racial issues. After touring housing in the Elm Street area and terming it "disgusting," the mayor announced that he favored building more scattered-site, low-income public housing units. Bowman conferred with New Haven officials and visited the Elm City seeking advice on how to attract federal funds to improve race relations. One important step taken during his administration was the incorporation of Community Action, an organization first headed by Democrat Bill Ratchford, as a vehicle to secure and spend antipoverty funds from Washington. But substantial progress in race relations did not occur until the election of the dynamic Gino Arconti to the first of three action-packed terms as mayor in 1967.

Not only did Arconti possess natural gifts – intelligence, energy, openness to change – that made him the strong mayor envisioned by the architects of consolidation, his life experiences also sensitized him to the particular problems faced by minorities and the poor. He had been born into a close-knit, Italian-immigrant family that had experienced economic struggles. The death of his father when Arconti was five years old placed the burden of raising five children on his mother, whose only source of income was irregular work as a seamstress. During the depression of the 1930s, the family was forced to accept some public assistance from city government. Family members contend that the memory of visiting City Hall to collect this dole never left the future mayor. As the eldest son, Arconti left school at age 16, after only a single year at Abbott Tech, to help support the family by working in a Danbury hat factory. Military service in World War II expanded his horizons and made him conscious of his considerable leadership qualities. He was drafted into the army as a private at the start of the war and emerged after duty in the Philippines and in occupied Japan with the rank of captain – an exceptional accomplishment for someone without a high-school diploma. Returning to his hometown, he made a reputation as an outstanding athlete in industrial softball leagues, built a thriving insurance business, and became the Democratic Party leader in the City Council. Arconti was elected mayor by a huge margin and led his party to a sweep of all 21 seats in the City Council.

Only months after his landslide election on a late December weekend in 1967, Danbury's new mayor set the agenda for his administration by sponsoring a Conference on Human Rights and Opportunities, the first city in the state to follow the example of the Governor's Conference on the same subject held the previous year. Robert Tomlinson, chief executive of Barden Corporation, a firm that was emblematic of the city's vibrant economy, served as co-chair of the meeting along with Sam Hyman, head of the Danbury chapter of the NAACP. Hyman was a protégé of Adams and was about to begin a 20-year career as an investigator with the Connecticut Commission on Human Rights and Opportunities. Even before the 300 participants took their seats in the recently opened Danbury Motor Inn on

Main Street, they were reminded that this was no routine gathering. Each participant received a copy of an anonymous paper with the provocative title of "Like It is In Danbury," in which many minority complaints were voiced. Next, they were treated to impassioned keynote speeches by Albert VanSinderen, the CEO of the Southern New England Telephone Company, who had chaired the Governor's Conference, and Homer Babbidge, the charismatic president of the University of Connecticut. Two days of earnest discussion followed in "an atmosphere, which at times became electric with emotion," according to a reporter from *The News-Times*. The conference agreed on a list of 99 goals the group pledged to strive to achieve, all of which Mayor Arconti enthusiastically accepted as objectives of his administration. Adams, from his post in Hartford, captured the significance of this meeting when he concluded, "Public opinion has been mobilized to the point where we can move."

But Adams was too optimistic. A series of escalating episodes of racial friction, centered around Danbury's high school, where fewer than 200 African-Americans stood out in a student body of over 2,000, marred the decade of the 1970s. Each outburst followed the same pattern: a sudden crisis, an emergency solution, and a return to the status quo. In 1971, after several weeks of tension between black and white youths on campus and in the community, violence erupted in the high school, leaving nine students injured. To inflame matters further, hate literature distributed in Danbury by Bridgeport members of the American Nazi Party was found in the high school. Police shut down the building and arrested four African-American students before surface calm could be restored. Mayor Arconti, safely re-elected to his third and final term, made a cursory investigation and concluded that no school or city officials were responsible for the trouble. In a token response, the Danbury Board of Education added its first African-American member.

Even more serious discord broke out at the sprawling Clapboard Ridge High School in April 1975. Simmering student resentment at changes in the school's attendance policy designed to reduce high absenteeism fueled an outbreak of fighting between black and white students. Principal

William Ryan's efforts to discuss grievances at class assemblies only prompted disrespectful outbursts by students and an increase in violent racial incidents. Once again police appeared and the school was shut down. When
it reopened the next day, as many as 800 students stayed home. This new
round of turmoil prompted a mixed public response. Board of Education
Chair Joseph Veccharino Jr. took a hard line blaming "some teachers" for
"shirking their duties." The head of the City Youth Commission, Danbury's
future Mayor James Dyer, urged the school board to improve communication by accepting a non-voting student member, an idea endorsed editorially by *The News-Times*. Sam Hyman called for a rejuvenation of the local
chapter of the NAACP, which he admitted had had "no voice at all" since
1970, when Ben Andrews, its flamboyant chief, had been chosen to lead
the organization on the state level.

A few months later, in October 1975, a flare-up of racial antagonism that
engulfed the school stunned all of Danbury. Two tense days of sporadic
hostility between black and white students exploded into a full-scale riot.
Ninety police personnel from Danbury and surrounding towns, along with
a crack state police unit, took several hours to impose order and evacuate
students on buses. Nine students and seven officers were injured in the
melee, and 16 students were arrested. Teachers voted not to return to the
classrooms unless their safety could be assured. The school did not open
for the rest of the week. And far beyond high-school grounds, sporadic
violence spread to the downtown area, where store windows were smashed
with rocks.

This time the community confronted rather than denied the existence of
an unpleasant reality. The current mayor, Charles Ducibella, was facing
re-election and quickly named a citizens committee to investigate and
make recommendations. The Danbury Board of Education, under a new
chair, welcomed the assistance of consultants provided by the state
department of education. The NAACP raised its voice and urged the
Connecticut Commission on Human Rights and Opportunities to help
root out racial prejudice in Danbury. A detailed and informed report
of the Youth Commission was not ignored. It had taken the "hatred,

prejudice, hostility, and violence" that a shaken Principal William Ryan testified he witnessed at the high school to fully mobilize the Danbury public for action.

A revived Ku Klux Klan tested the community's resolve to stamp out racial prejudice. In September 1979, when racist Klan leaflets appeared on the windshields of student and faculty cars at Western and were also found at Danbury High School, fear and anger gripped African-American residents. However, in a non-violent response the NAACP on October 21 staged a silent procession of approximately 500 citizens of both races from Kennedy Park to City Hall. Among the prominent participants in this "March for Racial Equality" was James Dyer, then in the final stage of a tight four-way contest for mayor, who had already asked the state attorney general and the U.S. Department of Justice to investigate Klan activity in Danbury. Little more than a month later in December 1979, then Mayor Dyer refused to meet with visiting Klan leader David Duke and instead endorsed the local NAACP's call for a city commission on racial harmony. After this rebuke Duke quietly slipped out of the city.

The Klan resurfaced two-and-a-half years later in April 1982, heralding its return to Danbury with a cross-burning ceremony ostensibly in retaliation for a classroom guide written by a local teacher, Dimples Armstrong, that outlined the bloody history of the secret organization. In the months that followed a series of Klan provocations drew increasingly firm responses from Dyer and the Danbury police. On August 7, when about 30 hooded Klansmen rallied on an isolated Spruce Mountain property, they were outnumbered by some 300 state and city police, with Mayor Dyer hovering overhead in a helicopter. In reality the Klan was an unsavory nuisance rather than an authentic threat. But given the background of decades of racial tension in the city, the mayor's adamant position that neither the Klan nor the racial prejudice it advocated were welcome in Danbury was a significant step forward. ♦

Interstate 84, completed in the Danbury area in 1961, was an important factor in the postwar economic boom in the region. Not only did it make it possible for new companies to discover Danbury, it also directed commerce away from the downtown, as this 1950s photo of the construction of the Seger Street interchange suggests.

Blue Collar to
White Collar

One day in 1975, Mayor Charles Ducibella summoned City Engineer Jack Schweitzer to his office to meet a "Mr. X," or "Mr. Gray," who represented an unnamed New York corporation thinking of relocating to Danbury. The secrecy surrounding the meeting, held to discuss the possibility of bringing city services to a remote wooded site on Danbury's west side, was necessary. The anonymous corporation turned out to be Union Carbide, the 25th largest in the United States. Its proposed move to Danbury would be a serious blow to New York City. At that time, Union Carbide had 110,000 employees worldwide, over 3,000 of them working at its landmark corporate headquarters at 270 Park Avenue, in Manhattan. Mainly a supplier of chemicals to other businesses, the company also owned such familiar household consumer brands as Glad Wrap, Prestone Antifreeze, the STP line of automotive products, and Eveready batteries. The decision of this behemoth to settle in Danbury and its actual move in 1980 marked the culmination of a second period of corporate growth to transform the economy of the city since the end of World War II. This time Danbury would go from a factory-floor to an office-cubicle economy manned by a workforce that went from "blue collar" to "white collar" in character.

It would seem this progression was inevitable. By the end of the 1960s, Danbury had completed a successful shift from a fragile single-industry economy to a robust base of diversified manufacturing. It had become a factory town with sophisticated industries that offered skilled jobs at good wages – though below those paid in southern Connecticut. By mid-decade, unemployment stood at a paltry 3 percent. The 1967 Plan of Development, written for the Planning Commission chaired by William Goodman, called for the city to continue to seek this type of high-tech industry that would bring with it higher-paying jobs.

Still, Danbury could not escape the impact of powerful national economic forces. The "stagflation" (high inflation, low economic growth) of the 1970s pushed local unemployment up to 12 percent. Vacant storefronts began to appear in the once bustling downtown. "Jobs aren't and won't be keeping up with the number of persons looking for work," warned a report prepared by the Connecticut Manpower Executives Association in 1973. "The greatest surplus of labor supply during the 1970s will be in the younger age groups, specifically those under 30 years old," the gloomy document went on. "Danbury is definitely not a place for young people to seek jobs in the future."

Events proved the report's author wrong. During the 1970s, Danbury benefited from a mass exodus of major corporate headquarters out of New York City, perceived by many as a place plagued by crime, high prices and ineffective government. Beginning with the Olin Corporation's move to Stamford in 1969, Fairfield County became a favored destination for the relocation of prominent corporations, quickly accumulating the largest concentration of corporate headquarters in the country outside of New York.

A parade of corporations to distant, inland Danbury began in 1970, when the parent company of Ethan Allen Furniture – formerly the Baumritter Corporation established in New York City in 1932 – purchased 16 acres of the Everett Keeler farm on Mill Plain Road. By August 1973, the company had erected both the Ethan Allen Inn and the company's executive offices on Route 6 (Mill Plain Road) overlooking the Danbury Fairgrounds and the airport. The furniture showroom on the property also served as a classroom for training employees. The company hired locally to staff the 190-room inn and restaurant but the headquarters alone brought 350 employees to Danbury, many of them designers and decorators.

Grolier Enterprises, a publisher specializing in mail-order books, opened a distribution center in a large warehouse on Old Turnpike Road in northeast Danbury in 1970 in a facility built for the company by Seymour Powers, developer of Commerce Park. In 1976, Grolier consolidated its domestic operations and moved its headquarters out of Manhattan to a new building next to its Danbury warehouse, bringing with it 200 staff members. (By 1980, with a total of nearly 1,000 employees in both facilities, Grolier would be one of Danbury's three largest employers and one of five local companies that were among the 300 largest in New England.) Earlier, in 1971, another of Danbury's corporate pioneers, the Berol Corporation (Eagle Pencil), had added an international headquarters building next to its 1958 manufacturing plant on Eagle Road. And in September 1974, the German pharmaceutical firm Boehringer-Ingelheim, after a search of possible sites in Virginia, New York, Maryland and Massachusetts, announced its decision to move its growing North American Division from cramped quarters in White Plains to the Danbury area. The company's building plans included a headquarters, a manufacturing facility, a research and development arm, and a distribution center – all on 193 acres straddling the Danbury-Ridgefield border. (By the early 1980s, the company would employ over 800 people at locations in both towns.)

Finally, in January 1976, Union Carbide Corporation made public its intention to leave Manhattan and move its world headquarters to an isolated tract on the edge of Danbury. The corporate parade to western Connecticut had reached a stunning climax.

While each of these companies had unique reasons for coming to Danbury, all were influenced by three broad factors. The most basic draw was the expanding transportation network that brought the area into closer contact with New York City. The existence of the Interstate highway system, the promise of a re-engineered Route 7, and the hope of a major airport were tantalizing parts of Danbury's attractive location. In addition, all corporate executives were impressed by the energy of state government officials in selling the assets of an area with a growing university and without a state income tax. Finally, the traditional strengths of Danbury, epitomized by favorable zoning regulations, a productive workforce and a welcoming attitude of city officials, were persuasive.

As noted, it was the I-84 segment of the federally financed Interstate highway system that helped make possible Danbury's corporate boom. When construction began in the 1950s on what was then labeled the Yankee Expressway, the road was viewed by locals primarily as a long-promised antidote to Danbury's decades-old downtown traffic congestion. Most area residents simply looked forward to a new driving experience of traveling at high speed through a billboard-free landscape. However, it did not take long before the economic potential of the highway became apparent. Even during construction, developers and real-estate agents earmarked significant pieces of property located near the proposed exits. Shrewd observers agreed with *The News-Times*' 1958 prediction: "This highway will be to Danbury in the 1960s what the railroad was to Danbury in the 1850s."

The newspaper editorial writer was prescient. The opening of the first stretch of I-84 through Danbury in 1961, and the road's completion within the decade, produced a second surge of population and economic growth in the region. But one crucial piece of the highway network, a direct link to New York, needed to be added. In 1970, the newly finished I-684, one of nine interstate "spokes" radiating out of New York City, connected with I-84 in New York State a few miles west of the Connecticut border. It was now possible to reach both Hartford and New York from Danbury by automobile in an hour. Not only could Danburians find employment in once-distant places like White Plains, restless corporations contemplating leaving New York now had a practical route to Danbury. By 1980, virtually all of Danbury's major employers were positioned along the Interstate, from the New York line in the west to the Bethel line in the east.

Nevertheless, while Danbury's prized Interstate highway connection was its critical asset, the city had several transportation weaknesses that many believed needed to be addressed to ensure continued economic growth. It would take a widened and straightened Route 7 to make Danbury a complete crossroads hub as it had been in the railroad era. Some city promoters also argued that modern corporations required access to an expanded airport. Both projects showed enough promise of realization between 1960 and 1980 to raise the hopes of supporters.

Danbury interests pressed the state hard for a new Route 7 for over 30 years. In the early 1960s, a movement was in the works to replace the winding two-lane road that led from Norwalk in southwest Connecticut all the way to northern Vermont. The General Assembly had authorized the rebuilding of Route 7 in 1962, but provided no funding for the project. Angered by the inaction, business and political leaders in the Danbury area formed the Route 7 Association to urge construction of what became known as "Super 7," a new, limited-access, high-speed expressway paralleling the existing Route 7 between Norwalk and Danbury. Adopting the slogan "New 7 Now," and led by Barden Corporation President J. Robert Tomlinson, the group hired 15 buses to ferry almost 1,000 advocates for a new highway to Hartford, where they besieged the governor and the General Assembly's Roads and Bridges Committee. The delegation argued that the economy of western Connecticut was missing growth opportunities due to the limitations of the current highway. Legislators agreed and, in 1965, allocated funds for a new road, with construction scheduled to begin by the end of the decade. The prospect of a completed "Super 7" helped interest companies from southern Fairfield County and New York City in coming to Danbury.

Twenty years earlier, as World War II ended and Danbury's economic renaissance began in earnest, many in the local business community had begun to view the Danbury Airport as an untapped resource. To promote use of the facility, the Connecticut General Assembly in 1946 established the Danbury Airport Commission headed by Paul Annable, manager of the Genung's Department Store on Main Street. Annable was pleased that key manufacturing companies expressed interest in taking advantage of the airport for parts delivery, executive flights, and visits by salesmen from other companies. The Barden Corporation even considered acquiring its own planes and building its own hangar. To raise revenue, the Airport Commission leased space to aviation-related businesses like air charter services, flight schools, and a defense contractor, Doman Helicopter. During the late 1950s and 60s, three short-lived companies experimented with service to business travelers by offering daily plane and helicopter flights to New York. However, the prime function of Danbury Airport was as an active general aviation facility. Once the field installed lights in 1962, a steady stream of private and corporate aircraft used the runways from 8 a.m. to 11 p.m. By the mid-1960s, the small airport recorded over 100,000 takeoffs and landings annually despite its lack of a control tower. By the time the field was equipped with a federally-funded control tower in 1973, it was rated in the top 10 percent of the busiest general aviation airports in the country.

Despite its heavy use and financial stability, the airport did not serve as a magnet to attract large corporations to Danbury. Annable highlighted the problem when he told the Danbury Rotary Club in March 1967, "Our present airport is adequate for planes using twin engines and planes of smaller size, but with the coming of the new short-haul jets, we will need longer runways." The Airport Commission hired Metcalf and Eddy, a prominent New York consulting company, to remove what seemed to be an intractable obstacle. In 1968, the firm submitted a two-fold plan of expansion. First, a runway 6,500 feet in length would be built through the flat wetlands of Mill Plain swamp to the shore of Lake Kenosia. This route would eliminate the steep angle of approach over the surrounding hills and remove the Wooster Heights residential neighborhood from most flight paths while allowing commercial and business jets to use the airport, although large jets would still be unable to land there.

The second recommendation was bold and imaginative. It urged the city to set up an "air industrial park" in the space between the new and the existing runways where the city could sell or lease industrial lots, each with access to the runways. The report estimated that up to 3,000 people would be employed by companies that located on airport land, making it Danbury's major industrial hub. In 1969, a state airport survey enthusiastically endorsed the Danbury expansion plan.

Nevertheless, opposition to both highway and airport plans emerged. The momentum behind the drive to build Super 7 stalled in 1972, when Wilton residents who feared the impact of a major highway on their bucolic suburb mounted a legal challenge, claiming that failure to prepare an environmental impact statement violated federal regulations. Howls of protest came from public officials and business leaders in the Danbury area. *The News-Times* joined in by labeling the existing narrow and crowded Route 7 as a dangerous "killer highway." By 1980, when the court finally

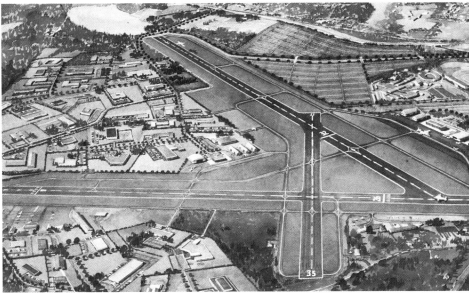

Courtesy of Danbury Municipal Airport. Photo by Stephen Flanagan

The 1968 expansion plan for Danbury Airport never got past the architect's rendering shown here. Major elements included the new mile-long runway for jets pictured here reaching through the Danbury Fairgrounds parking lots to Lake Kenosia in the upper left hand of the image, and an "air-industrial park" consisting of lots sandwiched between the runways.

settled the issue of the missing environmental study, construction costs had risen so high that even members of Danbury's legislative delegation began to back away from their previously united support of the project. In frustration, a coalition of 20 companies and institutions, eight of them based in Danbury, formed a group called Employers for a New Route 7. Led by executives of the Perkin-Elmer company, whose facilities were located along Route 7 between its headquarters in Norwalk and its key optical division in Danbury, the pressure group backed a compromise: immediate improvement of the existing route with the construction of the superhighway to come later. In 1981, the chief executives of Danbury and four of its neighboring towns, calling themselves the "Forgotten Five," lobbied Governor William O'Neill on behalf of the phased-in approach. The state deferred action until finally abandoning the Super 7 concept in 1999.

The airport expansion plan, featuring the "air industrial park" and the mile-plus runway through the Kenosia swamp, also ran into stiff opposition from neighbors and environmentalists. Without backing from the financially-strapped state government, the plan gathered dust until it was replaced in 1976 by a more modest approach that depended primarily on local resources. During the 1980s, the Airport Commission's chairman, businessman Ervie Hawley, managed to fund incremental improvements such as resurfacing existing runways, placing hazard beacons on towers located on the surrounding hills, and installing blue landing lights. Jack Thompson, founder of the Danbury Trojans football team and former mayoral candidate, served as the airport's first full-time administrator from 1974 until his death in 1983.*

As corporate migration to Danbury began in the early 1970s, both a Route 7 superhighway and an expanded airport were attractive proposals with enough public support to help convince new companies to come to the city. Ethan Allen's executives, for example, considered proximity to the airport a major reason for the company to move to Danbury. Surprisingly,

---

* So unappetizing did the idea of airport expansion become that when NASA offered to pay to double the size of the field in 1984 to accommodate a giant plane to transport the mirror for the Hubble Space Telescope, city officials swiftly declined the offer.

though, even when Connecticut's fiscal woes ultimately forced the derailment of both these state-funded initiatives, the pace of corporate settlement in Danbury did not slacken.

While the grand plans for the airport and Route 7 lost momentum in the 1970s, the creative use of planning and zoning regulations opened to corporate development a huge tract of land in western Danbury that bordered Ridgefield and New York State. Shortly after I-84 crossed this area in the early 1960s, the Town of Danbury Zoning Commission designated the land as a special zone designed to attract research facilities and light (non-polluting) industries. This matched an identical zone set up by the adjacent town of Ridgefield. The two "neighbor" towns thus guaranteed that interested corporations would be spared the complications and expense of a zoning-change application. In addition, Danbury's 1967 planning document and the comprehensive sewage study completed the same year urged construction of water and sewage lines on the west side to accommodate anticipated growth.

The designated "West Side Light Industrial Zone" occupied most of the Danbury districts of Mill Plain and Ridgebury. Sparsely populated Ridgebury had been a part of Ridgefield until 1846. Mill Plain was historically a semi-autonomous hamlet with its own general store, mission church, railroad depot and school. After the Civil War, native Yankees and Irish immigrants had coaxed a living out of farming in both districts. A major change in land use took place in the early 20th century, however, when large chunks of farm acreage were assembled into estates by people like famed singer Marian Anderson, whose country retreat was located on Joe's Hill Road in Mill Plain, and hat mogul Harry Mallory, who bought up over 100 acres in Ridgebury, where he sometimes hunted woodcock with Babe Ruth. These estates paled in comparison with the 1,500 acres accumulated in the 1920s by Harold Farrington, a reclusive engineer and head of the Southeast Gas Producing Company. Despite the existence of these large holdings, the area had a reputation as a sleepy and far-from-affluent corner of Danbury.

When the Interstate highway intruded on this space in the 1960s, no other part of Danbury, nor indeed any other section of western Connecticut, could offer interested corporations the rare combination of an entrée to a major highway system, large undeveloped tracts of land, and favorable zoning. Union Carbide was able to easily and quietly acquire more than a square mile of real estate for its corporate campus, much of it from the Farrington estate. The company candidly admitted that it sought a secluded and undeveloped site so its employees, freed from the distractions of the big city, would be more productive. The very wildness of the surroundings – tumbling stonewalls, mature woods, the occasional farmhouse – appealed to some executives. "No countryside could quite compare to Connecticut's," said Harvey Sadow, chief executive of Boehringer-Ingleheim, in explaining his company's choice to put down roots in Ridgebury.

In several critical ways, state government helped entice corporations to Danbury's west side. As early as 1970, the Connecticut Department of Transportation agreed to redesign the I-84 exit at Old Ridgebury Road, then designated as Exit 1, which could not adequately handle even the modest development already taking place near the New York State line. At the same time, Connecticut spent $1.5 million to construct a rest area near the existing Exit 1 (now Exit 2) that opened in 1971. Relocating corporations would be able to connect to the sewer line that served the brick welcome-center building.

In the shaky economy of the 1970s, Connecticut, in competition with other states, lobbied aggressively to attract businesses disenchanted with New York City. With land costs at a premium in crowded lower Fairfield County, state agencies steered corporations to the little-known Danbury area. State and local officials, including Connecticut State Representative Robert Steele who flew to Germany as part of his sales effort, worked for more than a year to convince Boehringer Ingleheim to explore Ridgefield and Danbury. Governor Ella Grasso personally escorted Union Carbide executives on a tour of Danbury that featured the fledgling Westside campus of Western Connecticut State College. The state willingly agreed to make improvements to I-84 in order to facilitate Union Carbide's move. Finally, the lack of a state income tax, an influential factor in all relocation decisions, gave Connecticut a temporary advantage over many rival states.

A cast of local actors played important roles in bringing prestigious corporations to Danbury. City government subsidized needed utilities such as the 1.6-million-gallon water tank atop Spruce Mountain and a 4.6-mile pipeline network that brought water from Lake Kenosia and the city reservoirs to industrial users on the west side. Well-connected individuals helped orchestrate corporate moves. Jack McCann, for example, a business executive who had chaired the citizens committee that sparked flood control efforts after the 1955 floods, formed his own consulting firm in the late 1960s. His client list included both Boehringer Ingleheim and Union Carbide. *The News-Times* kept quiet about early relocation discussions, championed them editorially once known, and trumpeted them elaborately when negotiations were completed. The high quality of Danbury's work force remained a powerful asset. Local people, testified a satisfied General DataComm executive, "give a day's work for a day's pay." His company was a maker of computer modems and one of the city's largest employers in the 1970s. But other firms wanted something more. As Union Carbide Vice-President James Freeman told *Barron's Magazine* in an August 1976 interview, "We wanted a city rather than a village, a place with an ethnically diverse makeup from which to draw our labor pool." Few places could meet this requirement more fully than Danbury.

Union Carbide executives left Manhattan with condemnations delivered by Episcopal Archbishop Paul Moore from the pulpit of the Cathedral of St. John the Divine in Manhattan ringing in their ears. The prominent clergyman echoed the frustrations of New York City and New York State officials who had battled to keep the chemical corporation in the city, seeing its departure as a monumental betrayal. The corporate giant's relations with its new home, however, were cordial. There were those who feared that "Carbide," as it was called, and other big companies would dry up the area's secretarial and clerical labor pool, further tighten its already stressed and expensive housing supply, and pour vast numbers of children into its schools. Ridgefield resident Paul Morganti, the area's largest contractor, warned the Danbury Kiwanis Club gathered at a luncheon that "Danbury is going to be overwhelmed."*

Anticipating the challenges associated with a move of such magnitude into a relatively non-urbanized area, however, Carbide officials had planned well. To soften its impact, the corporation's workforce was phased into its new headquarters gradually over a two-year period between 1980 and 1982. Three quarters of the 3,200 New York staff – overwhelmingly middle-aged men with small families – remained with the company during the move. The influx of children to area schools was diffused throughout several communities and about 1,000 people were hired locally, mostly in secretarial and other ancillary positions.

For its part, the city also worked to accommodate the move. Danbury's formal emergency plan, developed in 1970 following the Pardue bombings, proved successful when a major fire broke out in 1982 in the still-under-construction parking garage at Carbide headquarters. Some 2,000 office workers already on site, along with the alarmed Danbury mayor and Connecticut's lieutenant governor, watched firefighters over-come a series of obstacles to battle the blaze.

Despite Danbury's long history of welcoming new companies, it had scant experience with the kind of sophisticated corporate culture that Carbide represented. Housatonic Valley Council of Elected Officials Director Jonathan Chew, who arrived on the job in 1976, remembered one of Carbide's first outreach gestures: inviting area elected officials to a cocktail party. The invitation flummoxed local leaders, some of whom had grown up on farms and been educated in one-room schools. "Nobody did cocktail parties here!" Chew exclaimed in his recounting of the council's reaction.

During the late 1970s and early 1980s, "We were so busy you could

---

* Prior corporate moves had already produced unexpected impacts. Grolier's mail-order operation, which generated more mail than the rest of Danbury combined, was a major factor in building a new, larger post office on Backus Avenue in the early 1980s.

practically see the cranes at work everywhere you looked," recalled former Mayor James Dyer. Elected to the first of four terms in 1979, he understood the impact of this activity on city finances. When Carbide received a building permit to begin site preparation in February 1978, the Grand List evaluation of the city's taxable property soared to $1 billion for the first time. While attention focused on Carbide, established Danbury firms also expanded. Perkin-Elmer's work-force grew from 1,000 in 1970 to 1,700 in 1981; General DataComm's from 700 in 1978, to 1,300 five years later. Perkin-Elmer alone produced so many spinoff enterprises that there was speculation about Danbury becoming a new optics hub. Realizing that Carbide headquarters and the proposed Danbury Fair Mall would each account for 10 percent of the city's tax base when in full operation, Dyer hiked city taxes by 5 percent during his first year in office and began an aggressive program of public works. Famously, he drove (or was driven) around Danbury noting any deteriorating road conditions, which he then ordered repaired. After the initial boost, tax increases were minimal in subsequent years as the large new projects began paying their share.

Danburians took full advantage of the multiplier effect triggered by the arrival of large corporations. Union Carbide officials, for example, estimated that every 100 positions in the company headquarters generated 59 additional jobs in needed local services. Arthur Najamy had understood this relationship when, in the mid-1960s, he concluded that the growing community needed a modern banquet facility and established the Amber Room that became a fixture for testimonials and wedding receptions. Richard Jowdy launched a two-agent real-estate firm in 1968 that specialized in finding housing for corporate and other business transferees and, in fifteen years, his firm grew to be the largest real-estate company in the area, with a 100-person sales staff. By 1985, seven national-chain hotels with a total occupancy of over 1,000 rooms had replaced the forlorn Danbury Motor Inn and a handful of small motels. Specialized companies, ranging from cleaning services to a firm that supplied decorative plants for corporate offices, benefitted from the heated economic atmosphere.

Ordinary citizens felt the corporate impact primarily in soaring real-estate prices. Between 1977, the year Carbide began construction, and 1981, when a national recession briefly dampened the local boom, home prices in Danbury increased by 18 percent annually. Union Carbide employees alone purchased 403 homes in the Danbury region in the 1981-82 sales year. According to the Connecticut Census Data Center, a state government agency, the median price of a Danbury home more than tripled during the decade of the 1970s from $27,300 to $90,504.

The presence of a critical mass of prestigious corporations altered land values and uses in less direct ways. The rapid settlement of Ethan Allen, Boehringer Ingelheim, and Union Carbide on Danbury's west side caused a spurt in commercial development along the previously bucolic Mill Plain Road. Land prices there reached an unprecedented figure in 1984, when a New Haven investor paid $2.5 million for property near I-84's Exit 1, where he intended to erect a terminal for limousine service to New York City airports. The escalating home prices and interest rates of the 1970s sparked a boom in condominium construction as a more affordable housing alternative, particularly in the city of Danbury. In the early 1980s, *The News-Times* used the term "frenzy" to describe the pace of condominium building. The housing boom continued for five straight years, until the 1987 stock market crash brought it to a halt.

As Danbury approached its 300th birthday in 1985, its economy seemed to have little relation to its past. The combination of corporate construction, especially the Union Carbide complex; the growth of high-tech companies tied to the computer industry, such as General DataComm; a commercial boom; and surging institutional expansion of both Danbury Hospital and Western Connecticut State University lifted the former hat city into what many considered to be a permanent state of prosperity. Governor William O'Neill was so impressed with the city's economic health that he referred to Danbury as "the land of milk and honey" and held the 1984 meeting of the state's mayors in the city. *Money Magazine* went further: In 1983, the publication saluted the once-fading manufacturing city as the one of the best places in America to live.

Others were more cautious in their appraisal of what had happened in Danbury's second corporate revolution. In 1984, business reporter Ariane Sains of *The News-Times*, searching for a less utopian explanation, wrote:

> Carbide was perceived by some as the answer to all of Danbury's problems. The company would ensure the city's tax base for years to come; provide guaranteed employment for the area; generate new restaurants, hotels, and bars; and turn the city into a kind of upscale, professional community that would shuck off the last of the "Hat City" image that some found old-fashioned.

History confirms that Sains' mild skepticism was also on track. Union Carbide never fully recovered from public shock at the disastrous leak of poisonous gas from a chemical plant owned by the Indian subsidiary of the company in Bhopal, India on December 2, 1984. As many as 25,000 people died and another half million sickened in the worst industrial accident in the history of the world. Although the corporation denied direct responsibility for the accident, holding that it was caused by a disgruntled worker who deliberately mixed water with a deadly chemical, its fortunes swiftly declined. Following a failed takeover attempt in 1985, Carbide sold its landmark headquarters building to an outside investor in 1987, and leased space from the new owner. The once-proud firm left Danbury in 1999, when it was acquired by Dow Chemical Company and moved its corporate base to Michigan.*♦

---

* Union Carbide did leave behind several spinoff companies, the most prominent being Praxair, formerly its industrial gas division and as of this writing the biggest private employer in Danbury.

Courtesy of Roche Dinkeloo & Associates

Union Carbide's corporate headquarters on Danbury's west side quickly gained the local nickname "Battlestar Galactica" from its spaceship-like appearance. The structure consisted of 16 four-story pods of offices constructed around a central parking garage built on a former farm meadow atop a ridge.

Chapter Fourteen Spotlight

Designing "Battlestar Galactica"

For the Union Carbide headquarters architect, Kevin Roche, the project was equally about the people and the land, especially the trees. The firm of Roche Dinkeloo and Associates, heirs to the architectural practice of the renowned Eero Saarinen, amassed an impressive record of highly visible projects: the IBM Pavilion at the New York World's Fair of 1964-65; the New Haven Coliseum; the Richardson-Vicks corporate headquarters in Wilton, Connecticut, and many others. Roche himself, a soft-spoken and down-to-earth person, had grown up in a place much smaller and more rural than Danbury: a town of a few thousand residents in County Cork, Ireland.

Roche's firm began planning Carbide's headquarters in 1976. The 640-acre site that Carbide had assembled was typical Connecticut terrain: hilly, largely wooded, full of mature maples and oaks. There were three high points, two of them ridges with open farm fields and, in the low spots, small wetland areas. To Roche, one challenge of the project was to disturb as little of this natural terrain as possible.

Another challenge was correcting the dysfunction of Carbide's then-current physical headquarters. The corporation's Park Avenue tower had been completed only 15 years earlier, but its interior resembled a jerry-rigged maze of cramped, lifeless cubicles. Improvised work areas for secretaries were crammed together amid crossing wires and piles of paper and long, monotonous, even spookily Kafkaesque, corridors. Employees' places in the corporate hierarchy were indicated by the size of offices and the size of their windows, or whether there even were windows. Most employees labored in windowless chaos. The basic office unit had to be subdivided by movable cubicles. As a result, Carbide executives were finding that moving and rearranging them was costing the company millions of dollars every year.

Roche's egalitarian solution was a basic square office measuring 13.5 feet on each side that would be standard for all employees, executives or clerks. The room could easily be subdivided without the use of cubicles, and could be customized by a choice of furniture, rugs and other furnishings. The rooms were flexible; they could be used equally as small meeting or conference rooms or for stationing a pair of secretaries. These basic units were grouped in modules of 32, with access to a core area that resembled a small shopping mall, featuring services and amenities that included a dry cleaner, tailor shop, several cafeterias, an exercise room, even a bank. Most offices – about 80 percent – had a window with views of the woods that surrounded the building. To preclude the need for venetian blinds to control the light, Roche had each window fitted with glass awnings that diverted the light, softening glare.

Arranging the large number of office modules needed for Carbide's 3,000 headquarters personnel in a straight line would result in a building over two miles long. Surrounding it with acres of barren parking lots would require massive clearing of mature trees. Roche avoided both these eventualities by grouping the office modules around a central parking garage. Employees could park and walk to their offices only a few hundred feet away.

Nevertheless, the resulting structure was still massive. To minimize disturbance to the heavily wooded area, Roche planted the new building on the fields of one of the farmed ridge tops. The building was lifted off the ground on tall, concrete piers to further reduce alteration of the natural setting. The piers echoed the trees around the building, offering visual reinforcement of the woodland theme. Looping access roads from Old Ridgebury and Sawmill roads, totaling a half-mile, followed the contours of the land, then ended in security gates. Cars descended into the parking garage as though entering a tunnel.

The public areas inside were imposing and represented a new experience for Danburians who worked or had occasion to visit there. Access was restricted; visitors had to check in at an airport-like security desk while the lobby, up a flight of stairs, revealed itself as a vast horizontal space that glowed with large open windows and reflective metal. At the same time, the green and brown carpeting and colors of the interior piers and columns further reinforced the woodland theme. Shops and stores in the core area created an urban feel, almost as if a piece of New York City had literally been dropped into the woods. Of course, this was the company's intention: to ensure the transition to working in "the woods" wouldn't be overly jarring for its employees.

But that wasn't its popular image. It so commonly impressed most people with the image of a freshly landed spaceship that it quickly acquired the nickname of "Battlestar Galactica" after the then-popular science-fiction television series. This comparison was reinforced by the main cafeteria, an extravaganza of mirrored glass and shiny geometric metal that truly looked like it could have been on the "Battlestar." The cafeteria featured many small alcoves where groups of employees could have privacy while eating. In effect, Carbide had brought the city to its employees.

Company employees, no longer tempted by long lunches out in Manhattan, found themselves working longer. "Even diehard New Yorkers admit

Courtesy of Roche Dinkeloo & Associates

Union Carbide's futuristic cafeteria.

that, in Danbury's serene atmosphere, they work harder," reported *The Wall Street Journal.* Employees, by and large, appreciated the building; one former employee, interviewed by *The News-Times*, called it "perfect." Another said, "It was like working in a city [business headquarters]. Everything was available in that building. They didn't want you to leave."

And, indeed, the move did not foster any close ties to the host community. Located in a remote area of the city, physically closer to New York State than to downtown Danbury, Carbide was a place apart, tied to its umbilical cord, the Interstate highway. Its employees could easily live a distance away, commute into the closed complex and drive home at night without ever coming into contact with any Danburians save those who worked at the company. Carbide had left New York City; but in a sense it had brought the city along in tow. ♦

The bustle of Danbury's traditional Main Street is evident in this snapshot of a sidewalk sale in front of the John McLean store on the east side of Main Street in the early 1960s.

Retail
Revolutions

In 1965, Danbury retailers reported their best Christmas sales in years. Store after store along Main Street claimed gains of up to 20 percent over 1964, particularly for high-priced goods like the newly available color television sets. For interviews about the retail surge, the reporter for *The News-Times* hardly had to step into his car. Virtually every business he surveyed was located either on Main Street or somewhere close-by in what could be considered Danbury's downtown area. A multitude of all of the kinds of stores that today one would find in a mall were then located on Main or White or West streets. Though truly an urban environment, Danbury's downtown was small enough that most people still knew one another. Merchants and salespeople in these businesses, most of them local residents themselves, forged long-term relationships with shoppers not only from Danbury but also from every town in the surrounding region. As in earlier days of the city, downtown business people continued to play leading roles in many aspects of public life.

Few areas of community life would change so rapidly and so profoundly between 1965 and 1985 as did retail commerce in Danbury. Main Street,

the solid anchor at the town's geographic core for almost 300 years, was
no longer the focus of Danbury's life. By the mid-1970s, downtown had
assumed an almost eerie air of emptiness and quiet. *The News-Times* and
City Hall were as concerned about "saving" the decimated downtown as
they were jubilant about forecasts of new corporate growth and the boom
times ahead. It had become clear that redevelopment could not solve all of
downtown Danbury's problems. Conceived when this part of town was the
de facto shopping center for the entire region, the federally funded project
did not anticipate developments that emerged later. Downtown's inherent
problems were not the only reasons that the Main Street area lost its
traditional role as regional retail center. The lack of a direct connection to
the new I-84 highway; competition from new shopping centers on the
outskirts of town; and the Interstate highway itself, which now offered
quicker access to other cities – all of these were prime contributors to the
decline.

People had learned to live with downtown Danbury's drawbacks when it
was the sole major shopping area for miles around. Main Street was an
integral part of a state highway system that not only created congestion but
meant that any proposed street improvements like traffic lights or paving
had to be approved by the state and could become stalled in Hartford,
tying the hands of city officials. Most of the limited parking spaces near
stores on Main and White streets were metered and hard to find. Plenty
of parking existed to the rear of Main Street buildings in private and
municipal lots, but this parking was disconnected from the street and
impossible for the motorist on Main to see. Moreover, railroad tracks
bisected two of downtown's main thoroughfares, White Street and Main
Street, so that passing freight trains frequently disrupted traffic flow.

Modern shopping centers on the outskirts of the city offered relief from
these hassles. Built on sprawling tracts of what had been farmland, they
took advantage of the announced route of the new Interstate 84 as well
as existing state highways. Like the one-story, horizontal model, post-
World War II factories surrounded by large parking lots, newly appearing
shopping centers spread their stores around one-story "plazas" in the midst

of acres of asphalt. This allowed potential shoppers to swoop in from a major road and quickly find convenient, free (and well-marked) places to park near their destination. On land purchased from dairy farmer Edwin Ericson, city chemist Ellis Tarlton and his partners of the Mt. Pleasant Corporation erected the first stores of the North Street Shopping Center in the midst of 1,000 parking spaces in 1959, just as construction of I-84 was getting underway in the city. Two years later in 1961, the larger Berkshire Shopping Center was built in northeastern Danbury and the large discount department store, Caldor's, opened in nearby southern Brookfield. Capitalizing on easy access from by car major roadways, the chain stores that populated the shopping centers were usually owned by out-of-town interests. They frequently stayed open till 9 p.m. and offered more sale merchandise than traditional downtown retailers. Clearly, the Danbury area welcomed such attractive shopping opportunities. The Robert Hall chain's opening of its men's clothing store in an unassuming concrete block building on Federal Road just over the Brookfield line in 1958 proved that point. Some 7,000 visitors thronged the store on its very first day.

The most prolific developer of local shopping centers in Danbury was Ervie Hawley. Hawley had grown up in the 1930s and '40s in Germantown and on a farm in the Great Plain district that had been operated by his family for generations. His uncle Elbert Hawley ran the small Cloverlawn Dairy, with a mid-sized herd of 40 or so cows along with some horses for plowing and raking. Growing up, Hawley helped out with farm work and deliveries. Not wanting to spend his life milking cows, he eventually turned to building houses around the Danbury area in his spare time. But a chance remark by the manager of McCrory's department store on Main Street, whose lunch counter was part of Hawley's Cloverlawn milk route, that someday someone would build a shopping center that would take business away from the downtown, stirred Hawley's imagination. "Why not me?" Hawley asked himself. He turned to the Danbury Public Library to research how to finance and market a shopping center to prospective tenants. After a year of work, he finally received a favorable response from a suitable anchor store, S.S. Kresge, which also had a store on Main Street. "The real estate agents of these large stores usually arrived without notice and often while I was delivering milk," Hawley told *The News-Times* in a 1961 interview. "The only thing I could do was call on Uncle Elbert to deliver for me … [later] I would drive these fellows around and show them the spot I had in mind from the highest point of the Top-stone development. Then they'd start counting roofs [to get an idea of the potential customer base]."

With funds saved from the dairy and provided by lower Fairfield County investors, Hawley was able to raise the $1.25 million he needed to construct the Berkshire Shopping Center on a tract of open land near Commerce Park that had once housed a slaughterhouse. It opened in October 1961, accompanied by a breathless "gee-whiz" spread in *The News-Times* that described its wonders: 128,000 square feet of "shopping pleasure," 10 acres of parking that would accommodate 1,450 cars, and "merchandise in its stores worth millions … " The center con-sumed enough electricity to light and heat the equivalent of 1,480 homes. Its biggest draw was the Bradlee's discount store. One reporter resorted to making analogies to football fields and baseball stadiums to illustrate the center's size, spinning an anecdote about a child who was "awed by its vastness." If anyone in the area wasn't reading *The News-Times*, they almost certainly saw the skywriting airplane that flew overhead on two consecutive days, advertising the opening. The new enterprise created 300 jobs, half of which were in Bradlee's. Berkshire also duplicated many of the services that were already available on Main Street, including a drugstore and a men's clothier. The shopping center even had its own Merchants' Association.

Hawley expanded the plaza to the north in 1972, then created two more shopping plazas on Route 6. He and his company remained active throughout Danbury, erecting strip malls in his native Germantown dis-trict, building Nutmeg Square on Main Street; developing a subdivision of large homes on the former Landseidel property on Stadley Rough Road, and completing many other projects. Despite a low-key approach, Hawley Construction by the late 1980s was the sixth largest taxpayer in the city. Like the local business leaders of Danbury's past, Hawley filled several

Courtesy of Ernie Hawley

The scope of Danbury's post-Interstate development is seen in this aerial view of northeastern Danbury in 1972. Berkshire Shopping Center is in the foreground after its first expansion. Interstate 84 near Exit 8 runs diagonally from the right-hand corner of the photo, and the industrial buildings of Commerce Park are across Route 6 from the shopping center. Residential subdivisions carpet the former farmland outside this bustling hub, while Candlewood Lake beckons in the distance.

public positions, including service on the Danbury Hospital Board of Trustees for 14 years, and as chair of the city's Aviation Commission. In 1991, he received the community's Cecil B. Previdi Award for his contributions.

Another major commercial area took shape on Danbury's section of Route 7 near Exit 7 on I-84, close to the Brookfield town line. There, the D.M. Read Company of Bridgeport opened a large, two-story department store in April 1969. With 177,000 square feet of floor space on two stories – more than Genung's or any downtown Danbury store, and even more than the original Berkshire Shopping Center – Read's stood alone like a castle fortress amidst a large parking area. North of Read's, on a strip of Route 7 where Val's Hamburger stand had stood alone since 1957, commercial development began to fill in the low-lying properties. Stores and businesses lined Route 7 between the new Read's and the established Caldor store in southern Brookfield, with rocky Beaver Brook Mountain providing a rural backdrop. By 1970, the people of the region had become so accustomed to massive new commercial developments that Read's opening barely merited a passing mention in *The News-Times*, in contrast to the newspaper's gushing greeting of the Berkshire Shopping Center only eight years earlier.

In 1964, the city's redevelopment officials were shocked when the North Street Shopping Center announced an expansion, including a 1,200-seat movie theater named the Cinema. This development seemed to confirm that, notwithstanding agency efforts, downtown was not destined to resume its former role as the regional retail hub. But competition from outlying shopping centers was only one of several setbacks sustained by the traditional downtown during the early 1960s. The stalled redevelopment project, when it finally got underway, left the traditional city with a hole at its center. Displaced small business owners who wanted to relocate in the downtown area were forbidden to do so. One of these, Lou Ginsberg, whose Ace Industrial Supply on White Street was heavily damaged by the floods, desired to return to the still-busy downtown. Instead, he had to move to Starr Street on the city's southern edge.

Downtown Danbury faced another challenge: its awkward connection with I-84. State engineers decided to direct all traffic exiting the new Interstate and bound for downtown onto North Main Street through tiny, steep Downs Street. Vigorous but belated protests from the city planning commission about the hardship this inconvenient route would inflict on the central business district, along with heavy lobbying that included a mayoral trip to Hartford to push for a more accessible link, failed to budge state officials. In late 1960, the Connecticut State Highway Commissioner Howard Ives put an end to consideration of alternatives when he told Danbury businessmen at a Rotary Club luncheon that because the number of Interstate exits in Danbury already exceeded federal guidelines the state would not finance another. If Danbury wanted a downtown connector, he insisted, it would have to pay for it by itself.

As referred to in Chapter 12, with the planned downtown redevelopment project on the horizon in 1960, the city and the Chamber of Commerce hired an engineering consultant to plot a more direct link to the Interstate lifeline. Although Thomas Walbert of New Haven produced a design for a $5.8 million, four-lane, divided highway west of Main Street between North and South streets, no action was taken on the plan. A later state proposal for a six-lane Danbury-Bethel connector between I-84 at North Main to White Street and a four-lane expressway extending to Bethel, with a full interchange at White Street and a new street that would run through the southern section of the present railroad yards all the way to Greenwood Avenue in Bethel's business district, also failed because of lack of funds. Different configurations of this road would have demolished the Danbury Railroad Station, the Bethel Library or parts of Rogers Park, besides multitudes of homes. Only a small section was built, completed in 1976.

To further compound the downtown area's problems, fires wiped out buildings at important downtown locations. In 1969, a blaze consumed the J.C. Penney building at the key corner of Main and Liberty streets, creating an awkward vacant lot that exposed to view a row of once-respectable but now rundown wood-frame Victorian houses on Liberty Street. A few years later in 1972, the three-story Feinson building that anchored Wooster Square fell to another blaze. The Feinsons rebuilt, but replaced the landmark block with a single-story modern commercial building they later realized would have been more at home in a shopping center.

Investments in major downtown businesses seemed to yield little or no profit. Genung's, the major department store in the region since 1927, was sold to Howland-Steinbach Company of Bridgeport in the mid-1960s and proceeded to decline. The Hotel New Englander, opened in 1962 on the site of Main Street's demolished Hotel Green, sought to replace the land-mark with an automobile-oriented building that offered "the luxury of an overnight visit in a first class home." But despite hosting the studio of radio station WLAD on its top floor, the venture failed after only seven years.

All of these developments seemed to dampen faith in the downtown area, just as Danbury's wave of corporate relocations was about to begin. Many downtown merchants would agree with the sentiments of Charles Bardo, owner of Bardo-Platt Men's Wear, who noted in his memoir some

Courtesy of Ervie Hawley

Ground-level view of Berkshire Shopping Center on Route 6 in the early 1970s. Abundant parking was a large part of the appeal of such retail plazas.

years later that "downtown Danbury was over as a retail center." From a near-monopoly on Danbury's retail trade in 1960, the downtown's share of the city's retail revenue had shrunk to less than 25 percent by the time of the 1970 Federal Census. Downtown merchants who had relied on simple attempts to boost sales with promotions like dollar days, sidewalk sales, extended evening hours during holiday shopping seasons, and the popular Christmas street-lighting ceremony that took place every December, now faced more complicated marketing problems. Accustomed to operating on their own, merchants gathered in groups, but their efforts were unproductive. Four different times between 1973 and 1980, clusters of merchants attempted to organize, but "never got much past the talking stage," in the words of men's clothing store owner Robert Feinson.

In the late '70s, another threat to both the surviving downtown businesses and the new shopping centers alike appeared. A high-stakes competition developed to build a massive shopping mall that would serve all of western Connecticut and adjacent parts of New York State. The spectacular demographics of the area: the 11th highest rate of population growth in the country during the '60s; the wave of corporate settlement in the '70s; an affluent suburban rim; and the region's traditional high level of disposable income and retail sales, made it in the eyes of investors the "hottest real estate market east of the Rockies." Potential mall developers saw nearly half a million people within a 20-mile radius of Danbury who were not being served by an enclosed regional mall. Their cumulative income at the time may have been as high as $9 billion. As inevitable as the flurry of strip shopping centers had been in the '60s, the only question about the establishment of a mega-mall in the 1980s was where was it going to be built.

What *The News-Times* liked to call a "horserace" began in 1978, shortly after Union Carbide had begun construction in Danbury, and continued for over a year as different developers proposed regional malls at sites in Brewster, Brookfield and Danbury. Some support also surfaced for another downtown Danbury mall - this one on the large tract of redevelopment land behind the east side of Main Street - but quickly died when the city's redevelopment agency decided that more modest mixed uses were better suited for the downtown location than a traffic-generating behemoth like a regional mall. The "Holy Grail" of potential mall sites was the Danbury Fairgrounds that stood at the exact crossroads of the major north-south and east-west roads in the region, routes 7 and I-84. Real estate professionals considered it to be the most desirable commercial location in the state of Connecticut, possibly in the entire northeast. Danbury city officials and *The News-Times* were receptive to the mall proposal if not downright enthusiastic, but neither the Brookfield nor the Brewster developers were able to secure much cooperation from local officials. The mall contest ended in May, 1979, when the trustees of the Leahy estate, the Fair's owners, after turning down more than a dozen offers from a range of eager developers, selected the proposal of the Wilmorite Corporation of Rochester, New York to build the biggest enclosed mall in New England. Six anchor department stores and 150 to 200 other stores were to occupy over 1.2 million square feet, surrounded by parking for 7,500 cars. The mall would equal all of the retail space in downtown Danbury and exceed that in existing outlying shopping centers. Wilmorite felt such a potential justified the site's $24 million purchase price that made the actual sale of the property in 1982 the highest-priced real estate transaction in the city's history up to that time.

The horse race may have been over, but Wilmorite still had some serious obstacles to overcome. A large proportion of the fairgrounds site was wetlands – not much of an issue when it was used by the fair for a few weeks a year. However, with wetlands regulations in place since the early 1970s, the substantial parking and drainage areas that needed to be built on the floodplain of the Still River and over an aquifer to accommodate a huge mall required both local and state environmental approvals. The necessity of changing the zoning regulations from light industrial to commercial presented another hurdle. Not surprisingly, the mall proposal stirred up significant pockets of public opposition that coalesced into a protest organization calling itself SCRAM - Some Concerned Residents Against the Mall. Downtown merchants were alarmed, aware of how competition from nearby mega-malls had decimated downtowns in other cities. Environmentally conscious citizens questioned the enormous impact the project would have on vital wetlands. Nearby residents feared their neighborhoods would quickly be urbanized. Other locals shared former Mayor Charles Ducibella's concern that the mall would fail, leaving a gigantic white elephant on the city's west side.

However, Wilmorite had powerful supporters. Important local and state officials embraced the proposal. Newly elected Mayor James Dyer saw the mall as an inviting source of tax revenue and a natural outcome of the city's corporate makeover. He therefore worked diligently to improve highway access to the former fairgrounds location, particularly from Route 7. *The News-Times* printed editorial after editorial asserting the inevitability of the mall and its advantages for Danbury. Steve Collins, who wrote most of these articles, believed – as did many others – that the Danbury Fair he had known in his childhood had degenerated into a commercialized carnival and that replacement by a world-class mall would secure Danbury's economic future.

Disagreements about the mall were as bitter and divisive as over any issue in Danbury's history. When the Danbury Chamber of Commerce came out in favor of the mall, the action prompted Main Street jeweler John Addessi, among others, to resign from the organization. In March 1981, the Zoning Commission held its first public hearing on the requested zone change, at which more than 400 angry citizens blasted the mall proposal. According to one newspaper account, people "booed and shouted until after midnight while the chairman pleaded for order." A second, quieter hearing lasted until 3 a.m.

Wilmorite and its allies speedily cleared the way for construction of the mall. Only five weeks after the explosive hearings, the Zoning Commission approved the change of the land's status to commercial. The courts rejected the legal challenge brought by SCRAM. Compromise solutions removed environmental barriers. The fairgrounds property overlaid one of the city's aquifers and contained the Still River wetlands and its floodplain, plus the almost impenetrable swamp through which it flowed. The mall buildings were situated on the highest area of the property, several retaining ponds were built, and the lower roadway that circled the mall was designed to flood, which has indeed occurred numerous times since the project's completion. Still other accommodations had to be made. For example, the height of the Sears building at the mall's west end and the location of light poles in the parking lot had to be staggered so as not to interfere with takeoffs and landings from Danbury Airport's north-south runway.

Ironically, it was the shaky performance of the state of Connecticut, one of the main boosters of the project, that most hampered the mall's construction schedule. Despite repeated guarantees from Governor William A. O'Neill and several commissioners of the State Department of Transportation, the building of Route 7 interchange connections to I-84 at the site was marked by delay after delay.

Groundbreaking for the mall came in July 1984, with Governor O'Neill and Mayor Dyer in attendance. The Danbury Fair Mall did not lack for interest from major upscale tenants, unlike Leonard Farber's earlier Danbury Mall in the redevelopment area downtown. The new mall's opening, along with that of most of its tenant stores, was scheduled for late September 1986, but state officials continually backpedaled on a date when the necessary roadwork would be finished. It took an extra million dollars from Wilmorite and a herculean effort by D'Addario Company workers, some of them putting in 70-hour weeks for 10 to 12 weeks in a row, to complete a temporary modified ramp south of the mall. Because roadwork wasn't completed, Wilmorite found himself having to move the opening date for the mall back eight separate times. The first date projected for the official opening, September 25, 1986, had roughly coincided with the traditional opening of the former Danbury Fair, appropriate since the mall's developers had adopted the old fair as their design theme. The ever-changing beginning date even threw off *The News-Times*, which published a special 26-page section, titled "The Mall Opens," nearly two weeks before the opening actually occurred!

Wilmorite's Danbury Fair Mall finally began operation quietly on October 28, 1986, with three major anchors: J.C. Penney, Sears and G. Fox.* Approximately 200 other stores joined these in support. In contrast with ownership patterns of the past, only one of the businesses was locally headquartered. Parking areas for the project had been scaled back from the originally proposed figure to 5,700 spaces, which included the spaces in a four-story parking garage. Despite the bewildering switches in the starting date, on the eve of the mall's actual opening on October 25, 1986, Wilmorite threw a party for 1,100 invited guests – what *The News-Times* termed "the largest private banquet in the city's history." Thousands more showed up to shop and gawk when the structure finally opened to the public.

Wilmorite described its new mall as "the contemporary merchandising exposition of the decade." Unlike some others of its kind, the Danbury Fair Mall was airy and filled with light. It consciously played on its fairgrounds theme. A big Italian carousel with 24 custom-made horses in the center of the food court, along with mounted photos of the old Fair (including John Leahy in his ringmaster's outfit), dotted many of its hallways. But its

---

* The fourth major anchor, Macy's opened a year later to great fanfare.

Courtesy of The News-Times

The Danbury Fair Mall under construction in 1986.

architecture also picked up on earlier antecedents, particularly the glass superstructure of the Crystal Palace, site of the first World's Fair in Britain, held in 1851. Despite gestures to the past, the mall was a modern techno-logical marvel. During peak power usage in the summertime, the mall used about as much wattage as the entire town of Bethel.

The mall's financial impact was most immediate on the coffers of the city and state governments, which had been so instrumental in getting it built, although not to its advocate, *The News-Times*, which added only one new advertising sales position due to its presence. The mall and its stores paid a bonanza in property taxes – $1.8 million by 1989, the equivalent of a general tax increase of 1.5 mills which would not have to be levied. This figure stood in stark contrast to $84,000 in property taxes the old Fair had paid the year before it ended. And sales tax paid in Danbury, mostly in mall stores, became the largest single source of this revenue type in the state, accounting for approximately10% of all state sales-tax revenue. In contrast, before the mall was built, Danbury had ranked seventh among the state's 10 largest municipalities in retail revenue. While the upscale mall was only one of several major projects that changed the face and the dynamics of Danbury during the 1970s and '80s, it allowed Danbury to reclaim its position of retail dominance in the region.

The glamour and financial success of the mall contrasted with the changing nature of Main Street and its surrounding neighborhoods. By 1970, only about 15 percent of Danbury's total population lived in the center of the city. Residents there were likely to be blue-collar workers, poor, elderly, or recently arrived immigrants. The proportion of ethnic minorities housed in this area was twice that of the rest of Danbury, as was the proportion of those living below the poverty line. Most dwellings were old; three-quarters of them occupied by renters, one-third in low-rent units. Downtown had become the center of social support systems for the entire region because of its central location, its compactness and the availability of public transportation. This function grew in the 1980s, as large elderly housing projects such as Danbury Commons and Kimberly Square were built along Main Street.

Into this situation stepped Joseph DaSilva, a former baker and native of the Azores. In the 1960s, he began buying up property, beginning with older houses and eventually including big downtown commercial buildings. In 1970, he set up headquarters on Main Street in the towered landmark building occupied for years by *The News-Times* that overlooked the Wooster Square intersection. The newspaper had moved into the large former First National supermarket on Main Street. DaSilva became known for subdividing older housing into smaller and smaller segments, which he rented to low-income tenants without requiring the customary security deposit. Like many Portuguese immigrants, he shunned any ostentatious display of wealth, legendarily collecting rents personally and placing the rent money in a cardboard box on his car seat. By the time he died in 1983, DaSilva's real estate empire included over 100 properties, most of them along Main Street and in the Liberty Street-Town Hill neighborhood.

Despite its decline, downtown proved surprisingly hardy. What took place in Danbury was not much different from what was happening elsewhere in the country as federally funded urban renewal and highway building, bad economies, suburban expansion and crime all took their toll on traditional downtowns. But in Danbury, despite problems, there was reason for hope. As a 1979 planning commission document pointed out, " … the longevity of many storeowners testifies to the fact that the central business district is an area where an entrepreneur can maintain a good business." Many merchants owned their own buildings, which helped them weather downturns that hurt larger chain stores. Moreover, people were still coming to Main Street to shop at existing businesses or for other services, including using the public library, the biggest and, in most ways, best library in the area, as well as the courts, City Hall, Western Connecticut State College, the museum, and to access lawyers, accountants and doctors who still valued locations on or near Main Street.

At this time, the monumental banks on Main Street served as sturdy anchors, opening networks of small branches in the suburbs. Union Savings Bank, in particular, invested in downtown, and its president, Charles Frosch, took an active part in revitalization efforts. Store vacancies that occurred during hard times were usually filled quickly when the economy improved. A few new businesses arrived or expanded specifically to take advantage of the foot traffic and the slightly diminished congestion on city roads. A functioning Downtown Council established in the early 1980s with the backing of the Danbury Preservation Trust finally succeeded in mobilizing the downtown's multiple interests and laid the foundation for future efforts that included a special tax district. The city during the Dyer administration backed sensitive re-use of historic buildings and created the beginnings of what became a thriving restaurant and entertainment district in the warren of gritty little streets and alleys near the Post Office and Ives Street.

The neighborhoods around Main Street, though damaged by the wholesale demolition of redevelopment, did not drain out or rot away completely as they did in other places. They remained full of people, including newcomers from Portugal and areas of Southeast Asia and Latin America. As in the past, the makeup of Main Street's retail businesses began to reflect the needs and wants of these new populations in the surrounding neighborhoods. Prominently absent now were the expanded populations from increasingly affluent nearby towns, which had developed their own shopping areas. And the most sought-after customers, the new corporate employees and transferees, were missing, as well. No longer the retail heart of the community, downtown Danbury nevertheless still provided opportunity and specialized services for a highly diverse population.◆

From the purchase of the Westside site in 1967 to the opening of the first building on the property in 1982, Western Connecticut State University struggled to expand its regional influence with a promised suburban campus. In 1979, exasperated students hoped to force state action by staging a mock funeral for "Higher Education in Danbury" on the normally padlocked entry road. Complete with hearse, coffin, and a 250-car procession that wound through the city, the procession received full television coverage.

Regional Core

In 1955, Ridgefield's Zoning Commission released the results of a questionnaire given to town residents about their work routines and shopping habits. They revealed that, although Ridgefielders of the time tended to work in their own town and buy groceries there, "Danbury was the No. 1 shopping spot for everything else." For people living in the other small towns surrounding Danbury in the 1950s, the situation was much the same. Aside from a handful of necessities like gas and groceries, hardware and haircuts, area residents had to come to Danbury to purchase "everything else." A few years later, a survey of Newtown residents yielded practically the same results.

But the connection between the city and the rural countryside was more extensive than commercial links. Danbury was a second hometown for virtually everyone in the region in part because medical, legal, and financial services were concentrated there. Until the early 1960s, students from Brookfield and New Fairfield attended Danbury High School, those from Brookfield often commuting by train. Even after these towns established their own secondary schools, regional educational institutions like Abbott Tech and the newly-established Immaculate High School (classes began in 1962) drew hundreds of out-of-town students to Danbury. Some remained in the area to attend Western Connecticut State College. In the 1950s and 1960s, Danbury was the center of the region's social life, particularly for young people, who could find movie theaters and a drive-in nearby and weekly dances at the Elks Hall on Main Street. Almost all residents of the western Connecticut region were familiar with and dependent on the bustling core of Danbury formed by Main, White and West streets.

That close relationship began to change in the 1960s as towns bordering Danbury grew at an even faster pace than did the city. Prior to World War II, almost two-thirds of the inhabitants of the region lived in Danbury, but that ratio began to shrink and eventually reverse in the postwar years. To serve the growing suburban population, doctors, lawyers, movie theaters and a range of other businesses moved into retail centers and office complexes often built by Danbury developers in towns like Brook-field, Ridgefield, New Fairfield and Redding. As a consequence, suburban residents no longer had much opportunity or need to interact with Danburians. Their image of Danbury was often limited to reports of racial strife and urban sprawl. The local newspaper responded to this changing dynamic by dropping the reference to the small city in its name, formally designating itself simply as *The News-Times*. During the decades following consolidation in 1965, Danbury itself went through a process of reshaping its role at the core of a rapidly growing, affluent, and increasingly anti-urban region.

It was possible for suburban residents who no longer relied on the nearby city for their economic needs, to view Danbury as a source of problems rather than a place of opportunity. The zoning codes that governed settlement patterns in towns in western Connecticut, written in some cases by transplanted New Yorkers, were designed to favor single-family home building on sizable acreage with individual septic systems, and to discourage rental property, small lots, and large-scale industrial develop-ment that the suburb-dwellers associated in a negative way with cities.

During the three decades from the mid-1950s to the mid-1980s, Danbury's position in the regional galaxy evolved from being the vital center to becoming an object of suburban suspicion and finally to being accepted as a valued partner of neighboring towns.

The struggle to establish regional planning illustrates the defiantly independent stance adopted at first by rapidly suburbanizing rural towns. After the Home Rule Act abolished county government in the state in 1957, the Connecticut Development Commission designated 15 planning regions in an effort to promote inter-town coordination of large projects. In 1958, the Danbury Chamber of Commerce filed a request to set up a 400-square-mile, twelve-town region centered on Danbury and extending as far north as Washington, Connecticut. However, area towns showed little interest and the idea died. The same indifference surfaced in the mid 1960s, when Danbury Mayor J. Thayer Bowman attempted to find partners for a regional incinerator.

In 1966, the newly consolidated City of Danbury along with area towns trying to finance expensive infrastructure projects, were blocked from obtaining federal funds because they were not members of an approved regional planning association, which was defined by state law as one representing 60 percent of a region's population. Danbury and tiny Redding were eager to join such an agency; in other towns, however, the idea met with robust opposition. Bethel, New Fairfield and Newtown rejected the concept. In Brookfield, the weekly newspaper crusaded against it as a threat to local autonomy. State Representative Benjamin Barringer of New Milford convinced five southern Litchfield County towns to join him in boycotting the proposed coalition, declaring that he didn't want New Milford to be "outclassed, outfoxed and outfought" in a regional planning arrangement that had Danbury as a core. Rumors also circulated that regional planning was a ruse meant to benefit New York City developers.

But in 1967, when a state directive went out to Brookfield and Ridgefield as well as to Danbury to stop polluting rivers and to modernize their sewage treatment systems, these towns realized they did not qualify for state and federal funds to help pay for such expensive improvements. Ten area towns, in a sudden turnaround, accepted a compromise proposed by Brookfield to establish a body of local elected officials with permanent staff. This group would meet regularly to discuss joint planning needs. The resulting Housatonic Valley Council of Elected Officials (HVCEO) became the only planning agency in the state with members who were town office holders. Danbury Mayor Gino Arconti, who also hoped to establish a regional health district, backed the planning agreement and attended the agency's first meeting along with Charles Ducibella, who would succeed him in office. The hastily formed organization accomplished its original purpose, permitting previously blocked federal money to flow to member towns for major projects. Even so, some area towns continued to resist joining. As late as 1985, New Fairfield and Sherman were two of only five towns in the state that didn't belong to any planning agency. Presently still in existence, HVCEO provides an essential planning database and a mechanism for cooperative action in the region.

The relationship between Danbury and its neighbors contained elements of rivalry as well as cooperation. Several rapidly growing suburban towns, especially Brookfield and Ridgefield, sought to offset the burden on their taxpayers who had to pay for expanded education, police and fire services by attracting corporations and 'satellite companies' – their suppliers – the types of businesses that had sparked Danbury's transformation. At the same time, they understood that the restrictive zoning that protected the bedroom-suburb environment had to be maintained in order to continue attracting affluent residents. These towns wanted no part of traditional industry, but welcomed office or research-oriented operations tucked in sheltered locations. When, in January 1985, Bethel opened up the Francis X. Clarke Industrial Park on land adjacent to the Danbury line, potential buyers camped out overnight in the freezing cold to purchase 10-acre lots. In the late 1970s, the Ridgefield Economic Development Committee made a concerted effort to boost the tax base by recruiting suitable light industry to the almost exclusively residential town.

Danbury's willingness to share its developed infrastructure helped bordering towns diversify their economies. Brookfield, under orders from the state after 1967 to stop stream pollution, reached an agreement with the city to send sewage to Danbury's treatment plant from new lines to be built along Route 7 in southern Brookfield. This made large-scale commercial development along the sewer line route possible. Ultimately, a continuous commercial strip stretched from I-84 in Danbury well over a mile into Brookfield. In 1983, the town of Bethel shut its own small, in-adequate treatment plant and began sending its sewage to Danbury's larger and more sophisticated facility. And this ability of the city to provide water and sewers was key to bringing Boehringer Ingleheim (and other compa-nies) to the Ridgebury district that overlapped Danbury and Ridgefield.

Efficient public transportation required a regional approach. After years of declining ridership and profitability, the struggling city bus line ceased operation in 1967, leaving western Connecticut without public transpor-tation. Thanks to an emergency grant from the city, the Danbury-Bethel Transit District began to operate buses in those towns in 1973. Under the leadership of longtime Civil Defense director Peter Winter, and with assistance from HVCEO, coverage expanded in 1978 to include New Milford. Renamed HART, for the Housatonic Area Regional Transit district (and rejecting the acronym HATS as too backward-looking), which reflected its wider reach, the organization consolidated dial-a-ride assistance for the disabled and elderly. As more towns were added to its service area in the 1980s, HART's district headquarters remained in Danbury.

The end of county government, which had designated the Danbury Superior Court as a branch of the Bridgeport Court, expanded Danbury's judicial influence. In the 1970s, the General Assembly's reorganization of the Connecticut judicial system into regional districts that roughly paralleled the state's planning regions, made Danbury the center of a district that comprised eight surrounding towns. However, before this promotion could go into effect in 1978 as scheduled, a modern courthouse had to be built. The existing facility, an 1898 classic-but-faded Beaux

Courtesy of Housatonic Valley Council of Elected Officials/Housatonic Area Rapid Transit

Danbury Mayor James E. Dyer and Fifth District U.S. Representative William Ratchford, a Danbury native, at center at the ribbon cutting for new HART buses in 1982. They are flanked by HART Chairman Emanuel Merullo (l) and New Milford First Selectman Clifford Chapin (r).

Arts structure on Main Street overlooking Elmwood Park, was painfully inadequate, with so little usable space that lawyers waiting for trials were forced to lay out their papers on the tops of radiators. The selection of a location for a new courthouse touched off a controversy when the Danbury Bar Association recommended a spot off National Place behind White and Ives streets – a choice that would eliminate 500 spaces in one of the major downtown parking lots. In December 1974, the Connecticut Judiciary Department ended the dispute by picking an acceptable site on White Street, although the building wasn't completed and opened until nine years later, in January 1984.

Besides its official institutional and economic roles, Danbury provided direction in dealing with emergencies that affected the whole region. In February 1974, area towns followed Danbury's lead in dealing with spiraling gas shortages. With long lines of cars at gas stations spilling into the roads and anxious motorists foraging from station to station searching for fuel, the leaders of eight area towns adopted Mayor Charles Ducibella's plan for voluntary gas rationing. First used in Oregon, the arrangement called for car owners to restrict their purchase of gas to alternate week-days based on whether the last number of their license plate was odd or even. Police patrolled gas stations to prevent motorists from obstructing driveways. In large part because the rules were applied to the entire region, Ducibella's plan worked. Within the month, gas lines had disappeared.

Control of the heavy pleasure-boat traffic on Candlewood Lake also demanded cooperation. With its shoreline shared by five towns, the number of boats using the lake in the 1970s reached a dangerous level, particularly on summer weekends. Residents of lakeside communities alone owned more than 3,000 registered powerboats. In 1971, the bordering towns, including Danbury, created the Candlewood Lake Authority that would employ a paid staff to enforce boating regulations on Connecticut's largest body of water. By the mid-1980s, the lake patrol devoted approximately 1,000 hours each year to this task. The Authority, under a full-time director after 1984, also used Western Connecticut State University students to monitor water quality and to update maps and charts.

Regionalism may have been an unfamiliar term at this time, but it was certainly not a novel concept to the hospital and state university, two long-established local institutions. Although physically based in the city, and linked by name, leadership, and support to Danbury, both always saw their mission as service to the entire Western Connecticut district. How-ever, to keep pace with the spectacular growth in the postwar years, even these historically regional organizations had to develop more encompassing links to the wider community. They succeeded: Today Danbury Hospital and Western Connecticut State University are two of the largest employers in the area.

The then tiny hospital had struggled in the decade following the end of World War II. A conflict between the professional staff and the board of managers mainly made up of local businessmen resulted in a brief loss of certification. The facility's only predictable income, usually less than

$20,000 annually – even then a small sum – came from Danbury's Community Chest. Even with special fund drives, most of its income came from charges to patients. In 1963, room rates were above the state average: $28 for a single room and $25 for a double room. Nonetheless, the institution frequently ran a small deficit and had to dip into its endowment.

Despite shaky finances, the hospital struggled to keep pace with the growth in the area. The number of doctors on the staff rose from 32 in 1954, to 77 in 1957. Yet the institution continued to have difficulty financing expansion. A 1956 fund drive chaired by John Douglas, president of Republic Foil, a major local industry, fell short by almost 20 percent of its $1.5 million goal earmarked for new construction. The shortfall exposed a chronic problem even though the hospital did manage to add a sixth floor to its main building, with longtime trustee Marian Anderson offering a song at its opening.

In 1957, the hospital took steps to widen its base of financial support. It reorganized as a non-profit corporation, hired a development director, and added board members who resided in area towns. The facility had become a regional institution. Between 1959 and 1963, hospital usage by residents of the six suburban towns surrounding Danbury increased by 56 percent, amounting to more than one-third of all patients. Future growth required an expanded regional focus in both leadership and financing.

The emergence of Bertram Stroock as a major force illustrates the importance of this shift. A Newburgh, New York, textile manufacturer, Stroock had developed new products that made him wealthy enough to retire comfortably to a Newtown farm to raise sheep at the age of 43. He then put his business acumen and philanthropic generosity at the service of Danbury Hospital. In 1958, at his urging, the hospital inaugurated an annual fundraising effort called the Progress Fund that, by the early 1980s, had raised more than $1 million per year, making long-range planning possible. Stroock's own regular gifts to the fund alone, usually made on his birthday, totaled more than $1 million over those years. Other wealthy area residents followed his example – individuals such as Jack Ward of

Ridgefield, who contributed $150,000 for what became the state's seventh intensive care unit and who, in 1968, funded the hospital's first nuclear medicine unit. When the hospital honored eight major contributors in 1972, six were residents of towns outside Danbury. Even more significant, seven suburban town governments in the same year agreed to make annual grants to the hospital in recognition of their dependence on and appreciation for what had become a major regional medical center.

The level of care provided by the resurgent hospital made an enormous difference in the lives of the residents of the region. In the area of coronary care alone, deaths due to heart disease were halved in a single year, after the hospital's coronary care unit was established in 1968. In the three following years, about 95 percent of patients admitted to the unit were saved. No longer was a heart attack necessarily a death sentence in the Danbury area.

The hospital's rapid growth sometimes necessitated improvised measures such as housing the first radiation therapy unit in a converted coal bin, but staff physicians became known for research as well as practical medicine. In particular, the work of Dr. Nilo Herrera, who developed contacts with the U.S. Atomic Energy Commission and the World Health Organization, led to the hospital's designation of "U.S. Collaborating Center for Nuclear Medicine." By the early 1980s, the hospital, with its award-winning, seven-story tower, was the largest solar-heated building in the state, standing proudly atop its hill as Danbury's tallest building. The small "village hospital" envisioned by its 19th century founders had evolved into one of the region's most important assets. In 1965, even before many of these changes, Danbury hospital could boast on the occasion of its 80th anniversary that "the richest person in the world in the 1800s couldn't obtain the medical care available to everyone today."

Like the hospital, Danbury State Teachers College had its own growing pains. From its establishment in 1903 as a two-year normal school, the school's mission was never exclusively local. It functioned to train teachers for elementary schools in the entire western and southern parts of the state, often in rural areas. In 1937, it became a four-year college and, until the end of World War II, adequately fulfilled its mandate on a tiny campus consisting of just two structures that stood side by side on White Street: Old Main – the original college building – and its companion, Fairfield Hall, a women's dormitory added in 1927 to accommodate a modest number of out-of-town students.

By 1947, age and use had taken its toll on both buildings. State Senator Alice Rowland of Ridgefield told her colleagues on the education committee that year that "no [educational] institution in the State of Connecticut that I have visited … has as bad conditions as I find in Danbury."

The surge of growth in the state in the 1950s and 1960s that forced a response from Danbury government and Danbury Hospital also challenged the college. Enrollment increased, programs proliferated, more faculty members were hired, and the campus expanded. In 1959, a concerned General Assembly approved a bill introduced by Danbury State Senator Norman Buzaid, who was angry that his constituents had to leave home to finish their college educations unless they wanted to be teachers. The bill authorized Danbury and its sister state teachers colleges to offer degree programs in fields other than education, thereby broadening the goal of embracing the multiple aims of a regional institution.

Removal of this barrier propelled the renamed Danbury State College into a new era. Full-time enrollment reached 1,000 in 1965, and soared close to 2,500 by 1970 as the school added faculty in unprecedented numbers, doubled the size of the staff, and tripled the number of courses offered. After 1961, the school offered undergraduate degree programs in six liberal-arts disciplines and began training secondary education majors in the same fields. At the same time, it moved to fill needs that were vital to the area's economy and wellbeing. When Danbury Hospital discontinued its nursing school in 1965, the college quickly inaugurated a four-year, bachelor-of-science degree program in nursing. In 1968, with so many companies flooding into Danbury, a business-administration program was added. The previous year, 1967, had seen another change of name for the school accompany the rapid pace of its growth: The state legislature eliminated the reference to Danbury in its title, allowing the broader label of Western Connecticut State College to reflect the institution's expanding regional ambitions.

The physical limitations of its downtown location, however, imposed obstacles to the school's continued growth. Unstable soil eliminated the feasibility of building high-rise structures. The cost of purchasing additional land limited expansion to a few parcels eastward along White Street, where two dormitories were added in the 1960s. The college did take advantage of the opportunity to obtain the neighboring former Danbury High School building in 1962, when the current high school opened on Clapboard Ridge. Convinced by President Ruth Haas' low-keyed persuasion, the General Assembly agreed to buy the superfluous building to provide valuable classroom space for the crowded college. White Hall opened in 1969, after five years of extensive renovations.

Several times during this period, outside forces threatened to throttle the school's steady advance and it took concerted action by city and regional leaders for the institution to survive. The first potentially lethal obstacle to Western's growth, and even to its existence, came from the independent board of trustees that assumed supervision of the four state colleges in 1965. From the start, a vocal minority of the board, convinced that the Danbury college was in the wrong place, objected to the projected cost of buying more downtown land to stretch the cramped campus. In 1967, a consultant's report recommended that the college be relocated as soon as possible to a more adequate site in lower Fairfield County.

To block this action, President Haas rallied political leaders from both parties. *The News-Times* editor, Steve Collins, launched angry editorials. To checkmate the opposition, Danbury boosters adopted a strategy of proposing the establishment of a second, suburban campus that would be easily accessible and offer plenty of room for expansion. A 232-acre parcel of hilly pastureland originally owned by the Gregory family for more than 250 years fit this description. Located near the intersection of I-84 and north-south Route 7, the property had been purchased in 1954 by former

Mayor John Previdi, who offered it to the state for the bargain price of $1.1 million to keep the college in Danbury. The state bonding commission did its part by quickly approving the sale.

A two-year burst of enthusiasm followed as the energized college community sought to seize the rare opportunity to fashion a coherently planned campus. In a bold move, Connecticut Commissioner of Public Works Charles Sweeney, a Danbury native, hired a prominent architect to draft a master plan for the campus that would give expression to the school's educational philosophy. The proposed design called for construction of 12 buildings in the first stage of a three-phase development, all connected in what resembled a covered shopping mall.

The ambitious plans for a second campus hit a roadblock in 1970, when newly elected Republican Governor Thomas Meskill imposed a freeze on state building projects in response to a growing budget deficit. A discouraged Haas, president of the school since 1944, continued to battle for the original concept, but only managed to persuade the state to build an access road to the vacant location before her retirement in 1975. Her successor Robert Bersi, a politically astute Californian, recognized Connecticut's financial plight and adopted what he termed a "more modest game plan" of lobbying for construction of just two buildings on the Westside property – a classroom structure and a dormitory.

Like Haas before him, Bersi had the benefit of a legislature whose leadership was well stocked with influential Danbury-area representatives. William Ratchford, later a United States Congressman, was Speaker of the House of Representatives from 1968 to 1974, where he and fellow Democrat Charles Sweeney had regular contact with Governor Dempsey. On the Republican side, T. Clark Hull represented Danbury in the state Senate from 1963 until he was elected lieutenant governor in 1970. Francis Collins, a Brookfield resident with a law practice in Danbury and a former Danbury State Teachers College student, was minority leader in the 1971 session and Speaker of the House in the following term. A. Searle Pinney of Brookfield was chair of the Republican State Central Committee from 1961 to 1967.

Even Bersi's scaled-down expansion package faced determined opposition in the General Assembly from legislators Irving Stolberg and Laurence DeNardis, both affiliated with New Haven colleges, who sought to block funding for the new campus. Governor Ella Grasso, elected in 1976, responded to intense lobbying by Western students stressed over the high cost of living in Danbury by promising to build a dormitory on the Mill Plain Road property.* In October 1978, Grasso went even further by directing the State Bond Commission, over the objections of Stolberg and DeNardis, to release money to erect a classroom building. Construction began in 1979 and the first building, home of the newly endowed Ancell School of Business, finally opened in 1982. Now accurately designated as Western Connecticut State University, the Danbury school with its two complementary locations, one urban and one suburban, could meet the expanding needs of a diverse region.

By the 1980s, Danbury had reasserted itself as the major employment, retail, transportation and institutional hub of northern Fairfield and southern Litchfield counties. Partially suburban itself, the city had avoided permanent antagonism with surrounding towns. Its relationship with its neighbors was now one of first among equals. Borrowing baseball star Reggie Jackson's colorful quote, Mayor Gene Eriquez boasted that Danbury had become once again, "the straw that stirs the drink."♦

---

* Construction began on the promised dormitory shortly before Governor Grasso's death from cancer in February 1981. The 230-bed structure, the second building on the Westside campus, was named in her honor.

From the early 1970s on the C. D. Parks property, the largest undeveloped parcel in the city with hundreds of acres of prime meadow and woodland and an elegant Shingle-style mansion (pictured here) became an increasingly more enticing target for private acquisition and development. However, in 1985 a citizens movement resisted this pressure and convinced the city to purchase the land, which is now a magnificent public park.

Dealing with Development

At the dedication of Danbury's upgraded West Lake water filtration plant in 1984, Danbury Common Council President Constance McManus issued a subtle warning when she asserted that "A community's character determines whether growth presents large problems or opportunity. Thus far, Danbury has seen only opportunity." Buoyed by its economic renaissance, its population growing between 1,000 and 2,000 people a year, city leaders had long ago thrown off their paralyzing belief that Danbury was a doomed backwater and embraced a commitment to unlimited progress. In practice, this meant welcoming the benefits of rapid development while tolerating such costs as compromised air and water quality, traffic congestion, lack of open space, urban sprawl, and the gradual degradation of Candlewood Lake.

At the time McManus spoke Danbury was at a crossroads. The optimistic faith in continuing progress had already been challenged on a number of fronts: Physical limits to further growth began to appear as well as new environmental concerns. Moreover, beginning in the late 1960s, public resistance to this bargain emerged. In particular, the city's new white-collar residents and its younger, largely college-educated generation put a higher priority on providing a combination of recreational opportunities and cultural amenities that would improve the quality of life in Danbury. Although far short of a backlash, this gradual shift in attitudes insured that future development would no longer take place in a regulatory vacuum and would provoke clashes with those who clung to the old model of urban development. In the end, enlightened city leadership and the actions of organized citizens along with a public perception that unshackled growth had run its course combined to produce a more balanced stance toward development and conservation.

In 1966, the worst recorded drought in the city's history afflicted Danbury. Five consecutive years of below-average rainfall created a cumulative rain deficit equal to one full year's normal precipitation – as if no rain or snow had fallen on Danbury for an entire year. 1965 was the driest year in a century with precipitation 17 inches below normal. The handful of farmers remaining in Danbury felt the emergency first as their usually reliable wells dried up. In July 1965, Mayor J. Thayer Bowman began a series of escalating steps to deal with the crisis in the newly consolidated city, ordering restrictions on water use, applying for federal funds to connect an auxiliary water supply, and tapping Tarrywile Lake for a half-million gallons a day. By July 1966, city reservoirs had shrunk to 17 percent of capacity, at best a two-week supply, while much of the water from the bottom of Margerie Reservoir, the city's largest, proved undrinkable because it was laden with anti-algae chemicals. Bowman declared a water emergency, tightened water use regulations, and appealed to the state for help. Governor John Dempsey responded by ordering over 17,000 feet of pipe along with six noisy but powerful Civil Defense Department pumps, a chlorinator and other equipment trucked in over a trail hastily blazed by public-works employees to pump water from Candlewood Lake into Margerie Reservoir, a mile away. But the five million gallons a day from the lake only replaced the amount the city used in an average day.

Heavy rains during the autumn of 1966 finally brought temporary relief, but nature could not repair the city's shattered faith in its reservoir system. Created primarily to quench the thirst of the hat industry and therefore one of the most extensive in the state, the reservoir system had always been an object of civic pride best expressed by early city water commissioners who boasted in 1910, decades before Margerie Reservoir was built, that Danbury had "enough water to supply a city of 75,000." As the population approached this figure, it was clear that civic leaders no longer shared this confidence.

A 1967 water study urged developing auxiliary sources of drinking water, citing the possibility of digging wells on city property near Lake Kenosia as well as at other spots around the city. The 1967 Plan of Development advocated the exploration of aquifers – natural underground water-bearing strata. Candlewood Lake seemed to provide an obvious emergency supply of drinking water, but this option was soon ruled out by the discovery in the early 1970s that the Housatonic River that fills Candlewood, was contaminated with PCBs, cancer-causing chemicals. These had been dumped into the river for decades by the General Electric Company's Pittsfield, Massachusetts, manufacturing plant. During a water shortage in 1981, Lake Kenosia fed water to the booming westside. When successive dry years dropped the reservoirs below half capacity, the Dyer administration purchased a $2 million apparatus to transfer water from Kenosia to the West Lake Reservoir except during the summer swimming season at the public beach. Despite these efforts, when asked in 1985 what the city's number one problem would be in the future, former Mayor Gino Arconti answered emphatically, "Water."

As Danburians struggled to fully understand the rapid growth going on around them in 1961, McKim Norton, a vice president of the Regional Planning Association, provided guidance when he identified the pattern of urban growth that was taking shape in the region surrounding New York City. What is today familiarly known as "suburban sprawl" was making its appearance, devouring large amounts of open land and changing the character of the community. Calling this a "spread-city" arrangement, Norton stressed that small cities like Danbury were not satellites of the region's central cities and were "neither suburb nor city in the usual sense … [they were] built up solidly, though not densely." They represented, he insisted, "a new form of urban settlement with jobs, shopping and houses spread across the land … sparsely populated in spots and with very few patches of open space." Norton aptly described what had happened to Danbury in the 1950s and 1960s when farms and other open spaces began filling up almost randomly with residential developments and commercial strips. At the same time, the city's traditional downtown population and retail center was beginning to fade in importance. Most of this change took place in a virtual regulatory vacuum. A plan of development was only drawn up when the city was forced to do so as part of its redevelopment efforts, as detailed here in Chapter 12. After the repeal of zoning in 1937, it wasn't revived until 1960, when the town government adopted regulations that sought to balance continued residential and industrial growth. Zoning decisions in the city portion of Danbury, and after consolidation, fell to a committee of the Common Council. In 1977, a major revision of the city charter authorized the Zoning Commission along with the current "strong major" form of government.

A few years after Norton presented his analysis, Mayor Gino Arconti's administration began to address these developments, particularly Danbury's lack of public open space. At the time such protected land was limited to Rogers Park, Wooster Mountain State Park, and the WPA-built Town Park on Candlewood Lake and amounted to fewer than 700 acres. The first city Conservation Commission, established by a 1964 referendum, found it difficult to overcome the conviction that the still largely rural nature of the Town of Danbury made it unnecessary to spend public funds to protect still abundant farmland. Despite this resistance, the 1967 Plan of Development pledged that "an increase in urban living must not destroy the beauty of the outlying areas" and, to avoid this result, recommended quintupling the city's open space.

The mayor quickly took advantage of this opportunity to establish a series of "land banks," which he considered "the greatest gift we can give to future generations." In 1967, the first year of his administration, Arconti convinced the city to purchase from the federal government 63 acres that were adjacent to the Federal Correctional Institution on Pembroke Road. This aquisition included a barn and small cottage and was the first step in creating Danbury's Bear Mountain Reservation. Four years later, the city accepted 33 additional acres of surplus land from prison authorities and bought 42 more from private owners to assemble a 140-acre unit. In 1971, the city also acquired the 58-acre Drska property adjacent to the King Street Intermediate School.

Arconti's greatest success as a land banker came in 1970, when he and Martens Goos, the first head of the Conservation Commission, assisted by realtor Robert Goodfellow, persuaded Irene Myers Richter, a widowed summer resident and daughter of a prominent philanthropist, to donate her 80-acre West Lake Farm estate to the city for recreational use. Richter agreed to the formation of an autonomous authority to manage the facility, which would be named after her late husband, and endorsed Goos' idea of a golf course as the park's main feature. The first nine holes of the Richter golf course opened on Labor Day in 1971. By the 1980s experts rated the facility as one of the best public courses in the country. The spacious house on the property became an arts center first put to use during the early '70s for outdoor summer Shakespeare productions directed by Wendell Mac-Neal. Tennis and basketball courts as well as hiking and cross-country ski trails were added over the years. Before leaving office, Arconti hoped to block private development of the only large piece of residential property remaining in the central city when he proposed to purchase the 500-acre C.D. Parks estate from its willing owners. However, a low turnout of voters rejected the plan in a 1973 referendum.

The initiative of private citizens also increased access to natural areas. Virginia Welch, whose husband William was an aeronautical engineer and pilot employed by Doman Helicopter at the Danbury airport, worked tirelessly to convert the old municipal dump in the granite and pegmatite quarries off Mountainille Road into the city's first nature center. With

Virginia as the volunteer director, the Old Quarry Nature Center welcomed community assistance: Abbott Tech students erected a small structure with donated materials; Rotary Club members painted the building; young adult volunteers blazed trails and cleared debris. Once the center opened, Virginia acted as instructor and guide and helped to set up the Outdoor Laboratory at King Street School. Until they moved out of Connecticut in the 1980s, the couple provided invaluable aerial photographs that documented the rapid expansion of the area.

Shortly after the drought of the early 1960s temporarily depleted Danbury's water supply, state government raised questions about the quality of the city's drinking water. With recommendations of a 50-member task force appointed by Governor John Dempsey, and including the Barden Corporation's J. Robert Tomlinson and Republic Foil's John Douglas, both leaders of key Danbury postwar industries, the General Assembly passed a Clean Water Act in 1967. Wasting no time, the Connecticut Water Resources Commission ordered Danbury and the neighboring towns of Newtown, Brookfield and Ridgefield to "launch immediate long range plans to construct new or expanded sewage treat-ment facilities to abate water pollution." The toxic Still River, subject of repeated lawsuits against the city, would be made suitable for fishing and boating. It was also to ultimately become an approved source of water supply. The commission directed 18 Danbury firms, including long-established hatting and fur factories and new industries alike – ironically Republic Foil among them – to modernize their waste-treatment procedures. Unfortunately, agency deadlines for cooperation were often vague and distant so that change came slowly. However, the pollution order closed Samuel Young's hatters-fur operation, forcing him to turn to a less dangerous venture, the manufacture of synthetic stuffing material, which he established in the former Mallory front shop on Rose Street. The new enterprise proved wildly successful, and the Young family became some of the area's leading philanthropists.

Encouraged by government activity, private citizens also began to address water quality. In 1969, a group of recreational divers, finding themselves afflicted with mysterious rashes after using Candlewood Lake, organized the Clean Streams Committee to locate chemical sources of water pollution in the city. Led by Joseph McCarthy of Bethel, an engineer at Perkin-Elmer, they confronted city officials with evidence of leaking chemicals. The group then organized a cleanup of the Still River and assisted the state Department of Environmental Protection by photographing the bottom of Candlewood Lake. Although the first Earth Day celebration in Danbury in 1970 was symbolic, featuring a simulated funeral march from Rogers Park to Western's Midtown campus to bury a car engine, it called attention to the importance of citizen involvement. Another private environmental organization, Connecticut Earth Action, formed a chapter in Danbury in 1971, and two years later established a recycling center at the town landfill.

In 1972, during the waning days of the Arconti administration, the Connecticut legislature enacted a Wetlands Protection Act that required all municipalities in the state to safeguard their wetlands. Once derided as useless marshes and swamps or considered to be land suitable for building, these wetlands were now legally recognized as vital for wildlife habitat, aquifer recharge and, especially, defense against flooding. Arconti proposed naming the Conservation Commission as enforcer of this law in Danbury; but as often happened in the pre-1977 form of government, found himself blocked by a Common Council committee that feared "giving the environmentalists the nod," as *The News-Times* put it. Instead, Arconti designated an advisory committee he had set up two years earlier to monitor environmental issues as the city's Environmental Impact Commission in charge of enforcing wetlands regulations. The professional group was comprised of city employees such as City Engineer Jack Schweitzer and representatives of the health, flood, erosion and conservation boards, as well as knowledgeable private citizens such as Dr. Donald Groff, a soil scientist on the faculty of Western Connecticut State College.

Of necessity, the mayor created a unique organizational structure that some in business-friendly Danbury criticized as a threat to unhampered growth. At two boisterous Common Council hearings on the proposed regulations in late 1973 and early 1974, attorneys representing developers denounced the wetlands ordinance as "an unfair burden" that was identical to "stealing land." Even after the law passed, Judge Louis DeFabritis, a developer as well as a jurist, brought an unsuccessful lawsuit against the city for allegedly violating state law in drafting the ordinance. Despite a growing reputation for competence and fairness, the Environmental Impact Commission had to constantly defend its rulings from attacks by builders who were particularly suspicious of the objectivity of Groff, even though both Republican and Democratic mayors reappointed the outspoken professor.

Development issues roiled city politics. For decades, the brunt of residential growth in Danbury had taken place on the outskirts of the city and in rural areas. Before consolidation, this area had been served by the town government. During the 1970s, unexpected consequences of the consolidation process brought Danbury close to a split between city dwellers and suburban constituents. In order to satisfy those residents who did not use city sewers and water, the Consolidation Commission created a three-tier tax system that levied the highest rates on city residents who benefited from all municipal services. Councilman Joseph Pepin and several of his urban neighbors challenged this preferential approach in Superior Court. After several lower court defeats and two citywide referenda on the issue, the Connecticut Supreme Court ruled in May 1976 that Danbury had indeed infringed on the state's exclusive power to tax. This decision provoked a rebellion among suburban residents, who formed an organization called the Equitable Tax Association (ETA) to protest what they now felt was discriminatory treatment. Taxpayer "associations" and "leagues" that advocated limited government had been active in city politics since the 1930s and, during the 1950s and 1960s, had supported Sarah Rothkopf's multiple mayoral campaigns. But the ETA enjoyed a broader base of support. A product of the suburban expansion of the postwar era, the group also had a credible spokesman in Pat Cicala whose earnest rhetoric sometimes implied that those citizens living outside the city were like pioneers in the wilderness. The rebels unsettled local politics by lending crucial support to Republican candidate Donald Boughton, whose victory in the 1977 mayoral race ended a 10-year Democratic hold on the post. However, when the former Perkin-Elmer draftsman balked at slashing the city budget, the ETA withdrew its backing and ran Cicala as their candidate for mayor in 1979. The split helped boost Democrat James Dyer into office by a narrow margin.

Growing public skepticism about the unalloyed benefits of economic growth greeted the new mayor. The familiar problem of congestion reappeared in a new form as automobile traffic on the Danbury portion of the I-84 corridor, where most large employers were now located, tripled in only a decade to a flood of 11,000 cars each day. Beginning with the bitter reaction to the airport expansion scheme in 1969, neighbors, adopting a confrontational approach, challenged large-scale projects at public hearings. The condominium-building boom provoked especially loud opposition. When a developer proposed construction of more than 1,000 housing units on 139 acres in northern Danbury, nearby residents organized as Concerned Nabby [Road] Neighbors and pressured the city Zoning Commission to twice reject efforts to relax zoning. Sterling Woods, half the density of the original plan, was not built until 1983.

The youngest mayor in the city's history, Dyer would win three more terms in office, building an effective Democratic machine in the process. A former state legislator and the first student appointed to the Board of Trustees of State Colleges by Governor Ella Grasso, Dyer was well-traveled, well-educated, and well-connected at the state level, in contrast to many of his provincial predecessors. He also benefited from a 1977 charter revision that shifted power from Common Council committees and expanded the authority of the chief executive. Given this opportunity for leadership, Dyer used his new tools aggressively to control and direct growth in Danbury.*

Although Dyer considered his easing of racial tensions – particularly at the high school – as his most significant accomplishment as mayor, his land-

---

* Dyer's youth and progressive record as mayor earned him frequent mention as an attractive candidate for higher statewide office. However, in 1987 he was accused by federal prosecutors of receiving illegal payments from developers of several large projects that included downtown redevelopment and the Danbury Fair Mall. In a pair of trials in 1990 Dyer was acquitted of all charges, but his career in politics came to an end.

Courtesy of Western Connecticut State University Archives

James Dyer, the city's youngest mayor, takes the oath of office in 1979 for the first of four terms. Democratic Party stalwarts including former mayor Gino Arconti (next to Dyer) and future five-term mayor Gene Eriquez (right edge of photo) share in the jubilation.

use decisions left a more permanent mark on the community. With the exception of his defense of the Fairgrounds Mall as an inevitable consequence of the city's corporate transformation and his support for Waterbury developer John Errichetti's flawed scheme for the last redevelopment parcel, Dyer encouraged policies that restricted sprawl and promoted sensitive revitalization of the downtown. He bolstered the planning process by hiring three competent professionals and made the city's environmental-health officer a permanent position. In 1983, the Planning Commission, at the behest of chief planner Len Sedney and with the support of the mayor, imposed a yearlong moratorium on new Mill Plain Road development in order to cool what they considered chaotic growth. The following year, Sedney extended the restriction to Route 37.

Dyer and his youthful planners also imposed limits on the pace of condominium construction. High home prices and soaring interest rates that pushed people out of the suburban residential market made condominiums in Danbury an attractive alternative. In the late 1970s and early 1980s, condos were squeezed into tiny city lots, dangled off steep hillsides in Mill Plain, or replaced historic homes such as the E.S. Davis estate on Farview Avenue that overlooked downtown. Some complexes, such as George Davon's Lake Place on Lake Kenosia, won wide acclaim; others were shoddily built or on difficult terraine and began revealing problems only a few years after construction. To provide an opportunity to tighten city regulations, the Dyer administration imposed a one-year moratorium on condominium construction in 1983.

Dyer's willingness to enforce even temporary restrictions on development reflected a radical shift in outlook, as expressed most clearly in his October1986 speech to the Kiwanis Club. In the course of the presentation, he unveiled a planning effort that he labeled "Danbury 2000." The concerned mayor called for a slowdown in the city's explosive growth, a recommendation that would have been unthinkable twenty years earlier. "There's a growing attitude on the part of the community that enough is enough," he cautioned. "We've reached the extremes of our tolerance level as we go about building the city. I'm not saying no to growth. [But] we need some breathing room; we need to take a break and decide what we want to do."

The fate of proposals for high-rise buildings demonstrated this shift in attitude. The optimism of the late '60s had produced a tall modern office building, Stevanton Plaza, on southern Main Street that had sat empty for most of the following decade. High rise office towers were included in proposals for several of the downtown redevelopment projects of the time. In 1977, as Union Carbide prepared to begin construction of its new headquarters after several other large companies had already settled on Ridgebury Road, the Hilton Corporation applied for a permit to erect a hotel on the corner of Old Ridgebury Road and the I-84 entrance ramp. The building's proposed height of nine stories – taller than any in Danbury other than the hospital tower – troubled both the city Planning Commission and the owners of nearby Jensen Trailer Park, who contended that construction would impact the Still River nearby. Nevertheless, the hotel obtained a zoning variance and, with Mayor Dyer cutting the ribbon, opened in June 1981, providing an attractive venue for corporate events. Subsequently, planners treated applications for high-rise office and residential projects in the downtown area more harshly. By 1983, the Planning Commission was ready to reject a proposal for an 11-story office tower on southern Main Street, and specifications for redevelopment projects were scaled down to reflect the existing center-city streetscape.

No unresolved issue generated more passion among Danburians than the future of their city's downtown, which had long been the traditional economic and cultural heart of the community. Despite the failure of past redevelopment initiatives and the anticipated competition from the Fairgrounds mall, a handful of established merchants clung to the hope that customers could still be drawn to a more attractive and contemporary Main Street environment. Beginning in the early 1970s, building owners began to remodel their storefronts, often covering the exuberant Victorian-era details of the three-story brick buildings that dominated the downtown streetscapes with a variety of shiny metallic finishes, concrete aggregate panels, marble tiles or even Colonial-style details. John Addessi, businessman and member of the Redevelopment Commission, went further than most and, at considerable expense, modernized the facades of three adjoining buildings on the east side of Main Street, including his jewelry store, which resembled, on a small scale, the Tiffany store in New York City. Other older buildings were totally sacrificed with little or no knowledge of their historical meaning in an attempt to update the fading downtown. During the decade of the 1970s, Danbury lost the home of Revolutionary War leader Joseph Platt Cooke to a new banking enterprise and a hotel built by circus entrepreneur Aaron Turner – both historically significant Main Street buildings – to the wreckers' ball. *The News-Times* served as a cheerleader for the effort, hailing each facade alteration as evidence of the downtown area's resilience.

Another point of view, which had strong national support, surfaced in Danbury in 1976, when members of the Scott-Fanton Museum Board thwarted a plan to sell the decommissioned Fairfield County Jail at 80 Main Street to a car dealer who planned to level it for more vehicle display

Courtesy of Stephen Flanagan

Danbury's first historic preservation success was the former Fairfield County Jail on south Main Street. The classic 19th century Second Empire-style structure is pictured after restoration by the city in the early 1980s, followed by many years of service as a senior-citizen center.

and parking. Three years later a coalition of students, faculty and alumni of Western Connecticut State College launched the Danbury Preservation Trust, that quickly attracted people from diverse backgrounds, including politicians from both major parties, who believed that buildings that told the story of Danbury's unique past were the firm anchors of downtown reinvigoration. Adopting a strategy of simultaneously educating and advocating, the Trust sponsored speakers from cities that found fresh energy by building on their past. The Connecticut Humanities Council gave the organization a grant to produce a 16-page supplement to *The News-Times*, with the provocative title, "The Future of the Past." Steve Collins, who wrote most of the newspaper's editorials, in a turnabout became one of the Trust's strongest backers. Another ally was Mayor Dyer, who hosted a daylong conference on preservation at the Palace Theater. The Connecticut Historical Commission funded architectural surveys of major parts of the city, research that the Trust used to convince citizens in 1983 that a Main Street historic district should be included on the National Register of Historic Places. Thanks to a Trust connection, a

Washington-based foundation, Partners for Livable Places, selected Danbury as the smallest city in the nation to participate in a program that explored ways to use cultural resources as instruments of urban renewal. This foundation provided financial support for a study of how the Palace Theater could be transformed into a performing-arts center that would lure people back to the city center.

Dyer and his team embraced historic preservation as a tool to bolster downtown. By making Maple and Balmforth avenues one-way arteries, they improved access to I-84 without destroying an intact, historic neighborhood. Conversion of a 19th century fire-department headquarters into a restaurant provided a focal point for a lively entertainment district centered on Ives Street. Anticipating the replacement of the Main Street Post Office, the city turned little Post Office Place into an attractive open plaza and walkway funneling people to the new district and to a green newly constructed on what had been a large parking lot. Two restored, classic, city-owned Main Street buildings pumped new life into the city's center. The Second Empire-style (1855-1885 period) former jail, saved from demolition, functioned as a senior center while the old library, a Victorian Gothic masterpiece, housed meeting and performance space for cultural organizations. The Plan of Development, adopted in 1988, embraced the principles espoused by the preservation movement.

The forecast in the 1977 Plan of Development that predicted Danbury's population would soon reach a saturation level of 80,000 presented another urgent challenge to the Dyer administration in terms of recreational opportunities and the paltry amount of protected open space in the city. Although the Swampfield Land Trust, a private group, had begun acquiring land in the Long Ridge area in 1971, the city had failed to increase the amount of public open space since the Arconti years. To make matters worse, Danbury spent less on recreation than any Connecticut city of similar size.

Adding two important pieces of property in 1980 eased the situation. The city spent $1.1 million in 1980 to purchase from the Slovak Sokol organization some 32 prime acres adjacent to Lake Candlewood along with a restaurant, a duck pin bowling alley and skating pond on the site. The city renamed the valuable acquisition Hatters Park. After years of neglect, the Planning Department and a committee led by Councilwoman Carole Torcaso coordinated a volunteer effort that turned Bear Mountain Reservation into a legitimate park with 25 miles of hiking trails. It opened to the public in 1982.

The future of the C.D. Parks property – known locally as Tarrywile Farm, the name of the dairy that once operated there – reached a crisis point in the mid-1980s. Located close to downtown, it remained the largest single undeveloped parcel in the city and included 40 acres of meadows and pastures, a large pond, hundreds of acres of woodland, and two mansions – one a Shingle-style 1896 gem and the other a Norman stone castle structure with sweeping views of the region. Recognizing its potential, both the city government and private developers had made numerous efforts to purchase this attractive prize, including the Mobil Oil Company, which once considered the estate as a site for a corporate headquarters. In 1970, a Norwalk developer proposed building a "city within a city" on the property that would have included close to 3,000 residential units, 800 of them single-family homes, in a complex that would have left one-third to one-half the property in open space. This outsized proposal prompted the conservation-minded Mayor Arconti to hastily stage an unsuccessful referendum in 1973 that offered to buy the crucial land for $2 million. Later in the decade, Mayor Charles Ducibella rejected a $3.2 million figure set by the Parks heirs to transfer ownership to the city.

The city's reluctance only increased the eagerness of private investors to develop the property. In 1979, Otto Paparazzo, developer of Heritage Village in Southbury, sought to build 1,000 dwellings on a 300-acre segment of the coveted land, but was blocked by the Planning Commission's refusal to permit such tightly packed housing. Finally, in 1980, the aggressive BRT Development Corporation exercised a purchase option, intending to erect 6,000 condominiums – which would, the company argued, solve Danbury's chronic housing shortage. Again city authorities balked, citing heavy demand on sewer and water facilities and increased traffic that could overwhelm local roads.

The escalating scale of these projects provoked citizens to action when, in 1983, the Parks and Jennings families again offered the property to the city, this time with a $4.5 million price tag. Residents of city neighborhoods near the land in question formed the Parks Property Purchase Committee to make sure the sale would not be turned down. Led by neighbors David Coelho and Jane Keane, the 200-member band of aroused activists waged an educational campaign by publishing articles in the press, making statements at public hearings, and conducting a walking tour of the private and somewhat mysterious space. In addition, a natural partner, the Danbury Preservation Trust, enthusiastically backed the purchase. Ironically, Mayor Dyer, eager to keep taxes stable, at first resisted the deal, proposing instead to spend money on improving existing parks. Public pressure, especially the endorsement by the still-revered Gino Arconti, who broke a decade-long silence about public issues, forced Dyer to drop his opposition. In a referendum held on May 1, 1985, the grassroots effort scored a resounding victory when Danburians voted by a more than two-to-one margin to take ownership of the coveted Parks property.

Danbury's focus changed during the 1970s and 1980s. The community continued to embrace economic progress but not at the expense of its quality of life. The acceptance of historic preservation, the support of the Parks property purchase, and the Ives Center initiative signaled that economic development was no longer an exclusive goal. With a few exceptions, high-rise and high-density development proposals had been resisted and rejected. Residents deliberately chose a more human dimension for the city that rested on a foundation established a century or more before by its hat factories, hatters' neighborhoods and dairy farms. In 1986, Common Council President Constance McManus summarized this more-nuanced attitude when she said, "It's nice to see the tax base get larger, but when it affects the quality of life [such growth] is not worth it." ♦

Courtesy of the Danbury Museum and Historical Society Authority

The former Frank H. Lee Co. hat factory on Leemac Avenue burned on the night of September 9, 1968. This fire was the most spectacular of the blazes that destroyed the wooden reminders of Danbury's industrial past.

Chapter Seventeen Spotlight

Coping with Disasters

Fires, earthquakes (at least eight since 1890, all of them minor tremors), floods, crime and epidemics have visited every era of Danbury's history. But between 1965 and 1985, the city seemed to endure an unusually wide array of disasters that challenged its first responders.

The demise of the city's hat industry left behind a tinderbox "forest" of empty or near-empty wooden buildings that vanished one-by-one in spectacular blazes. None was more damaging than the fire that destroyed the city's largest hat factory complex. On the night of September 9, 1968, the call came in to Danbury Fire Department Headquarters on Ives Street: The old Frank H. Lee plant was on fire. Used as a warehouse, its 200,000 square feet of floor space sprawled between a hodge-podge of buildings filled with highly flammable materials that included 15,000 table-tennis and pool tables as well as rubber mats and boxcars full of foam mattresses. Firefighters who responded from all the city's paid and volunteer companies found the south end of the complex completely enveloped in flames, the fire having ripped through the open spaces of the plant in a matter of minutes. It was burning so hot that hydrants on Leemac Avenue couldn't be used. Plastic caps that covered the flashing lights on fire and emergency vehicles melted. In the blistering heat, firefighters had to abandon hoses and nozzles and began dropping from heat exhaustion, requiring a second wave of responders. Explosions could be heard from time to time as the fire sucked oxygen from the air. At one point, the fire hit an underground fuel-storage tank, sending flames roaring 200 feet into the air, dwarfing the 165-foot Lee smoke stack. "It felt like a hurricane came through for a few minutes," Gino Arconti, the mayor at the time, remembered in a 1993 interview.

"Leemac Avenue was a tunnel of flame," eyewitness Peter Mariano recalled. He was one of a thousand spectators who showed up to watch, wearing everything from pajamas to fur coats.

Concern spread that the huge smokestack would topple as radiant heat began to ignite buildings on the west side of Leemac Avenue and blew out all the windows of the nearby Bard-Parker plant. Firefighters employed by the surgical-suture firm scrambled onto the plant's roof to guide other firefighters to places where chemicals like magnesium were stored, which could explode if hit with water while burning. A fire block would have to be created by wetting down the nearby Leahy Company's oil tanks and boxcars filled with flammable rubber mats.

The blaze was visible for miles; even planes airborne in New York State reported it. Even though there was no wind, sparks landed as far away as Candlewood Lake. Soot flew all over the city; burning embers landed a mile away near St. Peter's Church on Main Street. An early morning drizzle helped the firefighters slow the blaze down, but it smoldered for days. Of the 21 buildings on the site, only the brick fur vault survived. It had been the most destructive fire in the city's history up to that point, as well as the most spectacular.

Thankfully, no one died in that disaster. A far more lethal event occurred on July 7, 1977, when a fire started in the washroom of the prison dorm of the Federal Correctional Institution. Killing five inmates and injuring 85, it was the worst fire in the history of the federal prison system. Panels used in the building were later found to be faulty, causing the federal government to agree to pay $329,000 to victims and their families while not admitting negligence or fire-safety violations.

A later fire would also prove tragic. On February 23, 1982, a young worker at the Awad Manufacturing Company, one of the city's last fur-processing plants, left a burning cigarette in an ashtray that ultimately ignited chemically treated fur fragments, producing an inferno. Engine Co. 23, stationed in Germantown, raced to the scene. Believing an employee was still inside, five firefighters charged into the burning building behind Lt. Martin "Butch" Melody and Joseph Halas, friends who had been fishing together earlier that day. The second floor, weakened by years of acid dripping onto the wood and rendering it unable to support the now-soaked bales of fur, collapsed with no warning. Melody and Halas were trapped beneath an avalanche of burning debris. Surviving firefighters were finally able to pull them out, but it was too late. The pair became the first Danbury firefighters to die in the line of duty. Melody, the colorful president of the firefighters' union local, and Halas were buried after moving funerals as Mayor Dyer, who had occasionally clashed with Melody, shut down city government for the day and proclaimed a 30-day period of mourning.

The fire department wasn't alone in having to respond to unique challenges. The Danbury Police Department experienced what came to be called "Black Friday," on February 13, 1970. Within a span of 20 minutes, bombs exploded at the police station, the Union Savings Bank and a shopping plaza parking lot. Each was located on Main Street and under the resulting cover of smoke, noise and confusion, two men robbed the bank and vanished with more than $26,000.

Police had barely begun to set up emergency headquarters at the War Memorial in Rogers Park when federal agents, state police and the national media descended on the city. With anti-Vietnam War activism and radical fervor simmering nationwide, initial speculation held that the bombs had been planted by some underground group. The FBI, fearing the coordinated attack had been an act of domestic terrorism, had as many as 40 to 50 agents on the case.

The perpetrators, two brothers, had concocted an audacious plan. John Pardue planted a bomb in a trashcan outside the front desk of the Danbury police station some time after 10:20 a.m. It went off 20 minutes later, crippling the alarm system tied into local banks and other businesses. When the two armed men burst into the Union Savings Bank at 226 Main Street two minutes later and ordered everyone to the floor, a bank official tried to call the police but there was no response. As the robbers left with cash and traveler's checks, they detonated another bomb in the bank lobby. They fled in a white Chrysler station wagon, abandoning it in the parking lot of the Danbury Downtown Mall on Main Street. At 11 a.m., a third blast reduced the getaway car to bits of smoking metal after the robbers took off in another vehicle.

Almost miraculously, no one died as a result of the three explosions. More than two dozen people were injured but the thick walls and huge windows of the bank building neutralized the full force of the blast. The bank reopened a few days later. The police station, however, housed in the former Danbury High School originally built in 1902 as the Main Street School, was so badly damaged it had to be razed.

State and local police, searching door-to-door along the suspected escape route, received a crucial tip from a Danbury resident, Virgilio Prebenna of Crane Street, who told them about a neighbor with two police dogs "trained to kill" and an arsenal of guns. The suspicious man, who had no apparent source of income yet owned several cars and paid a hefty rent, turned out to be John Pardue. On March 7, 1970, three weeks after the crime, police apprehended the 27-year-old as he left his Crane Street house. His wallet contained bills with serial numbers that linked them to the Union Savings Bank. Several hours later, officers in Maryland picked up James Pardue, John's 23-year-old brother and accomplice. While the crime stunned Danbury, it turned out to be only part of an almost nationwide spree by the Pardue brothers that included five bank robberies and five murders (two of these the killing of their parents.) The confusion surrounding the Danbury segment of the Pardues' bizarre criminal activity led the city to develop an emergency plan to coordinate its response to large-scale violence and disasters.

In addition to the more spectacular events of fire, flood, and crime, some in Danbury saw a quiet "disaster" festering in the lives of the chronically poor, many immigrant refugees, and others who were priced out of the booming local housing market. Dr. Ann Hines established the Hanahoe Pediatric Clinic in 1974 to provide free care for the children of the city's poor. Her efforts were honored by her receipt of the Jefferson Award, a national public-service award in 1979, and with her inclusion as one of "50 American Heroines" celebrated by the *Ladies' Home Journal* in July 1984. The clinic Hines founded continued in operation until 2008.

Hunger also affected Danbury. In the midst of a national recession in 1981, a group of volunteers founded the city's first permanent soup kitchen on Spring Street. In 1982, with homelessness a growing problem in the Danbury area as well as the nation, Dr. Paul Hines (husband of Ann Hines), a chemistry professor at Western, read in *The News-Times* about homeless people rousted out of heated train cars in the rail yard where they had been sleeping after a fire destroyed their makeshift shelters. Dr. Hines teamed up with Leo McIlrath, director of the Danbury Senior Center and one of the founders of the soup kitchen, and John Simonelli, owner of a kennel in Bethel, who possessed accomplished carpentry skills, and the three established an emergency homeless shelter. The Dorothy Day Hospitality House was named after the Catholic activist who founded the first communal House of Hospitality on New York's Bowery during the Depression. Day believed in treating the homeless as equals; the Danbury shelter continues this tradition, referring to those who come in as "guests." Simonelli supervised the work of converting an empty warehouse, garage and storefront adjacent to the soup kitchen on Spring Street into the only emergency shelter in western Connecticut. Four hundred volunteers provided help to the shelter and soup kitchen, which received donations from local restaurants. By 1985, homelessness in the mostly prospering city had grown to the point that the Dorothy Day House had to turn people away during cold weather, as did St. James Episcopal Church, which had also begun to provide temporary shelter. In 1986, the Salvation Army responded to the growing needs in this area by establishing its Good Neighbor House.◆

Courtesy of Mary and Hal Burke

Beginning in 1980, and continuing for 20 years, a volunteer group, the Greater Danbury Cultural Association, sponsored a summer weekend Ethnic and Cultural Festival at Rogers Park. National food, crafts and dances attracted large crowds. Here, a Colombian group performs a folk dance at one of the later festivals.

Changing
Demographics

In 1978, Mayor Donald Boughton told *The New York Times*, "I grew up in [Danbury] where I knew everyone. Now my town is a larger community and, though a lot of people recognize me because of my office, I don't recognize them." Boughton's sense of dislocation was shared by many natives as the city's population more than doubled from 30,000 at the end of World War II, to nearly 70,000 when Boughton was mayor. A survey conducted in the early 1980s found that 30 percent of city residents had lived in Danbury for fewer than five years. This population surge drastically altered the demographic profile of the city.

The influx had several dimensions. Since the 1920s, Danbury's accessibility by automobile had lured people for reasons other than traditional business or employment opportunities. The rural countryside attracted a small number of exurbanite writers and artists in search of privacy and an opportunity to live close to nature, like the author Rose Wilder Lane who practiced a lifestyle of rural self-reliance on King Street in the 1930s and '40s. In Long Ridge district in southern Danbury near the Redding town line, the old farmhouses, rocky fields and narrow, off-the-beaten-track country roads became the home of a small colony of people in the arts. Reminiscent of similar groups in Litchfield and in southern Fairfield counties, the colony began in the 1920s. Art collector Catherine Dreier and the gallery she had built (still standing in 2013) for her *Societe Anonyme* offered an early introduction of modern art to America. Dreier's houseguests included some of the leading names of the avant-garde movement, people like Marcel Duchamp. Performances by another of her friends, modern dancer Ted Shawn, bewildered neighboring farmers who showed up for the entertainment. Other new residents who worked outside of Danbury were drawn by the outdoor opportunities of Candlewood Lake. And in 1948, a group of Jewish firefighters from New York City established their own community at wooded Lake Waubeeka in the southern part of town.

By the 1970s, the mass of people employed by incoming corporations hailed from every state in the union and from many foreign countries as well. They included transferred corporate executives and middle managers; engineers and technicians working for the new high-tech companies; doctors and other hospital personnel; and university professors at the growing college. Their reaction to the area was mixed. In 1978 *The News-Times* found that for many it was "either paradise or the pits." Some of those interviewed felt the Danbury area was "quiet and friendly." They liked its countryside and the sense they had of being part of a community. Others found it difficult to adjust to septic systems, high prices and the lack of much nightlife. The article found that people who were transferred from large cities like New York favored the lower taxes and shorter commute time but missed the services and entertainment. The need to continue to attract and hold on to these often well-educated and highly-paid newcomers helped to gradually shift city policies away from unrestrained economic development and toward a new emphasis on "quality of life" that came to fruition during the Dyer era.

The influx of new people began to alter long-established patterns of Danbury politics as early as the 1960s, when the grip of the Democratic Party machine built by attorney Thomas Keating in the 1920s weakened.

In 1967, for the first time, voters who registered in Danbury as "independent" outnumbered the combined total of both Democrats and Republicans. This surge in unaffiliated voters correlated with the beginning wave of newcomers who worked for newly arrived companies. Gino Arconti, the successful mayoral candidate that year, told *The News-Times* that this altered electoral dynamics meant that a party had to have "a candidate voters could identify with," "substantive issues" to run on, and, finally, "an organization willing to exert the effort." Under the leadership of Town Committee Chair Norman Buzaid, the Democrats were able to field candidates that met these requirements until 1977, when Republican Donald Boughton won the mayoralty in part by appealing to issues important to independents and newcomers.

The concerns of new people, particularly those who came in with large corporations, also helped reshape the city's retail landscape. Unimpressed by either the downtown or by the strip shopping plazas, newcomers were practically unanimous in finding the shopping opportunities in the area inadequate, *The News-Times* reported in 1978. Democratic mayoral candidate James Dyer would learn this in 1979, when he campaigned in the traditionally Republican First Ward and heard about the limited shopping from corporate transferees and their spouses. He said later that the experience awakened him to the need to push strongly for locating a proposed regional mall in Danbury.

While Danbury's economic renaissance attracted residents from other parts of the United States, other factors contributed to the establishment of new ethnic communities and to the explosive growth of the city's existing Portuguese population. The numbers of Lebanese in the city had grown enough during the 1920s to make Danbury home to the state's largest population of Arabic speakers. But before changes in federal immigration rules in the 1960s, immigration's impact had been light, consisting mainly of a sprinkling of World War II war brides and Hungarian refugees sponsored by churches after the 1956 uprising against communism. Descendants of older groups like Italians, Poles, Lebanese and Slovaks grew up largely or totally assimilated into the mainstream of Danbury life, often intermarrying. Their ethnic organizations and churches changed with them.*

Beginning in the late 1950s, changes in federal immigration law caused some local ethnic communities to expand and encouraged others to form. These newer immigrants would follow the patterns of adjustment set by earlier groups, but there were some important differences. In 1959, immigration restrictions were relaxed to allow siblings of American citizens to immigrate, so families could reunite without a long wait. A few years later, in 1965, a federal law signed by President Lyndon B. Johnson eliminated the restrictive quota system of 1924 that had favored immigrants from northern Europe. These changes benefitted the local Portuguese, whose numbers increased dramatically from the small colony of 1,500-2,000 established in the 1920s to become the largest group of foreign-born in the city, numbering an estimated 10-15,000 by the 1980s. Migration to Danbury from Portugal increased dramatically through the 1960s and early 1970s. Portugal had escaped the ravages of World War II and the Cold War but, until 1975, the economy was stifled by a right-wing dictatorship. At the same time, the country hung onto its African colonies until 1975, longer than any other European colonial power despite tenacious guerrilla wars there. Young Danbury men who had been born in Portugal or were of Portuguese descent discovered draft notices from the Lisbon government in their mail in 1972. Immigrants in this later wave tended to be somewhat better educated than those who had arrived earlier; some also came from different parts of the country such as the Azores (the islands beyond the mountainous inland villages of the north.) Traditional divisions between the local Danbury community's two clubs (the Sons of Portugal and the Portuguese-American Club) remained in place. In fact it has been said that those Portuguese who emigrated to Danbury had already chosen which club they would belong to before they left home.

New Portuguese immigrants no longer needed to confine themselves to

---

* Evidence of ethnic survival decreased but did not disappear. Church fairs and festivals, Arabic and Portuguese bakeries, restaurants and radio programs like WLAD's back-to-back Sunday morning lineup of the Victor Zembroski's "Polish Eagle Show" and Kamil Saffi's "Lebanon Hour" helped keep cultural memories alive for some of Danbury's established immigrant groups.

hard laboring and construction jobs or dirty, health-threatening work in the fur factories. With large numbers of new factory jobs available in Danbury during the 1950s, 1960s and 1970s, Portuguese workers – along with other immigrants – raced to fill them. In some factories, most of the workers on the assembly lines were Portuguese. At the same time, more established individuals were starting their own businesses or moving into city jobs or the professions. Amerigo Ventura, son of one of the early grocers in the Little Portugal neighborhood, became the community's first lawyer, offering invaluable assistance in guiding individuals and organizations, often working pro bono. John Perry, a laborer who served as president of the Sons of Portugal during the 1960s, helped the first local residents of Portuguese background qualify for the Police and Fire departments.

With an already-established reputation as diligent employees, newer Portuguese immigrants and their families often were able to work more than one job. Thus they easily secured mortgages from local banks, and, in a short time, accumulated enough money to purchase a house and, in many cases, even rental property as an investment. A significant number reportedly saved up their earnings in America to enhance their intended return to the old country. Most, though, set down firm roots here. Names like Coelho, Carvalho, Costa, Boa, DaSilva, Dinho, Ventura, Andrade and others became not only common but prominent in many areas of Danbury's life.

A result of this combination of new and settled people from a common background was the formation of a true ethnic district in Danbury for the first time since the early 1900s. Little Portugal – an area at the intersection of Liberty and East Liberty streets and Town Hill Avenue now known as Portuguese Square – evolved into a recognizable ethnic neighborhood. The intersection received the name after the community rallied to respond to a March, 1984, blaze that destroyed a building at its heart, killing an elderly man and leaving seven families temporarily homeless. Dedication of a new brick building on the site in August 1985, capped a visit by the Mayor of Gouveia, Portugal, one of Danbury's "sister cities."

The Portuguese population, including those living outside this enclave, was especially cohesive. An annual Community Day in June honored a famous poet, Luis De Camoes. The colorfully dressed and usually young folkdance troupe of the Sons of Portugal almost always garnered a prominent photo in *The News-Times* following the parade and picnic that celebrated the event. Even as new arrivals struggled to learn English, they could keep in touch with events through local Portuguese-language media that included a biweekly newspaper, *Impacto*, and a radio station, WFAR, which broadcast from the Portuguese-American Club on Liberty Street and was the first daily Portuguese-language station in Connecticut. People continued the tradition of holding annual dinners with others who hailed from their home villages: places like Folgosinho, Ferreiros do Dao, Ribamondego and Vila Franca. In 1980, the small city of Gouveia, center of one of the regions from which most Danbury Portuguese originated, was designated Danbury's "sister city." It was estimated in 1985 that perhaps 40 percent of Danbury's Portuguese population had ties to Gouveia or its surrounding region. Mayor James Dyer and the Portuguese city's mayor exchanged visits in 1984 and 1985, as part of Danbury's Tricentennial Celebration. Soccer was another activity that unified and motivated the community – the Sons of Portugal teams won state championships in the 1970s and even produced a professional, Rui Caetano, who briefly played for a Lisbon team before returning to Danbury to coach. Finally, the Portuguese community grew so numerous that the Roman Catholic Diocese of Bridgeport assigned a Portuguese-speaking priest to say Mass in St. Peter's Church, and in 1979, established Immaculate Heart of Mary Parish, which acquired its own church only three years later.

Portuguese emigration to Danbury slowed after 1975, when a revolution displaced the Salazar dictatorship, and declined further after the country's entry into the European Union a few years later began to bring prosperity. However, by the mid-1980s, Danbury's Portuguese community was so well-established and substantial that it hosted the first meeting ever held outside the mother country of the worldwide Portuguese Communities Council, an organization composed of representatives of the governments of countries where their countrymen had settled.

Courtesy of The News-Times/Photo by Carol Kaliff

Danbury's first resident Buddhist monks, The Venerable Sambath Pon and the Venerable Sambo So, arrived in 1985. Danbury's Cambodian Buddhist community was the largest in the state at the time.

In the late 1970s and early '80s, Danbury received a sudden influx of refugees from a different part of the world. Following the 1975 Communist victories in Southeast Asia, Roman Catholic relief organizations in Hartford and Bridgeport began to receive hundreds of displaced persons from Vietnam, Cambodia and Laos who had been living in border camps in Thailand or Malaysia or who had escaped from their countries on rickety fishing boats. Local groups like the Association of Religious Communities (ARC) helped them find housing and employment in machine shops and factories. Jobs were plentiful in Danbury's booming economy in the late '70s, and rental or public housing was relatively inexpensive in the old neighborhoods near the downtown area. The refugees included people of several distinct nationalities, some of whom had been traditional enemies. By 1980, there were between 800 and 1,200 Southeast Asians in Danbury, about half of them Cambodian, the largest concentration of that population in Connecticut. Along with numerous Vietnamese and Laotians, a few mountain tribesmen known as the Hmong joined the mix. Once established, these "anchor families" attracted others, usually related, swelling the numbers of Southeast Asians living in Danbury to as many as 2,500 by the mid-1980s.

Southeast Asians faced challenges of cultural adjustment that were novel even in this multi-ethnic city, and they sometimes seemed remote and alien to local residents. These immigrants had been wrenched from a familiar, tropical world and transplanted to a place with a strange culture, language and climate. In addition, they were handicapped by a shattered social network. Broken families, many with members who had suffered wartime casualties or were still living in their mother country, strained the culture's traditional reliance on a Confucian value system that elevated family harmony and honor over the individual. Many of the refugees had worked for American-supported regimes in their Cold War-ravaged home countries, and relatives of some Danbury Laotians were still fighting as rebels against the Laotian Communist government. Danbury's social agencies and religious organizations, particularly ARC, organized clothing and food drives and assisted the newcomers in other crucial ways. In 1982, Mary Louise Brown of Danbury visited the apartment of a Vietnamese refugee family living out of cardboard boxes, with a crib tied together by rope. Moved by this visit, Brown founded the Clothing Plus Bank that distributed free clothing, furniture and household goods to poor residents. Donations valued at $125,000 were handed out in its first two years of operation.

Southeast Asians' struggles to adjust were both material and cultural. Social workers reported that to avoid shame some refugees were reluctant to seek help from social agencies because most problems were expected to be handled within the family. Most of the refugees who settled in Danbury were Buddhist, but there was no local Buddhist temple until one was established on White Street in 1990. Diet also proved to be a challenge, as few local stores carried ingredients used in Southeast Asian cooking. Social workers noticed immigrants with a variety of complaints related to adjustment to the American diet, including a girl at the high school suffering from anorexia-like symptoms who was losing weight because she couldn't digest the typical American food served in the school cafeteria. Fish was such an important part of the Southeast Asian diet and fishing such an important activity in all the Southeast Asian cultures that the state posted warnings in Khmer – or Cambodian – and Thai scripts about the dangers of certain fish caught in local waters.

Over time, conditions improved. By 1985, there were three full-fledged groceries owned by Southeast Asians available in Danbury to cater to the tastes of different Asian cultures, all started by people who had been told by friends that Danbury would be a good place to start such a business. Danbury's first Buddhist monks took up residence the same year. In addition, entrepreneurs were beginning to branch out into nail salons and other businesses, one starting a jewelry store specializing in the heavier gold preferred in Asian cultures over the 14-karat variety that was standard in the U.S. By the mid-1980s, stories were beginning to emerge of high-achieving students from the former refugee community. However, many of these residents of Asian origin were still struggling, looking for work when the economy was down, hoping to reunite with scattered family members who were still behind the "Bamboo Curtain."

Between 1965 and 1985, a local Hispanic community also put down roots. By the late 1970s, it was estimated to number about 3,000 in the city, between 5 and 8 percent of the overall population and about the size of several other city ethnic groups. In the early '80s that number began to expand. Most were originally from Puerto Rico, though towards the end of the 1970s and early 1980s growing numbers of Dominican Republic immigrants and a few Mexicans, Cubans and Central Americans began arriving, most of them coming through New York City. As Maria Cinta-Lowe, a native of Spain who by then had become director of the Hispanic Cultural Center, explained "among the Latino communities, Danbury has a good reputation as a city. Rents are low compared to the others, and it's considered a better place to live than Bridgeport." The Rev. Jose Fernandez, who organized Our Lady of Guadalupe Roman Catholic Church in 1976 to serve this population, described his flock at the time as mostly people who "put in 70 to 80 hour weeks at restaurant-related jobs, who have little time to learn the language and skills necessary for advancement." To meet some of the needs of this widely-dispersed population who hailed from an array of places in Latin America, the Hispanic Center was founded in 1967. Two years later, the organization established the multipurpose Spanish Learning Center, which received funding from the city's antipoverty program, Community Action of Danbury. Language training was one of its main emphases.

Not all of the members of this diverse group were working poor, however. Among DanburyHospital's most innovative figures was Dr. Nilo Herrera, a native of the Dominican Republic and a pioneer in the field of nuclear medicine who created that department at the hospital as well as its first residency program in pathology.

By 1966, the influx of immigrants speaking new languages posed such a significant educational challenge that Danbury's schools scrambled to inaugurate its first English As a Second Language, or ESL, program, in which the teacher helped foreign-language speaking students outside their regular classes. The field was in its infancy at the time, with few programs or resources available. Sharon Fusco, who began teaching in the Danbury program in 1969, was assigned to it because she spoke fluent Italian. To prepare she took courses in different majors at the University of Connecticut, and as the sole ESL teacher for the entire school system between 1969 and 1973, she traveled to different schools every day.

In 1978, a survey of the school population revealed 27 native languages spoken by Danbury students, including Tagalog from the Philippines, Albanian, Estonian, Hebrew and Hindi. That same year, the General Assembly mandated the inauguration of bilingual education in any language where 20 or more students in a building spoke the same dominant non-English tongue. Unlike ESL, bilingual programs provide instruction in the student's primary language while they learn English at the same time. Danbury school officials established bilingual programs in Spanish and Portuguese, the Portuguese program being the only one of its kind in the state, reflecting the large post-1960 Portuguese migration into Danbury. Schools in the city expanded their ESL and bilingual department to comply with the law and by 2004, the ESL program in

Danbury schools had grown from one with a single teacher instructing 100 students, to about 1200 students served by a department of approximately 35, including a director, staff and certified teachers.

The growing ethnic diversity of Danbury occurred alongside the racial tensions and disturbances of the '60s and '70s. Danbury native Andrew DiGrazia, a former teacher and worker in the court system, persuaded the city's Cultural Commission to endorse the idea of a festival incorporating all of the city's ethnic groups to celebrate the idea of harmony in this diversity. During 1979, he met with 20 organizations representing 14 different ethnic communities to line up support. A two-day Danbury Ethnic and Cultural Festival, later expanded to three days, premiered in 1980 on Western Connecticut State University Midtown's campus with dynamic leadership from Dr. Harold Burke, then dean of students, and was an immediate success. The next year it moved to the grounds of Rogers Park Junior High School during the second weekend in July, where it remained for two decades. The Greater Danbury Intercultural Association was organized as the actual sponsor of the event.

The festival's groups highlighted their distinctive cultures in creative ways, but almost all provided samples of ethnic foods that were the biggest draw for the general public. In its early years especially, the festival featured varied dance performances. The event had something of the colorful flavor of the Danbury Fair, which ended in 1981. In 1983, U.S. Rep. William Ratchford of Danbury called the festival "one of Danbury's newest traditions," and Mayor James Dyer added that he was "proud to be mayor of a city that has such a combination of ethnic pride and racial harmony." During those July weekends it seemed that people of good intentions and good sense had triumphed. Danburians could hope the rancor of the recent past was over, allowing their city to become known more for intercultural understanding and appreciation than for racial strife.♦

An excited crowd flocks around a parade through the midway of the Danbury Fair in a photograph taken from the grandstand's roof in the 1970s. The shot illustrates the statuary that was abundant throughout the Fairgrounds, including the giant statues of Farmer John, Paul Bunyan, a reindeer, and pixies perched on rooftops at left.

Last Days of Danbury's Mainstays

HATTING, FARMING, AND THE DANBURY FAIR

HATTING

After hatting disappeared from Danbury, some blamed its demise on President John F. Kennedy who, it was said, refused to wear a hat at his inauguration in January 1961. Presidents had long acted as unpaid endorsers for the nation's hat companies, who could then market the chief executive's favored style to the admiring masses. Hat manufacturers and unions, so often at odds with each other, worked together to present hats to incoming presidents. In fact, they gave Kennedy a Connecticut-made top hat to wear at his inauguration, plus a Danbury-made hat for his personal use. JFK actually did bring the top hat to the inauguration, but he wore it sparingly on that wintry January day; the fact is, he thought all hats made his large head look silly.

Had his rival Richard Nixon won the election in 1960, the hat industry would have been in no better condition. It is unlikely that Nixon would have sported a hat in the hoped-for way. Both Nixon and Kennedy came of age and attended college in the 1930s, part of the generation of young American men who stopped wearing formal hats as an everyday part of their wardrobes. Though men's dress at the time was becoming less formal than in the past, it was the automobile that sealed the local hat industry's fate. The earliest automobiles were truly "horseless carriages," open or canopied and designed like a traditional horse-drawn carriage. But the earliest enclosed cars introduced before World War I put the final kiss of death on Danbury's old favorite, the derby: The stiff hat was simply too easy to knock off when a man was getting in and out of an enclosed car. When auto designers began streamlining cars in the 1930s, lowering their roof height in the process, they also doomed the popular soft hat or fedora. Robert Doran, growing up in the hat industry as the heir to the Doran Brothers hat-machine business, did a study while attending Notre Dame University in 1941. He found that, as automobile sales increased in the United States, the sale of all men's rough-weather clothing, including not only hats, but gloves, overcoats, galoshes and scarves, declined in proportion.

In contrast, most of the hat industry entered a state of denial. Leaders and trade magazine writers refused to accept that the "hatlessness" epidemic among college-age men, first noted in the 1930s, was anything more than a temporary fad. The industry's Hat Institute led by Danbury's Harry McLachlan belatedly launched an educational campaign in the '30s, pointing out the health benefits and the inherent dignity and status a man projected simply by wearing a hat. However, the industry also resorted to gimmicks. The idea that men should wear straw hats only between Memorial Day and September 15 was one. There was even a serious proposal in the early 1930s that a huge gong be set up in downtown Danbury, to be sounded when anyone was spotted wearing a hat of the wrong season. As Stephen Collins has written, "Up until World War II and even afterward, no commercial salesman would try selling to a Danbury industry or store unless he wore a hat," lest he be summarily dismissed without an audience. However, despite well-intentioned pro-motional efforts such as an October 1950 Hat Parade that attracted an estimated 35,000 to 40,000 spectators to downtown Danbury to see floats in the form of giant hats, younger men in the 1950s no longer purchased the quantity of hats every year that their age group once had, nor were they following new fashion trends; a single dress hat could suffice for years. One by one, the big familiar Danbury firms – Lee, Mallory, McLachlan, Green – shut down in the 1950s and '60s.

By 1960, not a single Danbury company still manufactured complete hats. The industry's center of gravity had shifted to the West, where cowboy hats remained reliably popular, and by the 1970s, only a single firm continued the hatting tradition in Danbury. The Danbury Hat Company, a branch of the reconstituted Stetson empire under the supervision of local hatting veteran George Rafferty, survived in the former Mallory backshop by supplying rough bodies that were shipped to St. Joseph, Missouri, to be finished closer to the market. Despite the operation's limited size, it was still the biggest supplier of rough hat bodies in the country.

Occasional fads for particular hat styles inspired by movies like "Urban Cowboy" or the Indiana Jones films during the '70s and '80s stimulated runs for brief periods but could not prevent hatting's eventual demise on the East Coast. Stetson was in bankruptcy in 1986, when it was hit with a Department of Environmental Protection order to cease polluting the stream that ran behind its factory. Stetson decided to consolidate its operations in Missouri, and in December 1987, closed the Danbury Hat Company. Hat manufacturing in Danbury thus ended exactly 200 years after the founding of its first large-scale firm, Burr and White, making a convenient bookend of an anniversary.

FARMING

There were several reasons for the steep decline in dairy farming that occurred at the same time as hatting's long fall. Some former farms were swallowed up when Candlewood Lake was created, others were purchased by the federal government for the prison, still others were rolled up into country estates on the west side. Between 1920 and 1963, the number of Danbury's working farms dwindled from 170 to three, all of them dairies.

However, the majority of farmers were nudged off the land by market forces as it became increasingly clear to smaller dairy farmers that there were easier and more lucrative ways to earn a living. Dairyman Lawrence Swanson, one of the last to survive, gave *The News-Times* an idea of the discouraging economic realities facing dairymen in 1963 when he said, "We used to get half of the price charged to consumers and now we get only a third. They paid you about ten cents a quart thirty years ago and you get pretty near that today. And meanwhile, tractors and milking machines and all farm implements are getting more and more expensive." With residential development boosting open-land prices, it became increasingly difficult for young people to enter farming; the capital investment required for a dairy farm had more than doubled between 1930 and 1965. Federal milk orders, actively sought by farmers during the Depression years as price supports, established price subsidies for milk; but some farmers in later years believed they held down prices artificially at a time when costs were rising rapidly. Even local property taxes on farmland rose as residential expansion into the suburbs began. In 1950, Paul Ruffles paid $127 a year in taxes on his 100-acre farm on King Street; by 1965, that sum had quadrupled.

Some of the other reasons for the decline given by farmers were familiar ones: The lack of local labor to bring in the harvests and do other farm work was a complaint similar to those of farmers almost a hundred years before. City and farm youths alike could find higher wages and more regular work in the city's factories and other businesses during the '40s and '50s. A better-educated generation, they had aspirations that didn't include getting up at four o'clock in the morning to milk cows day after day with no vacation. Moreover, many farm youths had for decades been deciding to seek opportunities in the city or in other parts of the country. As Paul Ruffles recounted, he was the only one who remained on the farm out of the 18 sons of 10 dairy-farm families on his section of King Street in the 1920s.

Fields all over Danbury began to become overgrown with brush and scrub, particularly in depleted pastures where poverty grass, barberry, goldenrod and cedar succeeded meadow grass. Rabbits and meadow birds roamed where once cattle had kept the grass short and green. All over the former rural Town of Danbury, land began to revert to forest. Meanwhile, as farming became more mechanized, some basic farm skills were lost. When Tarrywile Farm's main cow barn burned in a spectacular blaze in September 1959, the dairy's milking machines were destroyed, creating a crisis as some of the farm employees had never hand-milked a cow. The next morning, according to witnesses, "farmers and ex-farmers from all over the area" showed up to milk Tarrywile's cows until emergency milking machines could be installed.

Only the biggest and most productive farms could survive. A breaking point for some dairymen occurred in the mid-1950s, when a new technology known as the "bulk tank" arrived on the scene. This innovation stored milk for longer periods, allowing farmers to do their own tests for butterfat content and eliminating the need to deliver milk to the Danbury railroad station in 40-quart cans. At the same time, the tanks were prohibitively expensive for some. When the dairy cooperatives that sold most of the Danbury farm milk and the state Department of Agriculture both began to require larger containers, dairy farmers faced a crossroads described by Charles Bardo in an unpublished memoir. Bardo, his in-laws and friends had started "Enterprise Farm" on Federal Road during World War II. He later wrote that "for a small farm like us [bulk tanks] would mean an expense … With our sale of land [to a newly relocated corporation, Eagle Pencil], new milk regulations and the proposed Interstate 84 and Route 7, it pretty much meant we were going out of the farming business." Many other small or struggling farmers made a similar calculation, choosing to sell off their land to residential developers or to corporations seeking to relocate.

During the '30s and '40s the Danbury area had as many as 50 or 60 small dairies and hundreds of milkmen, some with delivery routes through their own neighborhoods. Local dairies in Danbury included Rider (on West and New streets), Tarrywile, Marcus, Swanson's and Cloverlawn, among others. But home delivery of milk was also in freefall after World War II. As in other areas of American life, big national firms that marketed their product in large chain stores came to dominate the food industry. By

1985, only Marcus remained in operation and all but a tiny fraction of dairy products were being purchased in supermarkets and convenience stores.

Despite all the drawbacks and the growing list of obstacles, it was pull rather than push that got most Danbury dairy farmers out of the business. Howard Shepard, who maintained his farm in the Great Plain district for over 60 years, told an interviewer in 1963 that he'd "never seen a farmer pushed off the land. It was always the lure of something else." As the population of the Danbury area grew, the "something else" that tempted farmers to abandon agriculture was the rising price of suburban land. Paul Ruffles received offers of $3000 an acre from developers, a figure that equaled the value of his entire farm when he purchased it from his father in 1942. Some farmers were able to remain on the land by opening nurseries on remnants of their former property to supply the new residential developments with landscaping shrubs and trees. In 1965, Danbury had 22 nurseries, each operating on only a few acres of land.

By the mid-1970s, only a single major dairy remained in Danbury. Tarrywile Farm rebounded from its devastating 1959 fire by replacing its traditional barns with "open housing," which allowed cows to feed and then roam instead of being confined in pens. This modernization boosted milk production to 3,000 gallons a day. But rising fuel costs in 1974-75 doubled the price of feed at the same time that the Connecticut Department of Environmental Protection issued an order to restrict the movement of the herd to prevent manure from polluting a stream on the property, a hazard that had not existed when the cows had been pastured conventionally. In December 1975, Tarrywile closed down its dairy business, selling off its dairy herd.

Farming ultimately came to play a minor role in local life. State efforts to encourage agriculture by lowering local tax assessments on farmland, and by enacting the Farmland Preservation Program in 1978, came too late to benefit Danbury's farmers. The recent trend toward establishing vineyards, growing heirloom vegetables, and promoting tourist attractions like corn mazes and farmer's markets, however, did revive some interest in local agriculture. Several long-established roadside farm stands, such as the one operated by the Halas family in the Pembroke district, survived and for a time even flourished. An actual working farm – Danbury's last, as it turned out – was revived in the Great Plain district by Don Taylor Jr. and his wife Karen on ancestral land in the late 1970s. There, the family grew vegetables and other crops sold at regional farmer's markets.

An effort to preserve farming, or at least its memory, received a boost when the Danbury Jaycees took on a project in 1972 to renovate an old barn near the new Stadley Rough School, calling the effort "Down on the Farm." The property, which included a farmhouse built in the 1920s, had originally been a dairy farm, then an orchard and, finally, a riding stable until acquired by the city in 1970. The sponsors brought in livestock and a caretaker who operated a small, model working-farm as an educational facility well into the 1980s.

THE DANBURY FAIR

As the farms would disappear, so would the great Fair that had celebrated Danbury's agriculture for decades. It had been expanded and drastically transformed by John Leahy, who acquired it near the end of World War II. Born in 1895, Leahy grew up on Balmforth Avenue, close to the "circus lot" on White Street where traveling circuses pitched their tents every year. Buffalo Bill's Wild West Show, featuring sharpshooter Annie Oakley along with 200 expert riders that climaxed in a staged "buffalo hunt," performed there four times between 1896 and 1912. Leahy, fascinated by any and all forms of entertainment, also attended every Danbury Fair from the time he was five. He learned the machinist's trade at nearby Turner Machine, became acquainted with inventor Lewis Heim and followed his lead by establishing his own centerless grinding machine shop. He founded a financially successful fuel dealership in the 1920s. During World War II's difficult times, a customer behind on a fuel bill offered to pay Leahy with a share of Danbury Fair stock. The Fair was shuttered at the time, its worn buildings and grounds falling into disrepair. When Leahy met with aging

Agricultural Society Secretary G. Mortimer Rundle, he was told that the Fair was "basically out of business at this point." Ranging through the area's countryside, he bought up worthless shares of Fair stock from shareholders who mostly held them as keepsakes until, by 1946, he owned a controlling interest. He immediately had himself voted in as the Fair's new general manager.

At age 50, Leahy began a second career turning the venerable Fair into an "economy Disneyland," as he called it. Equal parts entrepreneur and entertainer, Leahy made the Fair his "full-time hobby." He began promoting the annual event as "The Great Danbury State Fair," and savored his role as master of ceremonies, dressing in full ringmaster's regalia for the daily livestock parades on the racetrack during Fair Week. He inserted himself into every detail of its operation, even handing out the checks to temporary crews hired to help clean up the grounds after Fair Week. He poured his own money into the Fair to fix up and repaint buildings and pave its rough dirt paths – loans that eventually amounted to hundreds of thousands of dollars. Particularly in its early years, the 1940s and '50s, the Fair seldom made a profit and during some of those years, Leahy took no salary.

Leahy's right-hand man in transforming the Fair was his assistant, C. Irving Jarvis, who had grown up with his family running the amusement park at Lake Kenosia. Before going to work for Leahy, Jarvis had also managed an Atlantic City hotel and amusement parks at Rockaway Beach as well as the famed Playland in Rye, N.Y. Like Leahy in his ringmaster's outfit, Jarvis also played the showman's role to the hilt, strolling around the fairgrounds in a huge hat, wearing a carnation boutonniere and carrying a walking stick. Jarvis provided practical know-how and flair to Leahy's ambition and drive.

The new management team inaugurated the re-opened fairgrounds shortly after VJ Day, in August 1945, featuring midget auto racing. Once used for trotting horses, the racetrack, which Leahy renamed the Danbury Fair Speedway and later the Racearena, proved a consistent draw over the years. After midget auto racing sputtered, Leahy introduced speedboats that

Courtesy of Stephen Flanagan

John Leahy (at right) poses with champion driver Chick Stockwell holding the Carradi Memorial trophy in front of his car at the Danbury Fair Racearena in the mid-1960s. Also pictured are William Carradi Jr. and his son William Carradi III. Beginning in 1951, the summertime Saturday night stock car races of the Southern New York Racing Association became as much a part of Danbury's identity as hats.

competed in a specially built tank in the middle of the track. Later, he turned the track over to stockcar racing.

Leahy's decision to run the Fair like a business initially generated controversy for which some locals never forgave him. To produce an income stream, he cancelled the free passes that shareholders in the Fair received each year in lieu of dividends. The passes had been distributed "from City Hall all the way down to anyone who had any kind of a title and any kind of political power in town," according to Jack Stetson, Leahy's grandson. Far more controversial was the 1946 decision by the board of education to cancel the longstanding prewar custom of "Danbury Day," a school holiday that allowed students to attend the Fair for free on Friday of Fair Week, a decision possibly made in reaction to Leahy's takeover of the Fair or perhaps prompted by Leahy's own policy. The board's decision, and subsequent rebuffs of student attempts at a compromise afternoon school closing, provoked a strike by some 800 Danbury High School students. They walked out of classes carrying placards and marched or road in army surplus jeeps to the fairgrounds on Friday, October 4, 1946, which would have been Danbury Day. School Superintendent Walter Sweet observed the spectacle while sitting in a dentist's chair in a building overlooking downtown as the crowd of students marched past. A large contingent continued to walk the three miles to the fairgrounds, where they milled noisily but peacefully outside the entrance gate. Finally, Leahy received word from Sweet that school was being cancelled for the remainder of the day. "It was the only decision that could have been made," Sweet said later. Leahy then announced that all Danbury students would be admitted free as his guests. "If there is anybody in Danbury today who is a hero in the eyes of the city's school children, it is John Leahy," *The Danbury News-Times* proclaimed. Beginning the following year, the school board reinstated Danbury Day as a school holiday, and Leahy made sure to distribute free Fair passes to city schoolchildren every year.

Whatever people thought of the new private regime and its changes, they came back to the Fair in droves. Attendance at the first postwar fair in 1946 rose to 163,456, a number that surpassed the previous record set in 1941 and that stood as the best year ever up to that point. Attendance swelled as the children of the baby boom began to grow up, averaging around 150,000 by the early '60s. Leahy was careful to maintain longstanding Fair traditions such as Governor's Day, Danbury Day and Out-of-town Day, as well as familiar Fair attractions like the Big Top and livestock exhibits. He blended innovations with Fair traditions, adding an attraction virtually every year. As Jack Stetson recalled, the management moved incrementally because "people came to the fair because they wanted to find what they expected to find, some of the stuff that had been there for many years. It was tradition and people would be disappointed when things disappeared."

To add new attractions, Leahy and Jarvis used creativity and ingenuity in expanding the Fair's physical footprint. A stage set with full-size facades

of "typical New England" buildings such as a white clapboard meeting-
house complete with a steeple, which had been on display in New York's
Grand Central Terminal, became the cornerstone of a picture-perfect New
England village, centered on a pond dug out of the endless wetlands on
the fairgrounds site. To add to the exhibit, Leahy transported the barn
and farmhouse from the old Backus place he'd acquired on the corner of
Kenosia and Backus avenues, and made the barn a center for handicraft
exhibits. A small steam-launch echoed the attractions of the old Kenosia
Park, chugging along as it carried passengers around the pond. It became
an iconic image of the new Danbury Fair.

Leahy and Jarvis used similar ingenuity to create other attractions. In the
late 1950s, with more than two dozen westerns on television every week
and the fad over Walt Disney's "Davy Crockett" in full flower, the Fair
opened Gold Town, a stylized replica of a California Gold Rush town
that Jarvis spent months researching for authenticity. The town came
complete with a twice-daily mock gunfight. In addition, youngsters could
pan for "gold" – in actuality, pebbles painted with gold paint – at a wooden
sluice under the eyes of an old "prospector" figure, while locals like coun-
try-and-western singer Carolyn Chase and dancer-choreographer Ona Mae
Hancock provided entertainment in a "dance hall" that overlooked the
stage set. In 1960, after seeing a print of colonial New Amsterdam, the Fair
hired a designer to study that city's Dutch buildings and convert some 35
rundown stables and other buildings near the racetrack into the "Dutch
Village" – an area full of shops and featuring a windmill, a courthouse
with a dungeon beneath it, and shop attendants dressed in Dutch-colonial
costumes. In another part of the fairgrounds, Leahy placed a simulated
1858 locomotive that became the foundation of a "transportation
museum," to which he added, over the years, stagecoaches, trolleys,
Conestoga wagons, carriages and early model autos.

Most memorably, Leahy peopled the fairgrounds with a vast array of
statues made of different materials, numbering over 400 by the time the
Fair ended its final run. The stationary figures were everywhere, perching
on rocks and rooftops and along the Fair's avenues. A giant farmer and Paul

Bunyan greeted fairgoers at points near the entrances, while a life-size Fiberglass Santa and sleigh pulled by reindeer raced perpetually in freeze motion along Backus Avenue. Pixies, dance-hall girls, the "Pirate's Den" inspired no doubt by Disney's "Pirates of the Caribbean" ride, and story-book figures of all kinds lent sheer exuberance to the place.

Leahy became adept at locating new display figures, seeking out closing amusement parks and maintaining contacts with suppliers of such crowd pleasers for parades and big department stores in New York City. From the 1965 New York World's Fair came a set of costumed figures made in Italy of special weatherproof plaster that Leahy set into niches on the outside of the grandstand. To create familiar landmarks around the fairgrounds, Leahy turned to the so-called "Muffler Men" – big fiberglass heads manufactured by the International Fiberglass Company. "They built these heads and we would convert 'em to Paul Bunyan, Uncle Sam or whoever Mr. Leahy decided they ought to be," Jack Stetson recalled. In addition to icons of the Fair's midway – the towering Paul Bunyan, the Viking warrior and Uncle Sam – there was a 22-foot statue of an American Indian that came to be called Chief Mohawk, which was posted at the entrance to Gold Town. At one of the annual meetings of the International Association of Fairs and Conventions held in Chicago, Leahy picked up nearly 60 papier-mâché pixie figures that had decorated lampposts in the city's downtown one Christmas season. Although a memorable addition to the Fair, they were fragile and in continual need of attention, so Leahy would shoo children away from them. "If John [Leahy] really wanted something, he'd spend for it," Stetson said. "A lot of it was beat up, so we'd refurbish it and it would become a fixture on the fairgrounds for a number of years." The figures were so important to the spirit of the Fair that Leahy employed full-time carpenters like Peter Reilly to repair them. Leahy was also willing to pay handsomely for such attractions as the Royal Canadian Mounted Police troupe that rode at the grandstand each day, as well as for daredevil auto shows, lumberjack competitions and comedy shows.

Despite its new commercial focus, the Danbury Fair remained a community institution. During its lengthy off-season, the fairgrounds were out of the public eye but far from idle. Behind the scenes, a small corps of skilled craftsmen toiled constantly in warmer weather to keep the Fair in shape and build up the new touches and attractions.

"It was a lot like farm work – constant repair," Stetson remembered. "The buildings were always falling down. Many of the crew were older men who didn't work during winter and then they'd work there at the fair all summer. It was pleasant and unique with no pressure. They got a little living out of it and were quite happy with it. It was almost like a summer camp for these people."

Carpenter Harold Kohler, John Leahy's cousin, worked at the Fair into his 80s. Jay Lavoie, a sign painter, painted the new creations. Work crews often included "rough guys from the streets of old Danbury," Stetson said. He and other members of Leahy's extended family occupied the old caretaker's house on the fairgrounds property, where early-morning rounds included looking after the Fair's resident livestock – llamas, ducklings (raised to mature in time for Fair Week and then sold off), and black Caracol Afghan sheep that Leahy kept for the wool he had made up into blankets.

The events of Fair Week meant a frenzy of preparations for the dozens of concessionaires whose small food and other booths lined the Fair's byways. By the late 1970s, about 4,000 people were working the Fair during its 10-day run, many of them familiar local faces. They included Dan Burke, who guessed people's weight at the Fair for more than 40 years, and Leonard Fletcher, a Derby farmer and pioneer of artificial insemination, who selected livestock exhibits for the Fair for more than two decades. Local musicians like organist Emile Buzaid, fiddler Al Brundage, and many others provided entertainment. About half of the concessionaires were local, what *The News-Times* once described as "a small army of local housewives, factory workers, policemen and small businessmen who converge on the fair each year to set up shop for ten days." A very few, like Nejame Catering, were companies or professional individuals, but most were not. Local people took vacations from their regular jobs to run small restaurants or craft booths at the Fair. And many of these were family affairs, generations growing up with the Fair as a part of their lives. Vincent Pannozzo, a detective on the Danbury police force, arranged his vacation so he could put in 14-hour days at the restaurant his family ran near the New England Village beginning in 1952. The Zinser family of florists from Westville Avenue operated their flower stand in the Big Top for over 45 years. Clare Maginley, principal of the Main Street School in Danbury, turned a hobby of making wooden toys into a retirement specialty, in part through selling at the Fair and at a summer craft event held at the fairgrounds. In 1977, Maginley crafted 2,600 handmade wooden toys during the off-season, slated for sale at the Fair and other shows. Although the concessions were no longer major fundraisers for local churches as they had been at the pre-Leahy Fair, some local groups, like the Kiwanis Club with its pancake booth, continued to operate stalls at the Fair.

The Fair also meant increased sales for a number of area businesses: hotels and motels; food distributors; the Pinkerton security agency that put over 200 employees on its payroll for the Fair; and the local stores that sold lumber and paint to keep the buildings repaired. There was so much activity that Fred Fearn, president and general manager of the Fair after Leahy's death, estimated in 1977 that Fair Week and its preparations pumped as much as $4 million into the local economy.

Maintaining the agricultural element of the Fair became problematic as the number of farms in the Danbury area declined. The prewar Fair had been organized around exhibits, with a day devoted to each kind of animal. Leahy changed that. He dropped livestock judging, a major attraction at pre-war fairs, and began to devote a single barn for an educational exhibit for each type of animal, with an array of representative breeds in each barn for the benefit of "people who had never seen a cow." Management began to have to pay stipends to farmers to continue to exhibit their best animals during Fair Week. By the end of the Fair's run in 1981, the bulk of its livestock came from Litchfield County towns to the north, or from New York state farms to the west. Still, Leahy kept up the daily parade of livestock at the grandstand as one of the Fair's highlights. Local farmers,

Courtesy of the Danbury Museum and Historical Society Authority

The basic elements of the Danbury Fair – racetrack and grandstand, Big Top and livestock sheds and barns – remained the same throughout the Fair's 112-year run, though structures were replaced and updated. Parking had to be expanded several times to the very limits of the airport as attendance soared in the 1960s.

4-H members and others throughout the Danbury area who didn't live on full-size farms, continued to raise and train oxen for the popular oxen pull, like Wallace and Richard Smith of Danbury and New Milford, the Ferris family of Newtown, and Bob Fisher of Brookfield. Others raised vegetables, livestock, poultry or pigeons, made jams and baked pies for the Fair's exhibits. Some farm families, like the Brundages of King Street, continued to exhibit at the Fair long after they sold their acreage to developers. Until the Fair ended, a visitor could spend hours or a whole day ignoring the teeming, frenetic midway to roam the acres of barns full of horses, cattle, thousand-pound hogs, the colorful array of sheep and poultry breeds, and exotic livestock such as Leahy's favorite, the llamas.

Americans had more leisure time on their hands in the '50s and '60s, and as the Fair's centennial approached in 1969, the "Great Danbury State Fair" became a legitimate tourist destination in early autumn. "Danbury remains perhaps the best example in the metropolitan area of what a country fair could be," a *New York Times* travel writer proclaimed in 1976. Completion of sections of I-84 and later, I-684 and I-87 in nearby New York state, boosted Fair attendance stratospherically in the 1960s and '70s. Previously during Fair Week, local traffic on the old routes 6 and 7 and along the Fair's local access roads was badly congested. Long waits, sometimes for an hour or more, were not uncommon during good-weather weekends. The new highways eased that situation. Capitalizing on the opportunity in 1964, Leahy instituted the Fair's first-ever ten-day run, opening on Friday instead of Saturday. In 1966, the Fair broke the 200,000-visitor mark for the first time, and only three years later attendance reached 300,000. By 1966, so many people were flying to the Fair in private planes from as far away as Arizona and California that the Federal Aviation Administration set up a portable control tower at the usually uncontrolled Danbury Airport for the two weekends of the Fair. It continued to do the same for the next few years. A factor in the swelling numbers of visitors was the inauguration of weekend bus group-tours from New York City that appealed particularly to church-related organizations.

By the early 1970s, age and ill health forced a change in Fair leadership. C. Irving Jarvis died in 1969, and Leahy suffered a stroke a few years later. Consequently, Leahy began turning more and more of the Fair's day-to-day operations over to his assistant, Fred Fearn, and his (Leahy's) step-grandson, Jack Stetson, who had been groomed to eventually take over and indeed had been promised the top job. The new management team made the Fair more profitable, raising ticket prices and expanding the fairgrounds' use off-season to spread the weather risk, with craft and antique shows and rentals to corporations for picnics.

Leahy had tried to make sure that the Fair would survive his death. In the mid-1960s, he established a nonprofit foundation, the JWL Foundation, which would operate the Fair and benefit his favorite charities like Danbury Hospital. Beginning in 1966, he donated shares of the Fair's stock to the Foundation and, in a will he filed in 1969, bequeathed the remainder of his Fair stock to it. However, within a year, a ruling by the

Internal Revenue Service that forbade a nonprofit foundation from owning more than 20 percent of a commercial entity, upset his careful planning.

The IRS ruling turned out to be a crushing blow to both Leahy and the Fair. Leahy had to pay cash at market value to buy back the shares he'd already donated. He also issued a codicil to his will in December 1970, which revoked his bequest of the Fair stock. At that point, with his health beginning to decline, he either procrastinated or else became so exasperated with the situation that he failed to take any further steps that would guarantee the Fair's continuation. On his death in 1975, the Fair's ownership passed to his estate, the trustees of which were his widow Gladys; Fred Fearn, who became head of both Leahy's fuel company and the Fair; Jack Stetson; and the Connecticut National Bank. As Stetson tells it, the bank had wooed Leahy for years, making him a bank director and playing on his ego. The bank stood to profit most by liquidating the Fair and investing the proceeds. "The bank was scared," Stetson said. "What do bankers know about the fair business? They wanted to turn it into stocks and bonds at a desk with a computer and not have to worry about weather and cows and carneys and all the rest of it." The law was also on the bank's side: Trustees were legally required to do with property what most benefited the estate.

Meanwhile, as Danbury boomed, so did the fairgrounds' worth as commercial real estate. Its assessed value quadrupling in 11 years. The influx of affluent new residents in the 1970s, coupled with Danbury's traditionally high retail spending per capita, made the fairgrounds a prime site for a regional shopping mall. Its 140 table-flat acres at the intersection of Routes 6 and 7 had always marked it as a valuable location; but with the completion of east-west I-84, and I-684 to the west in New York state, as well as an anticipated expansion of Route 7 southward, it became a magnet for commercial developers across the country. In 1978, *The News-Times* reported that at a meeting of commercial realtors in New Jersey, attendees had agreed that "Connecticut was the hottest growth area in the Northeast, that Danbury is the hottest growth spot, and the fairgrounds the hottest spot in Danbury."

Fearn told the press in October 1978 that the fairgrounds were not for sale, although he did acknowledge that developers, including representatives of Sears, had discussed with him the possibility of building a mall, corporate headquarters, or large factory on the property. He did, however, admit in the same interview that "the Fair alone cannot support the property right now." In May 1979, the inevitable happened with the announcement that Wilmorite, Inc., a Rochester, New York, commercial developer, had been granted an option on the fairgrounds acreage for $24 million.

The mall proposal was one of the most divisive issues in Danbury during this period of rapid and mostly welcome growth. There had been no real opposition to the coming of Union Carbide or the host of other corporate entities relocating in the area; but almost immediately there were outcries to save the beloved Fair. Politicians weighed in. U.S. Representative William Ratchford, a Danbury native, expressed his support for saving the Fair but realistically could offer no federal help. Even mayoral candidate Pat Cicala, running as a member of the usually fiscally conservative independent Equitable Tax Association Party, called for the state to purchase the Fair. A hostile coalition formed, made up of downtown merchants, nearby property members, stockcar drivers, racing fans and others. Calling itself Some Concerned Residents Against the Mall (SCRAM), it first unsuccessfully appealed a zone change that allowed the mall to be built on the fairgrounds; then it brought suit in Danbury Superior Court against the Zoning Commission, the fairgrounds owners and Wilmorite. The opposition had an important ally in Jack Stetson, one of the principals in the Fair, who viewed the sale of the property as a betrayal and claimed to have been responsible for initiating the protest group. The sides for and against the mall reflected a clash of lifestyles between the older, more rural and blue-collar Danbury and the new, more upscale and corporate one that was developing. On one side, some people wished for continuation of the seasonal Fair," … the one thing that was truly unique in Danbury, Connecticut," as Main Street jeweler Frank Cappiello called it, and its summer stockcar races. The position of the mall's proponents was voiced by *The News-Times*, particularly its editorial director, Steve Collins. He dismissed the Fair as an outdated and commercialized event that paid little in property taxes and represented an unproductive use of a large and strategic piece of real estate. "Agriculture has disappeared from this part of the state," he opined in a 1979 editorial, calling Leahy's Fair "a glorified carnival." In January 1981, Collins urged the zoning commission not to be "swayed by appeals to nostalgia or emotions that somehow the fair has to be maintained, even if it takes tax money to do so."

SCRAM's court case dragged on through all of 1983. In January 1984, a judge dismissed the suit on the grounds that none of the plaintiffs were eligible to sue because they were not abutting property owners. But by that time the Fair's continuation was a moot point.

The Fair's last 10-day run in 1981 recorded its highest-ever attendance, the imminent demise attracting over 440,000 visitors. It produced a massive traffic jam on I-84 as over 50,000 people showed up on the Wednesday of Fair Week. In the days following the Fair's closing , a three-day auction, some of it held in pouring rain, dispersed the statuary and other Fair memorabila around the Northeast. Rosy Tomorrow's Restaurant on Mill Plain Road in Danbury and a number of local individuals purchased figures or other pieces of the iconic Fair as souvenirs of good times past.

As inevitable as it may have been, the end of the Danbury Fair created a void in the community. As one Danburian said, "Some of the (community) spirit seemed to go out of Danbury when the Fair ended." ♦

Courtesy of David Vine

Leonard Bernstein conducts the American Symphony Orchestra at the Danbury Fairgrounds in a 1974 concert to honor the centennial of Danbury native composer Charles Ives' birth. The concert, held on July 4, was considered in the classical music world as one of the most important events of the Ives' centennial year.

Chapter Nineteen Spotlight

Honoring a Prophet

Composer Charles Ives, Danbury's native son, died in 1954 at a time when more and more people were becoming aware of his music. From songs to symphonies, his music was full of intentional "wrong notes," dissonance, wild swoops and intertwining musical lines. It was avant-garde, challenging to listen to. Ives was hailed as a rebel, a man of the people, an American original. In later years, musicians as disparate as the famed minimalist composers John Cage and John Adams and the psychedelic rock group the Grateful Dead claimed his music as an influence. Yet Ives' music was built on his memory of growing up on Main Street in Danbury. It was imbued with the band tunes and other sounds he had heard during patriotic parades or hymns from his churchgoing days in the small town's booming atmosphere of the 1880s.

The reclusive Ives had won the Pulitzer Prize for Music in 1947 for his Symphony No. 3, "Camp Meeting," a work completed in 1911 but performed for the first time ever in New York City more than 35 years later. Performances of his orchestral works led by the charismatic conductor Leonard Bernstein in the early 1950s helped bring Ives greater prominence. Local efforts to recognize the composer started out encouragingly in 1961, when his Redding neighbor and friend John C. Burnett led the Danbury Community Orchestra in the first New England presentation of Ives' Symphony No.2, reportedly the only major Ives concert since 1951. The music department at Danbury State College (later WCSU) made Ives' music the theme of its Connecticut Music Festivals in 1966 and 1968. The school's remodeled auditorium in White Hall, transformed into a first-class concert space, was dedicated to Ives in March 1970, and a bronze bust of the composer was stationed at its entrance. Ultimately, it would, in fact, be a member of the college's music department, Howard Tuvelle, who would be the driving force behind an exceptional concert celebrating Ives' centennial year in 1974. However, before this would happen, the community had to come to grips with saving the composer's birthplace for posterity.

1964 brought a crisis and an opportunity. Fairfield County Trust Bank, owner of the property where Ives' birthplace stood, made plans to raze it for additional parking. Members of the Danbury Music Center and the Scott-Fanton Museum approached the bank, which agreed to give the house to the Scott-Fanton if the museum would have it moved off the site. The museum organized a drive to save the building, led by its president, realtor and former Republican mayoral contender Robert Johnson. Despite Johnson's natural abilities as a salesman, local fundraising lagged embarrassingly and deadlines passed until, in 1965, *The News-Times* and community organizations such as the Junior Service League stepped up to publicize the cause. The city then provided a site for the structure in Rogers Park. Still, it took an infusion of cash by members of the Ives family to make the move a reality. On September 19, 1966, the Arthur Venning Building Movers sawed the house into two pieces and hauled it down Main Street to its new location in Rogers Park, as spectators lined the streets and pupils at the St. Peter's School rushed to classroom windows to gaze at the sight.

That wouldn't be the end of the house's travels, or its troubles. Johnson and others conceived of the Ives House as the centerpiece for a museum village on the 14-acre, city-owned site, and even had architectural plans drawn up. The project would begin with the Ives House, which would be joined by other threatened historic buildings. The one-room King Street schoolhouse, which otherwise would have been demolished, was transported to the site in 1972. The idea was that if and when the museum's Main Street property could be sold, the existing museum buildings there would be moved to Rogers Park as well. The Ives House might then serve as the focus of a concert series or an arts center for Danbury – features that might generate tourism dollars. The museum received a bequest from the estate of Ives' widow to begin fundraising for the project.

The museum had to move the house again a short distance when Rogers Park Junior High was built, and poured a large sum into site work to build a pond, around which the museum's buildings would be arrayed. Then Johnson died, funds ran short and the museum, though not quite rudderless, could not complete the project, leaving it with two separate campuses a half-mile apart. Worse, the unoccupied house saw more visits by vandals than by tourists and by 1968, a fire inside the house caused significant damage. Although the historic theme park idea wasn't completely abandoned until 1974, the new focus for those concerned became saving the house.

As the centennial milestone of Ives' birth approached in 1974, Ohio-born concert pianist and Western Connecticut State College music professor Howard Tuvelle, while brainstorming ways to publicize the Danbury composer, had a brilliant but audacious idea: produce an all-Ives concert in Danbury to be held on the Fourth of July – with no less than Leonard Bernstein conducting the orchestra! Tuvelle believed that such a concert could not only raise funds for restoring the Ives House, but could be the first step toward establishing a performing arts center in the city that would be focused on Western's music department. Enlisting the cooperation of colleagues like Western composer Richard Moryl, Tuvelle gained the backing of Mayor Gino Arconti and Connecticut Lt. Gov. T. Clark Hull, and assembled a centennial committee of locals that included light-opera producer Jean Dalrymple from the Long Ridge district. He even secured the use of the Danbury Fairgrounds, the only local venue large enough for such an event, from a skeptical John Leahy. Leonard Bernstein, on sabbatical from the directorship of the New York Philharmonic at the time, turned out to be intrigued by the opportunity.

The committee secured federal and state grants, but as happened with the Ives House move, fundraising locally proved slow until Nathan Ancell, president of the newly relocated Ethan Allen Furniture company, made a sizable donation. Ticket sales soon were brisk in all parts of the Danbury area.

Staging the concert itself proved a challenge. Committee members Alfred Zega, a former operatic singer, and Marian Anderson were able to secure baritone McHenry Boatwright, a friend of Duke Ellington's and a professor at Ohio State University, for no fee as a soloist for sung pieces at the event. James Furman, another composer and member of the college music faculty, helped Western's student chorus rehearse the choral pieces, which they shared with the Greenwich Choral Society. The American Symphony Orchestra, which had long experience with Ives' music, furnished the difficult instrumental sounds. However, in the weeks leading up to the concert, committee members were calling Bernstein's office so frequently that at one point he threatened to pull out of the project. Concert organizers had to scramble to find an adequate sound system, finally locating one only days before the event. Mayor Charles Ducibella persuaded the City of Bridgeport to loan a portable band shell that had to be transported by a company familiar with hauling extra-wide loads.

The day of the concert was both blistering and humid. The crowd of some 7,000 began arriving early. Some arrived having hitchhiked or walked; others were caught in bumper-to-bumper gridlock – as yet rarely seen in the area – on I-84 and other approach roads to the fairgrounds. As the evening concert's 7 p.m. start approached, the wax on the orchestra's string instruments was melting and fears arose that the musicians would not be able to keep their instruments in tune. Bernstein's manager urged Tuvelle to call off the performance, but Tuvelle remembers saying to him, "Look over there on the highway at those cars. It's now out of our hands. It either goes on or it fails, and there's nothing anyone can do but ride it out."

The concert included the "Second Symphony," conducted by Bernstein and, after a short intermission, Bernstein's protégé, Michael Tilson-Thomas, conducted a series of shorter works. As Tuvelle recalled later, it was "a true Ivesian moment: an American composer, an American traditional fairgrounds, an orchestra called the American Symphony led by American conductors, on a major American holiday." Called by composer Aaron Copland "the greatest tribute ever given to an American composer," the concert was followed by a champagne-and-hot-dog reception.

In all, the event was a financial success, generating a modest profit to begin restoration of the Ives House as well as seed money for Tuvelle's dream of a future Ives-themed music center in Danbury. But realizing that dream turned out to be quite a bit more elusive than the concert.

Tuvelle assembled another committee and, working through the college, got the encouragement of the school's new president, Robert Bersi, who saw the arts center as a way to help open up the long-delayed Westside campus. The group secured letters of interest from Leonard Bernstein, for whom a 6,000-seat main pavilion would be named, and from the American Symphony Orchestra, which had performed the Centennial Concert. Bernstein had already established a foundation to support music education, which Tuvelle hoped to tap. The center's main beneficiary, in Tuvelle's view, would be the college's music department, whose mission would be to nurture and promote the music of contemporary composers. Even though the center was to be funded by corporate and private donations, concert performances would be secondary to education.

Strong divisions arose among the committee members, however. In 1979 Tuvelle resigned from the committee, disappointed at how the project "wasn't going in the direction of the university." The board of the newly christened Charles Ives Center for the Performing Arts increasingly included corporate members who supported an arts center primarily for its tourism value. The concept of an educational foundation for nurturing young American composers evaporated.

Ex-Wall Street executive Donald Weeden ultimately emerged as the most important force in the Charles Ives Center. In 1984, concentrating on attracting a wide-ranging audience, the board announced that it hoped the center would become a "Tanglewood South" destination for summer visitors to New England. Instead of the Bernstein pavilion, its physical centerpiece became a gazebo-style floating band shell anchored in a small pond at the base of a natural amphitheater of woods and open space crisscrossed by stone walls. Concertgoers reached the bucolic setting after a long walk through woods from college parking lots and the access road. The inaugural concerts consisting of short programs that included the Hartford Symphony were held in the midsummer of 1980. The center was formally inaugurated on August 26, 1984. A month later, it hosted an Ivesian concert involving a panoply of folk, jazz and classical groups playing on five different stages. The Ives Center's first full season in 1986 featured classical works as well as a variety of other genres. For example, the featured "Musical Fair America" included the country-music duo, The Judds, and folksinger Richie Havens. Classical music soon faded from the program. More and more pop groups were added to the schedule as the center competed with other concert venues in the state such as the Oakdale Musical Theater.

Local efforts to capitalize on Charles Ives' legacy fell short of the expansive vision advanced by people like Robert Johnson and Howard Tuvelle. But Ives has not been forgotten in his hometown. In Danbury, "Ives" was to the twentieth century what "Wooster" had been to the nineteenth – the default name for local facilities. In addition to the Ives House and the Ives Concert Park, there is Western's Ives Auditorium, Ives Manor for senior housing on Main Street, and Ives Street – although this had already existed, having been named for the family, not the composer.♦

Past and Present

The way a community observes a significant historic anniversary reveals at least as much about its present as it does about its past. This was certainly true in Danbury in 1984 and 1985 when the citizens invested two years of intensive planning and an estimated half-million dollars to stage an extravagant celebration of the 300th anniversary of the city's founding. By extending the memorial festivities over two years – ostensibly to recognize the actions of the original settlers who judged the first winter too severe and returned to Norwalk before permanently settling on the Connecticut frontier the next year – the Tri-centennial Committee made possible a series of commemorative events, spread across the calendar, that built and maintained public enthusiasm. Hundreds of themed programs – from the formal Mayor's Ball to an ethnic festival – brought together all elements of the community to honor the past. Scheduling both the opening and the conclusion of the yearlong celebration in the month of September created an emotional link between the anniversary and the memory of the Danbury Fair, which had been a powerful autumn symbol of community pride and unity for more than a century.

The elaborate festivities began on September 16, 1984, with the largest parade Danbury had ever experienced. Revealingly labeled "The Parade of Progress," the march took its 15,000 participants, including 80 bands along with decorated floats, more than three hours to traverse the parade route from Western's Midtown campus on White Street to Rogers Park at the south end of Main Street. Deep ranks of enthusiastic spectators flanked the entire line of the march. "Danbury had never seen anything like it," boasted Donald Mellilo, the local businessman who planned the spectacle. An emotionally drained Mayor Dyer agreed. He had never experienced such a "charge of electricity of people waving and cheering," he confessed. "Talk about high. At the end of the parade I could have climbed clouds!"

The culminating event, on September 5, 1985, carried out the theme of cohesion. Close to 8,000 people flocked to Main Street, closed to traffic that Sunday for a massive community party. Three elevated stages were set up at spots between Elm and West streets, where a continuous stream of bands, magicians, clowns and other performers, including the famous Harlem Boys Choir, entertained the crowd throughout the sultry afternoon. Free food and beverages were served at this gigantic street fair. In order to promote civic consciousness, members of 60 non-profit local organizations manned sidewalk tables and distributed literature that publicized their activities. For the entire afternoon, the street that until recently had been the acknowledged core of the city once again became the focus of a shared celebration.

Danbury's prolonged and intensive birthday party expressed the community's pride and confidence in its recent accomplishments. The city was enjoying high employment, a robust tax base, a surge in population – and the knowledge that, as a former factory town, it had now become a magnet for dozens of prestigious corporations relocating from the New York metropolitan area. Two large-scale projects symbolized its recent transformation: The 1981 move of Union Carbide from New York City to a glittering new headquarters designed by a world-famous architect seemed to guarantee the continued prominence of the city as a corporate Mecca;

and, at the same time, a mammoth 150-store shopping mall was nearing completion on the site of the former Danbury Fair.

Nevertheless, beneath the sense of satisfaction produced by the vibrant economy lay concern that rampant development threatened the physical fabric and cultural traditions of the community. The massive new corporate headquarters of Union Carbide, located on the far western edge of Danbury, had little functional connection to the city. Most of its 3,000 employees did not live in Danbury and were linked to the self-contained workplace by a special exit on I-84 that eliminated the need to enter any other part of the city. The Danbury Fair Mall boosted the city's tax base and elevated its prestige, but as the largest shopping center in the state, it simultaneously jeopardized the economic vitality of the downtown, the traditional heart of the community.

Danbury's elaborate anniversary tribute used history in an effort to reconcile the underlying tensions present in a prosperous but rapidly changing society. City government played a crucial role in linking the past with the present. James Dyer, a youthful and dynamic mayor with a strong interest in history, took advantage of the bolstered executive powers of his office. He was willing to spend city funds on the celebration, convincing the City Council to approve two appropriations of $75,000 each for this purpose. He was careful to appoint members to the Tricentennial Committee who were knowledgeable about the community's past and sensitive to its cultural heritage. Aware of the key role of buildings as tangible reminders of the past, Dyer made preserving and reusing significant historic structures one of the main goals of his administration. Even before eventual total restoration, he refurbished the old library on Main Street, a Victorian landmark, so it could be used as official Tricentennial headquarters. This connection highlighted the core message of the 300th anniversary celebration: that change without respect for Danbury's unique historic qualities was not progress. ◆

Notes on Sources

Part One and Part Two

PART ONE: HAT CITY (1889-1945)

This account begins at a date (1889) that falls within the purview of the first formal history of Danbury, compiled by James Montgomery Bailey and others and published in 1896. Compiled is an accurate term, because Bailey's History – the name by which it is generally known – includes a series of historical reminiscences and accounts authored by Aaron B. Hull of Redding, Connecticut, in addition to segments written by the famed newspaperman Bailey himself. Hull's accounts first appeared in Bailey's paper in the 1880s. The volume was completed by Susan Benedict Hill following Bailey's untimely death in 1893. The book's description of "The Danbury of To-Day," probably written by Hill, is one important source for the "Portrait of a New City" section that begins this book. However, without a doubt, the pages of *The Danbury News* (sometimes referred to as *The Evening News*) mark the starting point of any meaningful research into Danbury history.

Small city newspapers during the late nineteenth century were comprehensive and boosterish, striving to make their city seem like the most interesting and lively place on the continent. In this task, Bailey's *News* succeeded to a greater degree than most. A daily paper since 1883, *The News* compiled its leading stories of the week into a Wednesday edition distributed to rural districts and towns surrounding Danbury. These comprehensive midweek editions are the chief source of material used here. *The News* also reprinted, in full, pieces published elsewhere, such as *The New York Herald's* Labor Day, 1892, article depicting Danbury as the "Model Workingman's Town," and the hat manufacturers' statement of 1909 that was also published privately by Charles H. Merritt. *The News'* lengthy obituaries of hatting-industry figures such as Ellen Foote, Harry and George McLachlan, Frank H. Lee, Charles H. Merritt, Charles S. Peck and others supplied information that was unavailable elsewhere.

The Prologue and Chapter 1 of this book draw on a broad range of primary sources. These include annual reports of the Town of Danbury and Danbury Common Council, and Danbury's city incorporation records. All of these documents and records are located variously at the Danbury Museum and Historical Society; the Western Connecticut State University Archives at the Ruth A. Haas Library; and Danbury City Hall. The 1886 Report of the State Board of Health quoted here is available in Danbury Hospital's Horblit Library. Additional primary sources include city directories, catalogs and photograph books of hatting firms, and a surviving copy of the Borough Water Rents Record Book for June 1888 that provided an opportunity to draw conclusions about the character of housing in Danbury at that time. These chapters and others throughout Part I are enriched by reminiscences of everyday life during this period in Danbury. Authored by Abraham Feinson, George Lepper and George Orgelman, these are located in the Western Connecticut State University Archives.

For an understanding of the process of hatting and the labor struggles of the late 19th and early 20th centuries, we owe much to the foresight of Stephen Collins, longtime editor of *The News-Times*, who taped an interview session with early hatters George Thorne, who came to Danbury in 1887; Thomas McNally, who participated in the Loewe strike of 1902; and veteran Hat Makers Union Local leader Jeremiah "Dee" Scully. More recent detailed interviews by hatting historian Debbie Henderson with Robert Doran and George Rafferty – both now deceased but two of the most knowledgeable modern hatters – appear in *Hat Talk: Conversations With Hat Makers*, published in 2002. Interviews with MacLean Lasher and John Cappellaro, conducted by William Devlin in 1983, were invaluable. Also useful was a 1951 printed program commemorating the centennial of the Hat Makers Union. The program, which is on file at the Danbury Museum and Historical Society, contains the reminiscences of long-serving union official Hugh Shalvoy. The Walter Gordon Merritt Collection in the Western Connecticut State University Archives documents Merritt's career fighting the union.

Important information about hatting came from the late 19th century trade magazines *American Hatter and Clothier* and *American Hatter*, archived in the New York Public Library, and the Ernest Hubbard collection of *Hat Life Magazine* now at the Danbury Museum. The best brief treatment of the subject of mercury use in the hatting industry is Robert Miller's November 2002 article in *The News-Times.* In writing this piece, Miller drew on interviews and the pioneering studies conducted during the 1920s by Dr. Alice Hamilton of Harvard University. The reports of the Connecticut Bureau of Labor Statistics quoted in these chapters, are located in the State Library in Hartford. An excellent and detailed description of Danbury's hat industry as it existed in 1917 is contained in the Danbury Industrial Survey commissioned by the Danbury Chamber of Commerce. Both the foundation of, and inspiration for, Danbury's industrial transition, the survey, after being unavailable for many years is now housed in the Western Connecticut State University Archives. This remarkable document, which includes data on every business then operating in the city, is also an important source of information on farming and all other aspects of local economic life. Raymond Trimpert's 1969 Western Connecticut State University masters thesis, "A Study of Danbury's Industrial Transition," furnishes valuable background on the survey. The thesis is available in the Western Connecticut State University Archives.

Two richly documented monographs provide important insights into the hat industry in Danbury. David Bensman, in his *Practice of Solidarity* (1985), explores the culture of hat finishers in Danbury and Orange, New Jersey. Robert Ernst, in *Lawyers Against Labor* (1995), details the role of the Merritts – father and son – and the American Anti-Boycott Association in the Loewe case.

The treatment of the 1917 Lee strike in Chapter 5 of this book is drawn from Herbert Janick's "From Union Town to Open Shop: The Decline of the United Hatters of Danbury, Connecticut, 1917-1922," in *Connecticut History* (November 1990). Research for this article, supported by this project, drew not only on interviews cited earlier but also on extensive ar-chival investigation into the War Labor Board manuscripts (Record Group 2, File 15) and the Federal Mediation and Conciliation Service manuscripts (Record Group 280, File 33/585), both at the National Archives and Records Administration in Washington, D.C., as well as from the United Hatters Papers in the Tamiment Library, New York University (Box 55); the Council of Defense Industrial Survey (Record Group 29, Box 64) at the Connecticut State Library in Hartford; and the Manufacturers Asso-ciation of Southern Connecticut records (Box 1) at the Bridgeport Public Library. A 1982 Yale University graduate history paper by Dana Frank, "Hard Times in the Hat City" (in possession of the authors), focuses on the 1893 lockout.

L. Peter Cornwall's *In the Shoreline's Shadow*, a history of the Danbury & Norwalk Railroad, and the Connecticut Motor Coach Museum's *Western Connecticut Trolleys,* part of Arcadia Publications' "Images of Rail" series, proved useful in understanding the transportation issues described in Chapter 4, "Making Connections." Information about Danbury's semi-pro baseball team sponsored by the local trolley line is from an 1993 interview with George Pawlush, local baseball historian. A very detailed August 30, 1967, *News-Times* article written by reporter Robina Clark and based on an interview with C. Irving Jarvis made it possible to understand the appeal of Lake Kenosia and its amusement park. The origins and early years of Danbury Hospital and of Western Connecticut State University (originally Danbury Normal School) are covered in two recently published books:

Pete Petersen's *Danbury Hospital: Challenge and Change* (2010); and Herbert Janick's *A People's University: Western Connecticut State University 1903-2003* (2002). Paul Estefan not only generously supplied valuable information about his own time as Danbury Airport administrator but also allowed us to examine the first Minute Book of the Danbury Airport Commission, which included details about early flying conditions at the field.

Chapter 4's "Diversity" section makes use of the town incorporation records at Danbury City Hall. These contain data about the founding of ethnic organizations in the city. Much of the information about the origins of the Portuguese in Danbury is from an interview with attorney Amerigo Ventura and a very informative, unpublished paper by Anna Marques detailing the history of the Portuguese in Danbury. 1983 interviews of Daniel Skandera and Anna Krizan provided background on Slovak immigration, as did Ancient Order of the Hibernians' historian Phillip Gallagher was especially generous with help on Irish immigration. The quoted comments from Lina Novaco are from the Western Connecticut State University history department's magazine, *Clio* (Vol. 2, No. 2, 1975). The recollections of Danbury native Alson Smith quoted here originally appeared in "Hometown Revisited," published in *Tomorrow Magazine*'s October 1949 issue. A copy can be found in the Truman Warner Papers in the Western Connecticut State University Archives (Box 26, Folder 55). The source of the story about Henry Kearney is William Cruse, Danbury's first African-American City Councilman.

Chapters 6, 7, and 8, which cover the period from 1920 to 1945, rest on a careful reading of the daily issues of *The Danbury News*, and, after 1933, when the paper merged with a short-lived rival, of its successor, *The Danbury News-Times*. Several manuscript collections provided details about the early Depression years. The records of the Connecticut Unemployment Commission (1931-1933), available at the State Library, contain brief accounts of worsening economic conditions in Danbury during those years. An agent of the state labor department visited Danbury in 1931 to mediate the fur union strike. Her letters describing the local situation are in the Federal Mediation and Conciliation Service papers (Record Group 280, File 170/6029) at the National Archives.

To write this history, the authors drew on research they conducted for the Danbury Preservation Trust, including Architectural and Historic Resources surveys that utilized land and probate records; and on nominations to the National Register of Historic Places – especially for information on the Main Street Historic District. In addition, Devlin prepared a series of feature articles for *The News-Times*, entitled "A Look Back at the Century," which appeared between July and December 1999. References to Charles Ives are supported by Devlin's research into local newspapers and town and city records conducted for the authors of two biographies of Ives: Stuart Feder's *My Father's Song* (1990) and Jan Stafford's *Charles Ives: A Life in Music* (1996). Interviews with local figures, such as architect Philip Sunderland, are contained in Vivian Perlis's book, *Charles Ives Remembered* (1971). Ives' profound influence on the Grateful Dead is discussed at length in Phil Lesh's memoir *Searching for the Sound*.

The contributions of the late Clarice Osiecki, who partially completed a draft of the history of this period, helped shape several chapters here, particularly Chapters 1, 4 and 5. The ideas of two other now-deceased, local historians who were also involved in this project, Truman Warner and Stephen Collins, influenced the intellectual framework of this book in profound ways. Warner's concentration on changes in energy use and the importance of geographic forces on history are evident in Volume 1 of *The News-Times Centennial Edition* (September 8, 1983) – material that was largely reprinted in Volume I and Volume 4 of the Tricentennial Booklet Series. Collins' knowledge, particularly his insights into Danbury's economic transition and political development, were expressed in scores of editorials written over his long career at *The News-Times*, and in his two booklets on hatting, *"Danbury Crowned Them All: Hatting in Danbury* (published by the Danbury Scott-Fanton Museum) and *Two Centuries of Hat Making: Danbury's Famous Trade* (Tricentennial Booklet Volume 5).

This book could not have been written without close attention to the daily coverage of the Danbury newspaper on microfilm available at the Haas Library. Dependence on *The Danbury News-Times* (after 1962, renamed *The News-Times*) for an understanding of this dynamic period is crucial for several reasons. In 1955 the Ottaway family, owners of a small newspaper chain based in upstate New York, purchased the Danbury paper and greatly expanded its number of pages and size and improved the quality of its staff. Reporters were encouraged to investigate and take stands on key local topics. Details of the acquisition are in Charles King's *Ottaway Newspapers: The First Fifty Years* (1986). The newspaper was an especially rich historical source under Ottaway ownership. We are indebted to Stephen Collins, the editor and the editorial director of his hometown paper from 1949 until his retirement in 1985, for his knowledge of Danbury history and the reform zeal that marked his clear and informed editorials. Finally, no matter how valuable, the un-indexed publication would have been more difficult to use without the sustained dedication of Dr. Truman Warner who, for years, made a nightly habit of clipping important articles from the newspaper and then saving and categorizing them – a practice that produced the basis of an enormous collection of Danbury ephemera, organized by topic. The collection is available under his name in the Western Connecticut State University Archives.

The newspaper was especially attentive to the transformation of the city's economy. In addition to regular coverage of economic issues, it published a special "Progress" edition that, each April, provided in-depth profiles of the companies that had recently located in Danbury. Box 3 in the vast Truman Warner collection at the Haas Library contains files on most of the large companies that settled in the city in the post-World War II era. A typed manuscript of a talk entitled "General Comments on Barden," delivered by company president Folke Ericson on January 15, 1954, treats the early years of the first large high-tech firm to come to Danbury. The manuscript is in the possession of the authors of this book. In addition, an oral-history interview with two original and long-time employees at Barden, Florence

Jednack and Jean Collins, brings out the importance of an available female labor force in attracting the firm to the city.

Later chapters of this book benefited from the continued expansion of *The News-Times* that earned it frequent regional awards for reporting and photography. During the late 1970s, the newspaper paid increasing attention to emerging environmental issues relating to pollution, regulation and development. Paul Steinmetz, environmental reporter for *The News-Times* in the 1980s and business reporter in the early 1990s, reflected on these areas in a thoughtful 2007 interview. The business coverage of reporters Bob Chuvala and Ariane Sains provided considerable insight into the rapid corporate and commercial growth of the 1970s and 1980s. The editorials of Steve Collins furnished perspective on such long-term subjects as urban redevelopment, land-use policy and historic preservation.

The campaign to modernize the local school system waged by the Citizens Committee on Education and the Committee of 1,000 is documented by letters, organizational material, handbills, booklets, and advertisements contained in the June Goodman collection in the archives of the Haas Library. The Goodman papers also contain a scrapbook of newspaper clippings related to the short life of the Fair City Foundation, as well as a copy of Harold Mehling's article, "How to Win the Fight for a New School," published in *Redbook* magazine (January 1964). Interviews with June Goodman, William Goodman and Rabbi Jerome Malino were invaluable.

Thanks to Steve Collins, the long struggle to consolidate town and city government into one unit is covered in detail in the news pages and editorial columns of *The News-Times*. Collins' own summary of the paper's role in convincing voters to support unification is in "Keeping Abreast of the Times," in *The News-Times*, Centennial Edition, Volume II, Part I (September 22, 1983). See also Devlin's 1983 interview with Collins in the Western Connecticut State University Archives. Materials relating to the citizens' campaign in favor of this reform are in the June Goodman papers. Interviews with A. Peter Damia, Hugh Morgan and John Murphy touch on this effort.

Many sources supplement the exhaustive newspaper coverage of the 1955 floods and subsequent urban renewal. Extensive oral history interviews, some video-taped, were conducted and a detailed abstract of the minutes of meetings of the Danbury Redevelopment Agency from 1956 to 1990 was prepared for the 1996 exhibit and catalog of "A River Runs Through It: The Urbanization of the Still River." The Danbury Preservation Trust Papers in the Western Connecticut State University Archives; the files of the Technical Planning Associates in New Haven; and the records of the New England Division, U.S. Army Corps of Engineers in Boston all contain pertinent material. A portion of a 1986 interview and Truman Warner's notes of a 1979 interview – both with Jeremiah Lombardi, the executive director of the Redevelopment Agency – are in the Warner Papers at the Haas Library.

A careful examination of race relations in Danbury, by David Wilder of the Bureau of Applied Social Research, Columbia University (October 1, 1966) is entitled "Assessment of the Community Needs of Danbury, Connecticut, and the Potential Role of Danbury State College in Community Service." Originally located in the files of the Technical Planning Associates, this document is now in the possession of the authors. "An Action Study to Improve Poverty Conditions in Danbury, Connecticut, Growing Out of the Wilder Report," Danbury State College (April, 1967), is in the Warner Papers, Box 1, Folder 25. Rich interviews with Richard Arconti, Lionel Bascom, Lena Eriquez, Gene Eriquez, Sam Hyman, and William Cruse were vital. Ken Hanna's piece, "Black and White," (a typed, undated manuscript in the possession of the authors) is an astute reflection on the life of William Cruse by a close friend.

Interviews informed a large portion of the "Fresh Energy" section of this book. Veteran planning professionals Jonathan Chew, executive director of the Housatonic Valley Council of Elected Officials, and Dennis Elpern, director, City of Danbury Planning and Zoning Department provided an invaluable overview of the growth of the city and the region. Chew also supplied the authors with copies of such key documents as Danbury's 1967

Plan of Development (the first such effort following consolidation of town and city) and the 1968 Sewerage Plan. He generously shared his agency's vast collection of land-use maps, most of which are now online.

The authors also profited from the foresight of Rick Asselta of the Alternative Center for Education. In 1985, Asselta had his students videotape incisive interviews with former Danbury Mayors Gino Arconti, Charles Ducibella, Donald Boughton and James Dyer. The authors conducted a lengthy interview with Dyer himself in 2010, a year before his untimely death and shortly after he donated a large collection of materials documenting his political career to the Western Connecticut State University Archives, where they are now available. The following also contributed helpful interviews and correspondence: former Common Council Chairman Joseph DaSilva; Judge Lloyd Cutsumpas, who served on the Consolidation Commission, was counsel for the plaintiffs in the Pepin v. Danbury taxation case, and was instrumental in the early development of Richter Park; Jack Schweitzer, chief city engineer during the 1970s; current airport administrator Paul Estefan; and former Environmental Impact Commission Chairman Dr. Donald Groff. We also made use of taped interviews filed in the Western Connecticut State University Archives with former state legislators in the 1970s, Clarice Osiecki and Francis Collins. The interviews were done for the university's centennial history.

Onetime prominent Main Street merchants Robert Steinberg, Robert Feinson and Charles Bardo provided first-hand observations about Danbury's commercial growth and the problems of downtown. Bardo's unpublished memoir, located at the Danbury Museum, also helps to explain the way commercial expansion brought about the demise of agriculture in the region. Ervie Hawley's recollections of his career in development also touched on his early life growing up on a Danbury dairy farm.

Several sources added to our understanding of Danbury's unusual cultural diversity. A taped interview, now in the Western Connecticut State University Archives, with Susan Fusco, one of Danbury's earliest bilingual and ESL teachers, proved to be an articulate guide to the school system's early response to the city's massive demographic changes. Sharon McQuade, in "Working with Southeast Asian Refugees," *Clinical Social Work Journal*. Vol.17, No. 2 (Summer, 1989), available online, described the cultural displacement faced by many of the Southeast Asian refugees who settled in the city in the 1970s and 1980s. Carlo DeGrazia of New Milford gave the authors information about his uncle Andrew DeGrazia, founder of Danbury's Ethnic and Cultural Festival, and offered a description of early festivals as did Hal and Mary Burke.

Key participants supplied invaluable and otherwise unavailable information on several important topics. Two interviews with Jack Stetson, both of them taped and available in the Western Connecticut State University Archives, provide a detailed inside look at the growth, operation and eventual demise of the Danbury Fair during and after the lifetime of John Leahy. Howard Tuvelle, retired music professor at Western, and the dynamic force behind the 1974 concert celebrating the 100th anniversary of Charles Ives' birth, shared the story of the effort to honor – and capitalize on – the fame of that Danbury native.

The move of the Union Carbide Corporation to Danbury provoked coverage in *The New York Times*, as well as in such national magazines as *Barron's* and *Time* – all of which can be found in the Truman Warner Collection in the Western Connecticut State University Archives. A 2010 Devlin interview with architect Kevin Roche was the chief source of information about the unusual design of Union Carbide's corporate complex. Herbert Janick's "The Carbide Corner: Changing Patterns of Land Use in Danbury, Connecticut" (1981) is helpful for its information on the history of Ridgebury and Mill Plain; a copy is in the author's possession. Kristin Nord's, "Partners in Progress" in William Devlin's *We Crown Them All: An Illustrated History of Danbury* (1984), presents profiles of Danbury companies and is a guide to the response of the local business community to the city's corporate boom.◆

Index

(n) for footnote;
(ph) for photograph;
(illus) for drawings, cartoons, advertisements, etc.;
(map) for map, and
passim following a hyphenated set of numbers;
passim is Latin for "... here, there, and everywhere..." within the range preceding it

Printed in the United States of American

Reynolds, Tim

The Green Beret Doctor's Get Fit Boot Camp: A Health Plan For Life, 10 Days to a New You by Tim Reynolds, M.D. with Tina Baiter

ISBN: 978-0-9844756-0-5

Editing by: Kate Benson, Pam Reynolds and Stephanie Baiter.

Cover Design and Layout by Dawn Teagarden.